I0570228

976-1313

HOW SPORTS PHONE LAUNCHED CAREERS AND BROKE NEW GROUND

HOWIE KARPIN

SCOTT ORGERA

FOREWORD BY
KENNY ALBERT

Copyright © 2024 by Press Pass Chronicles

All rights reserved.

No part of this book may be reproduced in any form or by any electronic or mechanical means, including information storage and retrieval systems, without written permission from the authors, except for the use of brief quotations in a book review.

Sports Phone Stories and *Quickie Quiz* designs by Ricardo De Leon

Sports Phone Stories concepts and sketches by Stepan Bybyk & Scott Orgera

Cover concept by Scott Orgera

Cover design by Castle Conrad Media

Additional artwork by Eric Egan, Carlos Martinez, and Valerie Zaremska

Visit us at 9761313.com

Howie dedicates this book to his wife and soulmate, Kathy; his sister, Carol; his nieces, Wendy Shore Rosano and Sharon Shore-Berrios; his daughters-in-law, Anita and Emmy; his granddaughter, Madeline; and his great-nieces, Rachel and Melanie, who is always in our hearts.

Scott dedicates this book to his parents, Betty and Rich; his brother, Dean; his sister-in-law, Lizzie; his nephew, Henry; and his niece, Abigail Rose.

CONTENTS

PREFACE

BY SCOTT ORGERA

When the idea for this book first began rattling around in my head there were only two certainties. First, in its heyday Sports Phone's roster was so jam-packed with notable names that there just had to be a tale or two worth telling somewhere in there. Second, there was no way I was heading down this road without my co-author getting involved. More on Howie later.

I've always been fascinated by origin stories. Whether it be Jeff Bezos founding Amazon from his garage or Mariano Rivera gripping a baseball made from wadded-up fishing nets, there's typically something uniquely inspirational in each.

In the case of Sports Phone, a cacophony of personalities set out to change the way scores and breaking news were consumed — and in turn, ended up setting the tone for the up-to-the-second updates we take for granted today. Of course, they didn't truly know what their collective impact would be at the time, but neither did Bezos when he sold his first book or Rivera when he unleashed that initial pitch.

While the roadmap of how Sports Phone got started, its evolution, and eventually where its revolutionary concepts showed up in the worlds of radio, digital, and beyond years later is covered in depth within this book, it was the stories of those individuals who made the service tick that made this a joy to write (and hopefully, to read). I was well aware that many of those erstwhile up-and-comers eventually became household names when I first pitched the concept.

Little did I know at the time that their collection of stories — equally hilarious, insightful, prescient, and occasionally tragic — would be so well remembered and captivating that they would become the heart and soul of the book itself. This became more than just a history lesson on Sports Phone and its mega-talented list of alums. It is a tapestry of lives planting their flag on the sports landscape: banded together in what was uncharted territory.

A key figure on that list happens to be my longtime friend, co-author, and former Sports Phone reporter Howie Karpin. A fixture in New York City press boxes for over 45 years and the Big Apple's senior MLB official scorer, Howie's radio broadcasting chops were first honed on the other end of the service's famous 976-1313 number.

His experiences at Sports Phone along with lifelong relationships with many of its employees allowed us to provide an unprecedented peek behind the curtain, one that we believe makes this book truly special. What started as another project morphed into a labor of love, one we're both excited to share with you!

FOREWORD

BY KENNY ALBERT

As I sat in class at Paul D. Schreiber High School in Port Washington, N.Y. during the 1980s, I couldn't wait until the final bell at the end of each school day. It meant one thing: time to head home and prepare for the Sports Phone "Quickie Quiz" at 3:20 every weekday afternoon.

What do I mean by prepare? Well, I would be in position by 3:19 to dial those memorable numbers — 976-1313 — to try and be the first to hear the quiz question on the 3:20 update. Occasionally, the one-minute sports report from 3:10 would still be on the loop, and I would have to redial (at the cost of an additional 10 cents on my parents' phone bill). I made sure I had various team and league media guides and record books nearby just in case I didn't know the answer to that day's Quickie Quiz off the top of my head. I was always so excited to hear the Sports Phone voices — my heroes — when they answered the quiz line. King Wally, Howie Karpin, and Pat Harris just to name a few. It was even more exhilarating when I learned that I was that day's winner, which meant hearing MY name mentioned on the next loop at 3:30. My biggest competition was usually the "Great Neck Connection." I recall winning prizes such as Dennis D'Agostino's *This Date in Mets History* and two tickets to a New Jersey Devils game.

I never worked at Sports Phone, but it's where many of my friends and broadcast colleagues honed their skills and received invaluable experience early in their careers. Al Trautwig, Howie Rose, Michael Kay, John Giannone, Steve Cangialosi, and Rich Ackerman (my NYU roommate) were loyal Sports Phone employees who became household names for countless sports fanatics in the tri-state area whose fingers were programmed to automatically dial 976-1313.

Their information gathering was archaic by today's standards. Reporters at every game (called stringers) would constantly phone the office to report the score. Then, every ten minutes (or two on football Sundays), the Sports Phone announcer would rattle off as many as 40 scores in 60 seconds, plus the top news stories of the day. It was part racetrack announcer, part auctioneer. It was frantic … chaotic … and remarkable! The demand for scores and information was so high that a second, 10-cents-per-call line was established. And I was one of its most frequent users.

A lot has changed over the last three-plus decades: the introduction of all-sports radio stations (the first: WFAN in New York in July 1987), the internet (early 1990s), and of course iPhones and other devices. It is so much easier for the younger generation to access scores, highlights, and live games with a quick click. I don't know about you, but for those of us who grew up in the 1970s and 1980s, there was something magical about picking up the rotary phone on the desk or wall at your house and dialing 976-1313. Enjoy reading the stories and anecdotes from those who lived it!

A GUIDE TO OUR BOOK

During the writing of this book, we interviewed over 100 people, many of whom are referenced more than once throughout its pages. These include dozens of alumni along with former callers to the service, as well as notable names across various industries that were impacted in one way or another by Sports Phone over the years.

To make things easier for you, the reader, we've created the following guide that details who many of these individuals are along with some of their key accomplishments, credentials, and where applicable their tenure at Phone Programs (Sports Phone's parent company). We hope that it will serve as a useful reference point while you enjoy the upcoming chapters and stories.

THE ALUMS

Found among those promising men and women of Sports Phone were some of today's most well-known broadcasters, reporters, public address announcers, and other prominent media figures. A veritable breeding ground for these now-polished professionals, many of whom are household names, the dial-up service that once handled 50 million calls in a year churned out talent at a level likely not seen before or since from a sports-related startup.

We were lucky enough to spend some time with these former employees and contractors, each of whom helped out a great deal in the making of our book:

RICH *ACKERMAN*

Longtime sports anchor and play-by-play broadcaster (CBS Sports Radio, WFAN, FOX Sports, and more); *1987 - 1990*

SHELLEY *ADLER*

First female sportscaster for AP Radio, where she has worked for 40-plus years; Played a key role in launching *CNN Headline News*; *1977 - 1978*

JIM *BERMAN*

In TV management for more than three decades; President and General Manager of NBC and Fox affiliate Dakota News Now; *1981 - 1982*

JOE *BOMRAD*

Long-serving letter carrier for USPS in Scranton, PA; *1984 - 1985*

STEVE *CANGIALOSI*

Television play-by-play announcer for Major League Soccer on Apple TV; Former TV voice of the New Jersey Devils; On-air at ESPN Radio and MSG Networks for several years; *1984 - 1992*

ROBBIE *CAPLOE*

Brand Director and Publisher for Cynopsis; Former executive editor for *Seventeen, Teen Beat, Tiger Beat, Ladies' Home Journal,* and other titles; *1985 - 1989*

FRAN *CAPO*

Guinness World Records Fastest Talking Woman; nine-time world record holder; Author, comedienne, radio host, and actress; *1987 - 1988*

CHRIS *CARRINO*

Radio voice of the Brooklyn Nets for 20-plus seasons; NFL broadcaster for Compass Media Networks and the Giants radio network; *1993*

JIM *CERNY*

Executive Editor with ForeverBlueshirts.com / Managing Editor NHL & PWHL with Sportsnaut.com; Former radio play-by-play for the New York Islanders, writer for *The New York Times,* and SiriusXM host; *1988 - 1996*

GARY *COHEN*

Long-serving television voice of the New York Mets and radio play-by-play broadcaster for Seton Hall basketball; Member of the Mets Hall of Fame; *1977 - 1979*

LINDA *COHN*

ESPN's longest-tenured *SportsCenter* anchor (since 1992); National Sports Media Association Hall of Fame member; Host and reporter for NHL coverage; *1984 - 1986*

CHUCK *COOPERSTEIN*

Radio voice of the Dallas Mavericks since 2005; Westwood One play-by-play announcer; *1982 - 1984*

RICH *COUTINHO*

Long-standing sports radio voice; Former New York Mets beat reporter for 98.7 ESPN and FiOS1; *1989 - 1993*

JACK *CURRY*

Sports commentator for the YES Network; Bestselling author; Former national baseball correspondent for *The New York Times*; *1985 - 1986*

JOHN *CWIKLA*

Long-term public information officer; Former executive producer at WXYZ-TV; News and sports director at WBRB; Freelance reporter for AP Radio and ABC Radio; *1980 - 1985*

GORDON *DAMER*

Established NYC sports broadcaster (YES Network, WCBS-AM, 1010 WINS); Co-host of *ESPN New York Tonight* on 98.7 FM; *1994 - 2000*

CHARLIE *DENATALE*

Media buyer for four decades; Part-time actor with credits in theater, film, radio, and television; *1978 - 1988*

CEDRIC *DEW*

Vice President of transitional housing at YMCA; Former freelancer for national Pro-Am city leagues; Seasoned audio and video editor; *1984 - 1987*

DREW *ESOCOFF*

Director of NBC *Sunday Night Football* since 2006; Previously directed *MNF*, *SportsCenter*, the NBA Finals, and five Super Bowls; *1981 - 1982*

MIKE *FARRELL*

Senior thoroughbred writer, harness racing writer, and handicapper who has covered the Triple Crown and Breeders' Cup for the *Daily Racing Form*, The Associated Press, and others; *1972 - 1984*

JOE *GAUCI*

Recording engineer; Sound effects editor for award-winning animated sitcom *Doug*; Worked with Metallica, REM, and The Who, among others; *1987 - 1990*

JOHN *GIANNONE*

Emmy Award-winning studio host and reporter for MSG Networks, covering the New York Rangers for over 20 years; Former sportswriter for the *New York Daily News*; *1982 - 1984*

BOB *GROCHOWSKI*

Former copy editor/proofreader for Business Wire; Worked for Bloomberg Business Radio and SportsTicker; *1982 - 1990*

PAT *HARRIS*

Engineer at TN. radio group; Former update anchor and host at WFAN, WNBC Radio, and ESPN Radio; Fill-in host for New York Rangers pre- and postgame; *1979 - 1982, 1999*

FRED *HUEBNER*

Retired sports broadcaster formerly with The Score and ESPN 1000; Ex-play-by-play announcer for the Chicago Fire; *1977 - 1990*

JIM *JOHNSON*

Sports media lifer with several decades' experience as a producer for Phoenix Communications and ESPN; *1982 - 1985*

BRIAN *KILMEADE*

Host of multiple shows on Fox News Channel and a program on Fox News Radio; Former sports anchor and play-by-place voice for UFC events; *1988 - 1990*

DON *LA GRECA*

The first voice heard on ESPN New York radio during its 2001 launch; Co-host of *The Michael Kay Show*; Radio broadcaster for Rangers and Knicks; *1990 - 2000*

STEPHEN *LEBOW*

Radio announcer and producer; CEO at New Spirit Broadcasting; *1976 - 1978*

AMY LENNARD *GOEHNER*

Contributing writer for *AARP Livable Communities*; Former senior arts reporter at *Time*, deputy chief of reporters at *Sports Illustrated*, and senior editor at *SI Kids*; *1981 - 1984*

JOHN *MARTIN*

Distinguished executive producer who was part of more than 4,000 sporting events over a quarter-century at ESPN Radio; Spent 40-plus years in sports broadcasting; *1977 - 1981*

TONY *MATTEO*

New York City Fire Department Captain; Joined FDNY in 1994; *1990 - 1994*

NAT *MAULDIN*

Screenwriter and film producer with TV credits which include *Barney Miller, Night Court,* and *Newhart* and movies such as *Doctor Dolittle* and *The Preacher's Wife; 1976 - 1978*

DENIS *MCNAMARA*

Former program director at WLIR; Worked with Billy Joel, U2, The Rolling Stones, and more; International A&R for artists including Van Morrison and the Bee Gees; *1975 - 1976*

JIM *MEMOLO*

Veteran sports talk host on SiriusXM; Former broadcaster on WFAN and Tribune Media stations; *1981 - 1982, 1985 - Unknown*

PETER *NEWMAN*

A leading producer of theatrical films, working with notable filmmakers including Robert Altman, Wes Anderson, and Jonathan Demme; *1975 - 1978*

JERRY *O'NEIL*

Former writer for *Soap Opera Weekly*; Day player on popular soaps including *All My Children, One Life to Live*, and *As the World Turns*; *1984 - 1988*

BOB *PAPA*

Radio voice of the New York Giants since 1995; Broadcaster on the Golf Channel; Boxing announcer for ESPN and HBO; *1984 - 1986*

CJ *PAPA*

Fox News Media anchor on SiriusXM; Formerly on SNY, FiOS1 News, ESPN Radio, WABC-AM, NBC, and MSG Network; *1986 - 1989*

HOWIE *ROSE*

New York Mets play-by-play announcer since 1995 (radio since 2004); Member of the Mets Hall of Fame; Former New York Islanders and Rangers broadcaster; *1975 - 1977*

ANDY *ROTH*

Has covered the NBA since 1979 for AP Radio, NBC Radio, Sheridan Hoops, and The Sports Network, among other outlets; *1979 - 1990, Returned part-time post-'90*

KEN *SAMELSON*

Formerly Editor of Macmillan's *The Baseball Encyclopedia*; Senior Editor for Contemporary Books, Triumph Books, and Skyhorse Publishing; Freelance editor, fact checker, and proofreader; *1982 - 1988*

ALAN *SANDERS*

Agent with over a quarter-century of experience representing on-air talent; *1983 - 1988*

DAVID *SCHUSTER*

Seasoned Chicago-based sports reporter and talk show host for multiple outlets including 670 The Score (WSCR) and ESPN 1000; *1978 - 1990*

PETER *SCHWARTZ*

Host and anchor for WFAN and CBS Radio; Play-by-play and public address announcer for multiple leagues; *1989 - 1993*

CHARLIE *SLOWES*

Radio play-by-play announcer for the Washington Nationals since their inception in 2005; Former voice of the Tampa Bay Rays and Washington Bullets; *1981 - 1984*

TOMMY *TIGHE*

Radio host for Miami Heat on 790 The Ticket; ESPN Radio *SportsCenter* anchor; Former Westwood One studio host; *1978 - 1981*

STEVE *TORRE*

Program Director for Mad Dog Sports Radio on SiriusXM; Former Sports Director at WINS; *1984 - 1986, 1987 - 1988*

MIKE *WALCZEWSKI*

"King Wally"; Public address announcer for the New York Knicks since 1989 and the New York Liberty since 1997; *1975 - 1987*

RICK *WALCZEWSKI*

Traveling sales seminar speaker; Formerly chief announcer at WRHU-FM and studio engineer at WABC-AM radio; Voiceovers for Al Italia, MTV, and Nissan; *1977 - 1982*

MIKE *WEINSTEIN*

EVP of Sales Planning & Distribution for Lionsgate; Former TV executive; *1979 - 1988*

LISA *WERNICK*

Director of CNBC's on-air promotion and scheduling; **Approximately** *1986 - 1989*

THE SUPPORTING CAST

In addition to those who worked at Phone Programs, our book would have never seen the light of day if not for this esteemed list of interviewees:

KENNY *ALBERT*

Five-sport broadcaster including the NFL on FOX Sports since 1994; Radio voice of the New York Rangers

JOE *BENIGNO*

Sports talk host on WFAN since 1994; Host of *Oh the Pain* podcast

LIZ *CALLAWAY*

Stage and film actress; recording artist; provided the singing voices in multiple animated films including *Anastasia*, Jasmine in two *Aladdin* sequels, and Odette in *The Swan Princess*

RICKY *COBB*

President of Super 70s Sports, including its popular Twitter/X account; Inspiration for VICE TV's *Super Maximum Retro Show*

ED *COLEMAN*

Veteran radio reporter who covered the New York Mets on WFAN and WCBS for nearly three decades, hosting several shows along the way

ROCCO *CONSTANTINO*

Baseball writer and co-founder of *BallNine*; Collegiate Athletic Director

TONY *CORDASCO*

Play-by-play broadcaster; Long-standing marketing manager and event planner

MARK *CUBAN*

Alternate governor and former principal owner of the NBA's Dallas Mavericks; Former star of TV's *Shark Tank*; Co-founder of audio and video streaming portal Broadcast.com

JOE *DELIKAT*

Internet handicapper for all four major sports and the horse racing Triple Crown; Former broadcaster and manager for Dial Sports and The Sports Network

SCOTT *ENGEL*

Inaugural member of the Fantasy Sports Writers Association's Hall of Fame; Longtime SiriusXM Fantasy Sports Radio host

JIM *FEIST*

Award-winning handicapper and sports information provider since the early 1970s; Creator of the Nevada Sports Schedule Scorephone

LARRY *FLEISHER*

Wire service writer for two-plus decades; SportsTicker, The Sports Xchange, AP

FRANK *FLEMING*

Blogger and vlogger for Barstool Sports since 2017; Creator of the Sports E-Cyclopedia

ZIG *FRACASSI*

Sports update anchor and host for over a quarter-century (SiriusXM, NFL Radio, NHL Network Radio, ESPNU Radio, and more)

JEFF *GARLIN*

Actor, comedian, director, producer, and screenwriter with over a hundred credits; Jeff Greene on HBO's *Curb Your Enthusiasm;* Former member of Second City comedy troupe

PHIL *GIUBILEO*

Play-by-play broadcaster for Quinnipiac Hockey on ESPN+; Former announcer and studio producer for multiple teams and outlets including WABC Radio

ED *GUEVARA*

Security director; Retired FBI Special Agent (25 years) for multiple field offices and divisions; Assigned to Boston College point-shaving case and Lucchese organized crime family

BILL *JAMES*

Baseball historian, statistician, and writer widely known as the father of sabermetrics; Senior advisor on Baseball Operations for the Boston Red Sox from 2003-19

ED *MCDONALD*

Senior counsel; Former federal prosecutor and Attorney-In-Charge of the Federal Organized Crime Strike Force in New York; Prosecuted Lufthansa robbery and BC point-shaving cases

RANDY *MCGUIRE*

Former Las Vegas sportscaster; Veteran Scorephone announcer and production supervisor in the 1980s

SWEENY *MURTI*

Senior Contributor for MLB Media; Former on-air anchor and producer for WFAN from 1993-2023, serving as their Yankees reporter for 22 years

PAT *O'KEEFE*

New York Knicks radio host and play-by-play announcer; ESPN and NBA Radio host

DANIEL *OKRENT*

Credited as the founding father of fantasy sports; Inventor of Rotisserie League Baseball; Author of several books; First public editor of *The New York Times*

EDDIE *OLCZYK*

TV commentator for Seattle Kraken; Analyst for NBC's horse racing coverage; 16-year NHL veteran; 1994 Stanley Cup winner with NY Rangers; Former head coach of the Pittsburgh Penguins

KEVIN *REECE*

Sports photographer for 40-plus years; AP and other outlets; Has covered 10 Super Bowls, 9 NBA Finals, and 24 Rose Bowls

HAL *RICHMAN*

Creator, chairman, and founder of Strat-O-Matic, which revolutionized the world of board games and sports simulations

CHRISTOPHER *RUSSO*

Mad Dog Sports Radio on SiriusXM; Host of *High Heat* on MLB Network; Contributor to ESPN's *First Take;* Former co-host of *Mike and the Mad Dog* on WFAN; Radio Hall of Fame inductee

DAVE *SIMS*

TV play-by-play voice of the Seattle Mariners since 2007; MLB Network correspondent; SiriusXM radio host; Three-time Washington State Sportscaster of the Year

LEIGH *STEINBERG*

Sports agent who has represented more than 60 first-rounders in NFL Draft history, including eight number-one picks; Real-life inspiration for Oscar-winning film *Jerry Maguire*

JEFFREY *TOWNES*

Along with actor Will Smith, one half of the Grammy Award-winning, multi-platinum-selling hip-hip duo DJ Jazzy Jeff & the Fresh Prince; Actor, producer, and lifelong disc jockey

SUZYN *WALDMAN*

Has covered the Yankees for almost 40 years, including 20 as a radio color commentator; Radio Hall of Fame inductee; First woman to broadcast MLB full-time; Former musical theater actress and singer

LAST BUT CERTAINLY NOT LEAST

There are several others not listed here who were also generous with their memories and insights, each adding their individual touch to the finished product. They are also referenced throughout the book, and we are profoundly thankful to them for being a part of this project.

———

SPORTS PHONE STORIES

Scattered throughout the following chapters are sections formatted a little differently from the rest. Labeled *Sports Phone Stories*, each features a tale from an era gone by.

For easy access to each story, simply reference the separate Table of Contents below.

"Bo Knows Sports Phone" (feat. John Cwikla and Charlie DeNatale), Ch. 4

"Fuck This Place" (feat. Don La Greca), Ch. 4

"Slumber Party" (as told by Don La Greca), Ch. 4

"Magic Shocks the Sports World" (feat. Cedric Dew, Howie Karpin, and Peter Schwartz), Ch. 4

"I'm Real and I'm Fantastic!" (feat. Chuck Cooperstein), Ch. 4

"You Fucking Moron!" (feat. Jim Berman), Ch. 4

"Captain Cutup" (feat. Don La Greca and Tony Matteo), Ch. 4

"Wheel of Miss-Fortune" (feat. Rich Ackerman), Ch. 5

"The Magic Number" (feat. Alan Sanders), Ch. 5

"Pardon My French Open" (as told by Ken Samelson feat. Steve Cangialosi), Ch. 5

"I Fought The Law (And The Law Lost)" (feat. Ken Samelson and Charlie Slowes), Ch. 5

"Fast and First" (feat. John Martin), Ch. 5

"Home Blown" (feat. Bob Papa), Ch. 5

"Touch 'em All, Joe!" (feat. Chris Carrino), Ch. 5

"Darryl Defends Dad" (as told by Jim Johnson), Ch. 5

"Subway Series, Sort Of" (feat. Hal Richman and Mike Weinstein), Ch. 6

"Miracle on Splice" (feat. Eddie Olczyk, David Schuster, and Bob Grochowski), Ch. 6

"Man or Mouse" (feat. Charlie DeNatale and Mike Weinstein), Ch. 6

"Arrested At Arlington" (feat. Fred Huebner), Ch. 7

"Killer on the Court" (feat. David Schuster), Ch. 7

"Holy Rejection, Batman!" (feat. Charlie DeNatale), Ch. 9

"Tire Trouble for The Fresh Prince" (feat. Mike Weinstein), Ch. 9

"Good Luck, Champ!" (feat. Pat Harris, Howie Karpin, and Mike Weinstein), Ch. 9

"It Pays to Drink" (feat. Jim Memolo), Ch. 10

"Lasorda, Lawrence, and a Lopsided Win" (as told by Howie Karpin feat. Dave Sims), Ch. 10

"A Reel Frankenstein" (feat. Don La Greca), Ch. 10

"'Boo' Ackerman" (feat. Rich Ackerman, Kenny Albert, Jim Cerny, and Andy Roth), Ch. 10

"Bunny Business" (feat. Tony Matteo), Ch. 10

"Mournful Meadowlands" (feat. Bob Grochowski), Ch. 10

"Big D and The Juice" (feat. Don La Greca), Ch. 10

"Tough Pill" (as told by Howie Karpin), Ch. 10

"What's the Fuckin' Score?" (feat. Tommy Tighe), Ch. 10

CHAPTER 1
THE BIRTH OF SPORTS PHONE

I n this age of instant information, it's hard to imagine waiting around for an updated score or the reason your favorite quarterback was pulled from a game. We stroll around with real-time access to the latest pitch, punt, or penalty shot right in our pockets, likely not giving a second thought to how truly remarkable that is.

Long before this treasure trove of up-to-the-second data was just a finger tap away, a group of upstart broadcasting hopefuls and sports junkies comprised the brains and voices behind a dial-up service that revolutionized the way results and news were consumed. Following a bumpy introduction in 1972 that ultimately failed, Sports Phone hit the ground running three years later and quickly gained a loyal following.

No longer did you have to wait for a newscast, or worse yet the next day's paper, to find out if a wager hit or if the local team notched a win. Just place a call to 999-1313 (later changed to 976-1313, the number most synonymous with Sports Phone's history) or one of the service's other numbers and you'd hear a recorded rundown of the latest scores and noteworthy updates, gathered by a team of reporters and stringers scattered throughout the country, and delivered by a collection of unique personalities who were unwittingly shaping how sports information is collected and disseminated for decades to come.

MIRACLE ON 34TH STREET

To truly appreciate the concept of Sports Phone it's important to understand how it all started, inspired by a jolly old fat man with a long white beard. In a tradition that dates back to 1861, Macy's department store invites tourists and New York City natives alike to a meet and greet with Santa Claus from late November through Christmas Eve each year — a heavily attended event that's been held at their flagship location in Manhattan's Herald Square since 1901.

Decades later in 1964, the retail giant set up a "Dial-Santa-Claus" program that allowed starry-eyed children to pick up the phone and hear a recording of Kris Kringle himself on the other end. The new line was a smash hit right out of the gate, tallying two million calls in a few short weeks but also placing such a burden on New York Telephone's systems that service throughout NYC was disrupted.

The popularity of Dial Santa, along with the near-disaster that followed, led Ma Bell to enhance its technology so that many simultaneous calls to a single number could be handled gracefully without putting a strain on phone service in the area. These upgrades didn't happen overnight and would cost New York Telephone approximately $10 million, but by 1972 they had a system in place that could handle a whopping 198,000 calls per hour.

SANTA'S SLEIGH TO THE STEELERS SCORE

Dating back as far as the early twentieth century, dialing a number for information such as the current time, and some years later the local weather conditions, was commonplace. These were basic, quick hits, however — offering data that often came from a singular source. Even a recorded line like Macy's Dial Santa did not require details gleaned from multiple locations, and perhaps more importantly didn't have to be updated very often to be relevant.

This is what made the idea of Sports Phone feel like a monumental undertaking at first, and in many ways, it ended up being just that. While the *Chicago Tribune* and some other publications had call-in hotlines for late-running games, in most instances, they only provided final scores from a select few contests. Scores from games taking place all over the country, updated several times per hour, certainly sounded like pie in the sky at the time.

Jack Goodfellow's vision was precisely that, and despite some early hiccups it eventually came to fruition. A New York Telephone employee for many years who was now a consultant, he attempted to launch a score line in 1968 but was thwarted by a system that simply couldn't handle the volume. Fast-forward four years later to when the phone company's advanced equipment was up to the challenge, and the dial-up service known as Sports Phone was born.

As with many fledgling businesses, there were early growing pains, some revolving around a revenue-sharing setup that wasn't sustainable. Sports Phone's first iteration in '72 featured a minute-long segment containing the latest scores interspersed with two commercials, the latter of which occupied an unwieldy 23 percent of the caller's time.

Many of these promotional clips were sold by Phone Time, Sports Phone's main sales representative run by Notre Dame Hall of Famer and former NFL star Dick Lynch. A defensive back for the New York Giants and Washington Redskins, Lynch led the league in interceptions in 1961 and '63 and was later inducted into the Giants' Ring of Honor. His post-playing career included finding buyers for this coveted portion of Sports Phone's recording time, a group that included airlines and Broadway shows along with several beer and liquor companies.

While not exactly the ideal experience, the 14 seconds of advertisements was an unfortunate necessity — as New York Telephone was not only pocketing the entire customer fee for each call but also charging Sports Phone every time someone dialed their number. Even with some ad money coming in, reaching profitability under these conditions seemed near impossible for Goodfellow — especially since many of the sponsors were existing clients who weren't willing to actually pay for those brief inserts.

The overall business model was too intriguing though, and the potential audience too massive. This untapped potential soon resulted in Air Time Inc. purchasing Sports Phone, and executive Fred Weiner successfully convincing the phone company to share a portion of the per-call bounty. This was a game-changing development for Sports Phone and similar call-in lines, leading to its full-blown introduction in 1975 under Air Time subsidiary company Phone Programs.

"Eventually what New York Telephone figured out is if we did a better job of segmenting out these programs and actually shared the revenue with the producers, we could have all of these various programs that would make us all sorts of money," explained Mike Farrell, who worked at Sports Phone from its initial launch in 1972.

"So there was Sports Phone, there was an OTB result line, there was Dial-A-Joke. They basically paid the producers of these programs x amount of money per call out of those [one-minute] message units they were collecting, or on a flat contract basis, and that's how the whole thing took off at that point in time."

DROPPING DIMES

For callers local to the Big Apple, ten cents could now get you what was mostly an uninterrupted barrage of scores delivered in rapid-fire succession during peak times — with the quicker-tongued announcers managing to read up to 30 scores in that New York minute. Those in other areas could reach Sports Phone via long-distance calls, many waiting until opportune times of day when rates were lower. Phone Programs even ran ad campaigns in other markets that detailed the long-distance costs as the clock turned, giving would-be callers a play-book on when best to pick up the receiver.

Being a 24-hour operation, there were of course slow periods where the slate of games was slim or even non-existent. It was during this downtime that the service pioneered yet another form of round-the-clock sports information by offering news stories, editorials, trade rumors, and even interview clips from various venues. Sports Phone even provided waiting times at public tennis courts and golf courses in and around NYC.

"We literally were a radio station that did its bidding through the phone company and not over the air," Chuck Cooperstein said. "We did everything that a radio station did, and in a lot of cases we did more because we covered everything."

Perhaps the most memorable time fillers were Sports Phone's Quickie Quizzes, which celebrated broadcaster Kenny Albert fondly recalled in the foreword to this book.

"I remember that Kenny Albert used to win the Quickie Quiz every day," recalled Drew Esocoff. "Whenever I see Kenny still joke about it."

Those listeners who called in with the correct answers fast enough were in turn given their 15 minutes of fame, with the top five getting their names read "on-air" and the first also taking part in a brief inter-view that was typically broadcast to the service's callers the following day.

"When I was a teenager I would call Sports Phone to take the Quickie Quiz, and then I would be thrilled if I got the correct answer because they would mention your name during their next update," Jack Curry reminisced.

Although legal restrictions prevented awards like cash prizes, in later years the service would mail sports magazines to the Quickie Quiz victors and occasionally give away other items including tickets to local games.

"I was a high school sophomore the first time I recall winning the quiz. I won probably two or three times. By that point I would try to win all the time, maybe not every day but as often as I could," Phil Giubileo reflected. "I remember winning tickets a couple of times to Knicks games and once to a Yankees game."

ONE BILLION CALLS

The attention to dial-in lines continued to boom, with Sports Phone near the top of the list in most categories following its successful relaunch in '75. By the following fall they were fielding 65,000 calls per day on average, thanks in part to an aggressive marketing campaign focused on the pages of several New York newspapers.

That number spiked around major happenings in the sports world, such as those fateful rumor-filled days in June of '77 that led up to the hometown Mets trading fan favorite Tom Seaver to the Cincinnati Reds. Fans of the Amazins were feverishly dialing to learn the latest news about the dominating right-hander they referred to as Tom Terrific or The Franchise, with many first learning details of the future Hall of Famer's heartbreaking departure through Sports Phone itself.

"I had to ask my mother permission to call because of the service charge. To this day I still know the 976-1313 number like a jingle you can't get out of your head," recalled bank financial auditor William Sherman.

"I remember calling, waiting for the Tom Seaver trade. I was crushed and was trying to figure out who the Mets might get. I remember hearing about the trade on 1010 WINS before I went to school. It was the end of the school year and we had finals. I called

Sports Phone because I needed the who. For what [did they trade Seaver]?"

The quartet of Doug Flynn, Steve Henderson, Dan Norman, and Pat Zachry left Sherman nearly inconsolable, his sentiments echoed throughout the borough and beyond.

"I wanted to vomit," he added. "Growing up in Queens as a Mets fan, it was disgusting and unthinkable."

By 1979 the service was handling about 100,000 daily calls, part of a banner year for New York Telephone's phone announcement numbers overall. In addition to Sports Phone's steady traffic, an off-track betting information line targeting horseplayers averaged 175,000 callers a day while old tried-and-true lines providing the time and weather each topped 125,000 per. Other notable numbers featured stock market quotes, horoscopes, and even Dial-a-Joke for those needing a quick laugh. When Pope John Paul II visited New York City for the first time that October, a papal information line was even put in place.

"The first night I'm there, they had the pope on the one TV where we have three TVs set up, and everybody was busting my chops," boxing maven Pat Harris shared. "They were putting the Yankee game on and the Met game, and I barely could even follow what the heck the pope was doing because everyone's joking around and goofing off but watching the games. I just did the best I could."

All in all, the system received a staggering 271 million calls that year at an average revenue of six cents apiece, netting the phone company over $16 million in 1979 alone.

The next few years saw continued growth for Sports Phone, whose 50 million calls in 1981 resulted in a $3 million revenue boost and vaulted the service into second place behind the oft-used OTB line — solidifying that dial-up sports scores and news had become more in demand than Dow Jones updates, the latest weather conditions, or even when the clock tolled. In 1984 the US hosted its first Summer Olympics in more than half a century, prompting Sports Phone to dedicate the lion's share of its programming to headlines and results from the Games in Los Angeles.

By the time 1990 rolled around, the company had moved Sports Phone's operations out of Manhattan to Elmont, Long Island, and the service had received close to a billion calls in total — an astronomical figure that may have once seemed a pipe dream to the visionaries involved in its inception decades earlier.

CHAPTER 2
HOW IT ALL WORKED

Sports Phone was an intrepid undertaking in every sense of the word, with the members of what could initially be described as a skeleton crew figuring things out on the fly, doing what was necessary to deliver accurate and timely info in what was often the tightest of time windows. The concept appeared promising and the phone company equipment was now ready to handle any challenge it faced in terms of volume, but how was this all going to work exactly?

WHAT'S THE SCORE?

The need for a service like Sports Phone in the first place was derived from the fact that updated scores and the like were not readily available elsewhere, aside from scheduled news broadcasts, etc. Now that the systems were in place, those announcers manning the broadcast booths at Sports Phone's offices in Midtown Manhattan needed a way to obtain all of this information — and to have it relayed to them regularly throughout each day and night.

"It's weird when you're sitting in a little [booth]. It's not even like at a radio station or something where there are all kinds of technicians. Air Time was a very successful, high-end business. They were in television commercials and they were just well-dressed, go-get-'em kind of people," Peter Newman described.

"In the corner, there was this little booth. If Sports Phone was created today the booth would be somewhere in Queens or the Bronx and it would be a ramshackle building, but we were in one of the most desirable buildings in Manhattan."

In the beginning Sports Phone operators would get the latest details from a Western Union Ticker Tape Machine, a relic of a device you might find in a museum nowadays. As time went on it became apparent that pulling scores off of the wire wouldn't do long-term, however, as they simply weren't updated often enough to satisfy the callers' needs.

What happened next was part stroke of genius and part jury-rigged problem-solving, as the gang at 919 Third Avenue found a way to clear another hurdle. It wasn't the first time and wouldn't be the last that Sports Phone had to make a major adjustment during its evolution, something the service proved very adept at doing in the coming years.

Rather than relying on the relative snail's pace of the ticker tape, staffers began calling press boxes at various venues and asking whoever picked up the phone for the latest score. In other cases, they'd pay reporters already covering a game for another outlet to call in with updates. If it was local to the New York City area, Sports Phone often sent employees to the games themselves to relay direct updates and occasionally file their own audio live from places like Yankee Stadium and Madison Square Garden.

"We had the Western Union ticker, but what we put together as we went along was a database of press box phones that we could call to get updated scores, which was faster than the ticker," explained Gary Cohen, who started at Sports Phone in the fall of 1977.

"That's what we really relied on, especially during the busy times like a college football or college basketball Saturday night. Those were the craziest times, when there were the most games going on, but even for the pro games we found that calling the press tables or press boxes — especially for basketball and hockey — was faster than waiting for the ticker."

Relying on press box denizens didn't always go smoothly.

"There'd be places where we didn't have stringers and we would call the press table and somebody, they'd give you the score," recalled Ken Samelson. "I was working during the day as the desk assistant during spring training games. There was nobody down there so you'd have to call the press boxes. One day I was calling for the Mets score, and by the third time I called the guy that was answering was really getting annoyed."

The voice on the other end was seemingly ticked off by the constant interruptions and decided to relay a fake score, one that made it into Samelson's copy and on the air.

There were other times when announcers were put in the awkward position of making up their own hoops scores if the onsite stringer was dragging their feet.

"We'd only do this with basketball, you couldn't do football or baseball or anything else, but when a stringer on a basketball game, college or NBA, was late calling in in the early going [we'd put the score on ourselves]," Alan Sanders revealed.

"To my recollection, if it was college basketball it was always tied at four. If it was the NBA, it was always tied at eight or 10-9, something like that. And I remember Celly [Mike Celentano] would look at me and say, 'Don't worry, it'll get there. It's all right.' I remember that as being pretty funny."

This creative approach was taken to another level when it came to other types of content such as one-on-one interviews...

 # Sports Phone Stories

Collect Call From Wayne Gretzky
(as told by Howie Karpin feat. Pat Harris)

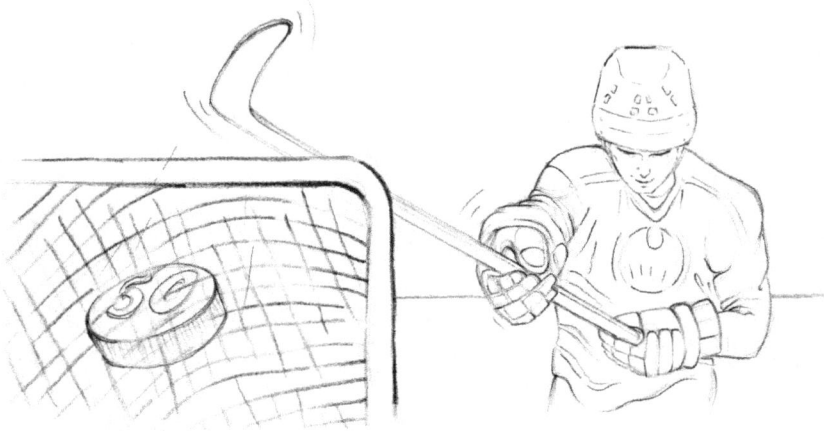

Sports Phone may not have made the impact that 24-hour all-sports radio stations like WFAN in New York would in later years, but it was still run just like those outlets were and are in many ways. Offshoots throughout the country deployed reporters to their respective local scenes to gather sound from games, press conferences, and other relevant events. Sometimes the in-office staff would use the phone to try to secure their own postgame interviews with players that made news on any particular evening, especially when an onsite reporter was not available.

On December 30, 1981, Edmonton center Wayne Gretzky scored five goals against the Flyers at the Northlands Coliseum in Edmonton. The memorable output gave Gretzky an NHL record by scoring his 50th goal in his 39th game. Pat Harris and I were working in Sports Phone's

Manhattan office that night. Harris said, "I'll try and get Gretzky [on the phone] and see what happens." I encouraged him to go for it.

Harris called the arena and asked if he could be connected to the Oilers locker room. A woman who answered the call said, "Yes, sir." The call was then transferred and a man picked up the phone.

"This is Pat Harris. I work for Sports Phone. Who am I speaking with?" "This is coach Glen Sather."

Harris said: "How 'ya doing coach? Great night there tonight."

"It sure was," Sather replied.

Harris said: "We just want to talk with Wayne for as briefly as we can, as long as we can get him."

Sather exclaimed: "Do you know how many people are standing around him in that locker room right now?!?"

Harris understood but refused to give up. "I can only imagine. I'm gonna give you my name, my phone number. Can you make sure you give this to him? At least give it to him."

Sather said: "I promise you. I will put this in his hand."

Of course, we never thought that Gretzky would get back to us but it was worth a try. Some of the other staff members that night decided to have a little fun with Harris, so they went to another room and called the sports newsroom — claiming there was a collect call from Wayne Gretzky. At first, Harris fell for it. When he picked up the phone, he'd hear the voice on the other end say something like, "You moron." After about three or four times it got tiresome, but the phone rang one more time. Harris said, "Hey guys, this is getting a little old."

"No, he really is on the line," they said. Harris, with some frustration, picked up the phone. I was standing right there and I could hear the voice on the other end say, "Yeah, hi. I'm looking for Pat Harris. This is Wayne Gretzky." Harris had the megastar on the phone for about five minutes.

After Harris left Sports Phone he had another chance encounter with Gretzky, while working for a cable TV company in New Jersey when the 1984 NHL All-Star Game was played at the Meadowlands.

Harris and a team went to cover the press conference that took place the day before the game. Gretzky was there, and after the formal press conference ended there were one-on-ones available for the TV crews. According to Harris, Sal Marchiano and Len Berman from Channel 4 in New York were there along with CNN, which was in its early days at that time. The PR representative said to Harris, "You're last in line. Whenever he gets to you, he gets to you."

After about an hour and a half, Gretzky comes over to do the interview. "I'm Pat Harris," he said to Gretzky.

"Hey, you're the guy that called me the night of the 50 goals in [39] games!"

"Yes, I was," a stunned Harris replied. Even Hall of Famers remember Sports Phone!

———

ON SCENE

Howie Karpin would later suggest that Sports Phone send anchors to the games to do their updates on-site, providing a real sense of ambiance. Instead of hearing the latest updates from the sterile environment of a recording booth, callers might experience the buzz of a Saturday afternoon at Shea Stadium or the roar of a Giants Stadium crowd. Armed with their own phone line and a seat in the press area, staffers began calling the Sports Phone office to get the latest scores — adding them to their slate before broadcasting a full update, similar to what the announcers did in the booth.

"Being able to go live from various press boxes, that was pretty unique and I think people appreciated it," John Cwikla suggested. "We always felt that gave credibility to it, that we were at the stadium in the press box and you could hear the fans in the background when you did reports. I think that gave credibility to it as not just being a score service, we were a sports information service."

Even if they weren't recording the full rundown from the venue, being on the scene also meant landing in-person interviews and grabbing pre- and postgame audio that enhanced the Sports Phone caller experience.

"Sports Phone taught me, better than any place I ever worked, that content is king in the business. You could do a two-minute report that's the greatest sounding report in the world, but without a sound bite in there from some player or manager or coach, it's not as good," opined Rich Coutinho.

"It's almost like that sound bite is the exclamation point of a sentence. A lot of things I took to other places I worked, particularly at ESPN when I was covering the Mets. I loved my own voice, but the fans want to hear David Wright's voice more than mine."

As can be the case with professional athletes, those sound bites weren't always on-air friendly.

"When I covered a Mets-Dodgers game as a teenager," Rick Walczewski said. "I got Reggie Smith on tape telling me he was going to 'shove a microphone up my ass.'"

READY, SET, GO

The staffers that made Sports Phone tick following its 1975 rebirth had a fairly basic structure in place when it came to the actual production process, one that functioned on a loop. Among that original crew was the estimable Howie Rose, veteran radio voice of the New York Mets and former hockey play-by-play man.

"It was on a loop and there wasn't much that we had to do. The original hiring plan was to have a guy who was the announcer, and he was working with someone that they called the manager. So the guy I worked with as manager was Mike Farrell, and he was the weekend evening manager which meant that he would help compile the scores and help with whatever needed help with — taking intake when it would be coming in from various places," Rose conveyed.

"The job wasn't really hard at all, technically. As I recall, we just went into the studio, you picked up the phone and as soon as it came off the hook I think you'd hear a beep."

Timing was key in the original system, and each announcer had their way of staying on target. In later years each booth had a digital clock prominently placed, but Rose and his early cohorts were essentially on their own.

"You had to go in with a stopwatch because you had, I think, 58 seconds, and you would hear another beep after the 58 seconds," he said. "That meant you were done and if you got cut off, you heard the beep while you were still talking, you had to do it again."

This technology had its advantages, though, as it also offered an easy do-over if you happened to fumble any part of your rundown.

"On Sports Phone you'd finish and I think you had to hang up the phone in within five seconds, and then it would loop into the system," John Martin described. "But if you didn't hang up the phone, then it would start to recycle and you'd get the beep and you could go and record again."

The loop-based system was eventually scrapped for a more modern approach. On a touch-tone phone, the announcer would dial an internal number to enter the system, next keying a series of digits which prompted a final set of beeps. The cue to start the recording followed those beeps. It was a quick sequence, so you had to be ready to go.

Although each transmission came to be known for lasting about a minute, the announcer actually had 50 seconds or less to squeeze in their updates because there was almost always an opening and closing to be read. Later developments in some of the out-of-town lines provided a bit more flexibility with timing, but for those narrating for New York Sports Phone, it was always a race against the clock.

"I think we all wanted to figure out who can get the most scores in clearly in this 59-second thing," Mike Weinstein mused.

On occasion the tapes were sponsored, so that took up even more time.

"I guess we eventually made a deal with the [New York] *Daily News*," he added. "So now we lost like two or three seconds because you had to go, 'Mike Weinstein for Sports Phone brought to you by *The Daily News.*'"

The announcer would read his or her update, and then close it out by inputting a code and pressing the asterisk key to lock in the audio. They would then call the respective line themselves to ensure it successfully made it on-air.

While games were in progress, Sports Phone started updating its recordings every fifteen minutes — which at the time seemed like more than enough, especially considering there was no viable alternative available to the public. Because of its rapid ascent in popularity, however, that frequency was soon shortened to every 10 minutes.

At times when there were an exorbitant number of games in progress the gap became even tighter, and the segments sometimes spilled over to a second line [976-2525] if all of the scores couldn't fit into a minute. On college basketball Saturdays, a third line was often needed. Some slates saw between 60 and 70 games in action across the major sports, a daunting task for the personnel on duty.

In other scenarios like NFL Sundays when callers — especially gamblers — demanded the absolute latest information, announcers updated the scores every two minutes. These days were so hectic that a quartet of announcers would be needed, working in 15-minute intervals to get through each hour.

"When we did the NFL, I don't remember who came up with the idea of instant updates, but instant updates were spectacular because there was really nowhere else to get the scores," Weinstein described.

"We'd have a guy sit in the booth for 15 minutes and somebody gives him a clipboard. Sometimes I was the guy doing the scores, getting the clipboard. Sometimes I was the guy [in the booth] doing the scores, but it was amazing. We were so ahead of our time and I really miss those days."

Going over that duration on any given Sunday wasn't a sound strategy, as the Sports Phone announcers had to preserve their pipes.

"Do a report, open the door, changes? No, do another one," Charlie Slowes noted. "You had one minute in between, and you would go for like a 15 or 20-minute segment, and then somebody else went in. You did like [four] people an hour to save your throat. That was crazy."

As the day-to-day processes evolved, so did the roles and responsibilities in the Sports Phone offices. What was once under the purview of a shift manager, a staffer designated as the writer became the person who made sure the announcers had the latest scores when they recorded their updates. At first, they simply gathered updates and delivered them to the booth either on paper or by relaying them verbally, but as the service's tech improved they would instead enter the scores into a proprietary computer system.

"There would be a list of all the games that were being played depending on the season. During college basketball, there were so many games but the writer's job was to answer the phones from the stringers. There'd be TVs on for the local games, so you keep your eyes on that," said Samelson.

"They didn't have a subscription to SportsChannel so we used to have the Met game or the Yankee game on radio, by the New York booth, so I would have to dash in there to find out the latest half-inning score and what was going on. And we used to have to call places where we didn't have stringers and we would call the press table."

The busiest shifts at Sports Phone amounted to a state of perpetual motion, one fueled by carbs and camaraderie.

"It was constant movement that day for six hours, pretty much one to seven, but it was a lot of guys so there were four announcers, two writers, and the supervisor. There were seven of us in what was a fairly small room for people that size. That was intense and I liked that kind of intensity," Rich Ackerman recounted. "We come in with bagels to start. We'd order a pizza or whatever the case may be. It felt like a clubhouse more than it did work."

NIGHT MOVES

If you worked the night shift at Sports Phone, you were required to stay until all the games were over and the final overnight update was recorded. Baseball season was particularly tough because of the late start times on the West Coast, and the sport's general unpredictability when it came to duration.

"So as I recall it, my shift was between five and midnight but the kicker was that you had to stay up till the last games on the West Coast were over, so you could end up staying a lot later than you signed on for, depending on how some of those games were going. " Rose said. "And you had better be accurate because that became a lifeline for gamblers. You gave a wrong score, it might have affected somebody's bet and you're gonna hear about that."

Sports Phone Stories

Stay With Us, For However Long It Takes
(feat. Pat Harris and Tommy Tighe)

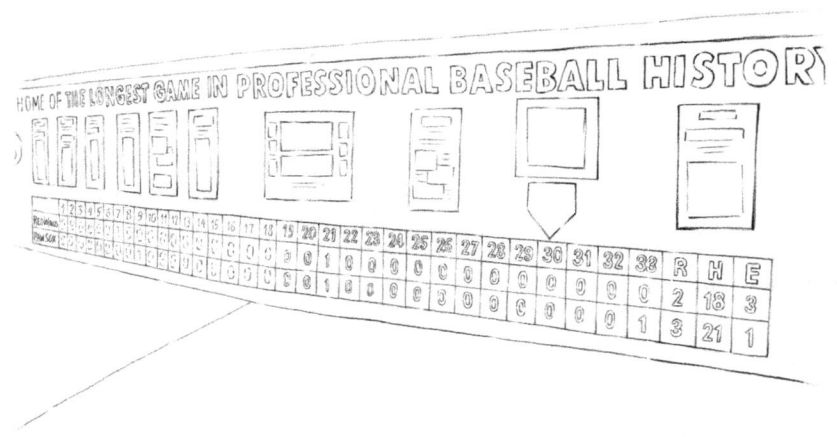

On the night of April 18, 1981, the visiting Rochester Red Wings and Pawtucket Red Sox kicked off the longest professional baseball game in history, which lasted 33 innings and was played over two days at McCoy Stadium. Pat Harris was on Rochester Sports Phone that night and had to update the game in real time.

"That was the night before Easter Sunday. The funny part about it is that Tom [Tighe] was gonna drive me home. He always did because he lived in Jersey. The game's going 10 innings, 12 innings, 13 innings," Harris recalled.

"So he was out in the lobby there, just laying there catching some Zs, and I go, 'Tom, you better go. Who knows how long this game can last?' He goes, 'It can't last much longer.' I said, 'You never know. I've seen games [go] 25 innings.'"

A team player and a good friend, Tighe decided to stick around.

"I'll never forget. I came out and he was laying on the couch. There was a table with a wild lamp on it, like a hard table, and he had his head pretty close to it. I said 'Tom, you're not gonna believe this,' because he wasn't paying attention. I'm doing the reports that come out," Harris explained. "I said, 'Inning number 20' and he went, 'Shit!' and put his head back really hard and he hit his head into the table. He got up and started cursing."

Tighe would settle back down, and Harris headed back into the booth with no end in sight. Knotted at 1–1 through 20 frames, Rochester plated a run in the top of the 21st but the home Sox tied it back up in the bottom. On they went, matching zeroes until play was mercifully suspended in the 32nd inning at 4:07 a.m. EST.

"Tom stayed the whole way and drove me home," Harris remembered. "We could see the sun coming up. That's how early it was."

The minor league matchup was resumed months later on June 23, ironically during the MLB players' strike, and ended in just 18 minutes when Pawtucket's Dave Koza singled home Marty Barrett for a 3–2 win. The total time of game was 8 hours and 25 minutes, with fourteen hurlers throwing over 800 pitches.

When it was all said and done, future Hall of Famers Cal Ripken Jr. (Rochester) and Wade Boggs (Pawtucket) had gone a combined 6-for-25 at the plate and had each manned all 33 innings at the hot corner for their respective clubs.

———

Jim Memolo opted to work on the nation's birthday in 1985, figuring he'd get out early enough to fit in some celebrating. Even if a game or two went a little long, the night could still be salvaged.

"There was a Fourth of July where I agreed to do the shift, because the latest game was going to end very early and it wasn't going to eat into my evening at all on the Fourth of July," he reminisced.

Holiday or not, Mother Nature had other plans, as did the Atlanta Braves and the visiting New York Mets. Following a 90-minute rain delay, the tilt got underway at 9:04 p.m. — still early enough for Memolo to take part in some post-midnight revelry, right?

Not so fast. The hometown club took an 8–7 lead in the eighth, courtesy of a bases-clearing double by two-time MVP Dale Murphy. Bushy-bearded Hall of Famer Bruce Sutter couldn't close it out though, with the Mets forcing extra innings on a trio of consecutive singles.

The game dragged on and on… and on… with each team plating a pair in the 13th and nothing but blanks until five frames later. Lenny Dykstra's sacrifice fly gave the Mets an 11–10 lead in the 18th, to the likely relief of everyone in the New York dugout, the Atlanta Fulton-County Stadium press box, and Memolo at 919 Third Avenue.

What happened next was a gut punch, and the reason history has since labeled this contest "the Rick Camp game." Out of position players and in dire straits, Braves skipper Eddie Haas was forced to send Camp — batting .060 for his career — to the plate against lefty Tom Gorman, who quickly got ahead 0 and 2 on the Atlanta reliever.

Camp drove the next pitch over the left-field fence, knotting the score yet again in this seemingly never-ending story. New York would score five in the 19th and Ron Darling, despite allowing two unearned runs, would seal the win fittingly by fanning none other than Camp at 3:55 a.m.

Memolo updated his final recording and was mercifully finished, as any thought of enjoying part of the night was long gone. His work wasn't done, however, as the Sports Phone announcer had some explaining to do.

"I know my girlfriend at that time was very suspicious that I showed up at her place in Manhattan five hours later than she expected," Memolo added. "And I said, 'Well, there was a ballgame.' That was met with some skepticism."

Whenever the slate featured only basketball and hockey, the games typically ended before 1 a.m. EST, meaning a reasonable checkout time for the night squad. Things didn't always go according to plan.

"I remember one night [Howie Karpin] got mad at me because the only game of the night was a 10:30 hockey game," said Bob Grochowski. "The Bruins in Los Angeles, they're playing the Kings, the only game at night. Usually hockey games, even in those days, by one o'clock, it's over. That particular night, the Kings decided to honor [general manager and former goaltender] Rogie Vachon."

Vachon became the first player in Kings history to have his jersey retired in a pregame ceremony at The Forum, which was unveiled next to former Lakers greats Elgin Baylor, Jerry West, and Wilt Chamberlain. The festivities weren't the only thing that would delay Grochowski and Karpin's exit that night in 1985.

"The LA stringer called and said, 'Listen, this game's not starting for a while.' So it didn't start until after 11," Grochowski recalled. "The game [a 3–3 tie in overtime] didn't end until after two o'clock and Howie got pissed at me because hockey was my favorite sport."

Whenever the night's last game was taking place in our 50th state, Steve Torre just crossed his fingers and hoped for the best.

"I was hoping I was gonna make the Long Island Railroad, which sometimes if I didn't make that last train I was basically screwed. They didn't have Ubers back then. That was always the thing that stuck in your mind," he explained.

"You were always keeping your fingers crossed that whatever late West Coast game, it wasn't gonna be Hawaii. You could take Cal Santa Barbara against Long Beach, which ended at like 1:15 a.m. That'd be fine, but if Hawaii was tipping off you knew you were in trouble."

For those scheduled for the next morning's shift, crashing at the office was sometimes the best move.

"I would work Friday night, Saturday afternoon, Sunday afternoon, so I was on three of the high-volume shifts back in the day. I wound up staying, sleeping over at the office more often than not on Friday night into Saturday," recalled Memolo.

"It's late night and it's Manhattan, P. J. Clarke's right downstairs. You'd go out for a couple hours, you'd come on back to the office, and you find a couch and sleep for four or five hours."

BRANCHING OUT

There were a number of different Sports Phone lines that initially came out of the New York office. At one time, Sports Phone in Atlanta, Buffalo, New Jersey, New Orleans, Buffalo, Rochester, and a few other locales were all originating from headquarters. Different markets demanded different content, such as the best spots to bait your hook on the Tampa Sports Phone.

"The first one that plateaued out was the New Jersey Sports Phone. Cory Eisner did a lot of that and Walter Burch was heavily involved in doing that. It was very similar, but every local phone company — and that was for New Jersey Bell — wanted to believe that they needed a customized product," Mike Farrell pointed out.

"So you had to emphasize certain things even though the markets were similar. So for a New Jersey Sports Phone, you had to pay attention to Philadelphia. Your home teams were the New York teams, any Jersey teams, but also Philadelphia. So you kind of changed up the order in which you reported scores. You treated them as your home teams."

The customization often went beyond just the local sports teams.

"We had a guy down there [in Tampa] who worked at a UHF station so he was our liaison reporter on-site," Martin shared. "He used to do fishing reports and all sorts of stuff."

As the number of remote dispatches expanded, so did each announcer's responsibilities.

"You would try and do them on an overlap basis," Farrell explained. "If the New York update was being done on the hour, 10 minutes after, 20 after, you could do another city at 5 after, 15 after, 25 after. So you could kind of double it up."

As demand grew nationwide, additional offices were opened. In 1977, one such hub was established in Chicago via Illinois Bell (312-936-1313), occasionally broadcasting motorboat racing results. Another followed in Detroit in 1979 (313-976-1313), which sometimes featured auto racing.

"What was happening is the phone companies around the country were seeing what New York Telephone was doing and the kind of money they were making, so Michigan Bell in Detroit and Illinois Bell for Chicago [wanted a piece]. We briefly did one for Ohio Bell in Cleveland. We also did one in Minneapolis briefly. They saw the money New York was making and they wanted their piece of the pie," Farrell said.

"Some of those we did remotely. I think Minneapolis, they did that out of Chicago. But we had an office in Detroit and one in Chicago. So my job was to go and set up the office, find the space, get the leases signed, do the leasehold improvements, build the little booths in the studios, and then find the staff. Basically, replicate the New York model in Chicago and Detroit."

Like in New York, the new locations eventually offered more than just the main numbers to its caller base. Detroit added a horse racing line, covering two thoroughbred and four harness tracks. They also had lottery, time, and weather hotlines, all managed out of the Sports Phone office — the latter of which was utilized to showcase 976-1313 to a larger audience.

"We had a line that did the weather update and the current temperatures. We hired a service that was well respected in Michigan to do the updates," Cwikla said. "I had some friends at the Detroit NBC affiliate, and they used it as the WDIV weather line. We said, 'We'll give you exclusive rights to that number if you promote Sports Phone so many times a day in your newscast,' and that boosted our numbers right away."

Similar to New York's roster, the initial Chicago staff included some up-and-comers as well as on-air vets.

"David Schuster was one of those young guys who came along at that point in time, but we also hired some veteran guys. Les Grobstein, who had been on the air for a long time in Chicago. Dick Gonski, who did the Bulls games, basically ran the office," Farrell added.

"You needed to have a veteran presence like the Guy LeBow figure to kind of convince all these teams when you came to town that A: you were legit and B: you weren't bookmakers."

 Sports Phone Stories

A Veteran Voice
(*feat. Gary Cohen, Mike Farrell, Stephen LeBow, Nat Mauldin, Peter Newman, Howie Rose, and Mike Walczewski*)

When Sports Phone relaunched in 1975, its staff was made up of mostly young broadcasting hopefuls, each virtually unknown to the public at that time. The powers-that-be realized that a veteran voice was needed to add some legitimacy to their budding operation.

"That whole crew then came into existence because New York Telephone was going to spend the advertising money to make this work. They bought a lot of newspaper ads, hired Guy LeBow who was an old-time TV sportscaster on Eyewitness News, and before that Guy had done a lot of other sports," Mike Farrell explained. "He was very big in the early days of television doing wrestling. He was the wrestling ringside commentator back in the early 1950s."

LeBow was well known in New York broadcasting circles, even recreating San Francisco Giants baseball games for WMCA radio listeners after the team had relocated to the West Coast. Offering Sports Phone callers a recognizable name wasn't the only reason he was hired.

"It was two things. They wanted a name that they could promote. It was a new concept, and there was always this weariness about, are you really just a front for bookmakers? So they wanted somebody with some name recognition and credibility to be essentially the frontman, to kind of calm those waters and reassure everybody that all we're giving you here is information," Farrell added.

"We're giving you scores. We're giving you home runs and pitching changes. We're not giving you point spreads. We're not taking bets. We're not operating as a front for some big bookmaking operation, so having a celebrity was part of that whole effort to legitimatize the whole process."

Often compared to the comedic actor who played a narcissistic anchorman on The Mary Tyler Moore Show, LeBow was an enigma — someone who had the ability to both irritate and inspire his Sports Phone colleagues.

"I cut my teeth really with Guy LeBow. He was the Ted Knight of his day. Big ego, bombastic, but the difference was that Guy really did have a background in journalism and reporting. He was a tiger and he taught me some stuff," Mike Walczewski reminisced.

"My memories of Guy LeBow are very fond. He did teach me a lot. He taught me about aggressiveness and those types of things that help you, and not to be shy when you're trying to work your way around something, and not to be afraid to be told off."

"Fred Weiner hired him to help us become incisive journalists and to get the story. So he [LeBow] would call, in those days it was so much easier, but he would call into clubhouses. We'd occasionally get interviews from the locker room after the game if he influenced the PR guy to do that," Walczewski added, elaborating on that aggressive nature.

As the sports media environment was undergoing both a culture and technology shift, Guy's presence harkened back to a foregone era.

"We all used to get our jollies telling Guy LeBow stories, but he was in a different world. He'd show up at six o'clock wearing a sports jacket, that tie, and have a folded handkerchief. It was crazy because he's going into a little booth," Peter Newman recalled.

"Then he would always go down to P. J. Clarke's and hold court with what he thought were famous people afterward. It was kind of bizarre, because on the one hand you had kids, and an unknown technology or medium or platform just sort of having fun like in the schoolyard and making things up, but everyone loving sports. Then at night you had a guy who used to be on ABC, thinking he was in front of two million people on camera and he was in this little booth. [He had] this really weird voice he would put on, and this man-tan and this orange dye in his hair. It was strange."

Attire and affect differences aside, LeBow had an impact on most who shared an office with him.

"He was Sports Phone's primetime main event, conducting interviews and issuing commentary with a voice that was, inexplicably, both booming and silky at the same time. Guy was also a snappy dresser who wore ascots and used a bronzer, and seemed to behave as if there was always a TV camera in the room with its little red on-air light illuminated," Nat Mauldin elaborated.

"Every night he called the same local restaurant at dinnertime. 'Hello, Chimes, this is Guy LeBow!' would resonate in the hallway, and within minutes an enormous meal was ferried upstairs, which he would proceed to slice in half with surgical accuracy. The first half was his and the second, which he would carefully rewrap night after night, he would bring home to his wife. They spoke on the phone often and it was obvious how much he cared about her, and not just because she was his greatest audience."

"He started out driving me crazy and I ended up genuinely liking him. It was hard not to," Mauldin added.

There was much more to LeBow than old-timey suits and a camera-ready complexion, a fact Mike Walczewski (King Wally) discovered early on.

"Guy was a piece of work. The first night, he was going to Jahn's, which was the ice cream shop on Queens Boulevard. He was heading out there and he goes, 'Say, Wally, I'll save you some cents. I'll give you a ride home,' because he knew I lived in Sunnyside [Queens] and that was on the way. The first night I got dropped off in his friggin' Cadillac boat by Guy LeBow at two in the morning because we were there until the last game ended," Walczewski said.

"Because he had polio as a kid, he walked with a significant limp. He was a remarkable, very gutty man. When he got into the office he would sit. He wouldn't move around a lot. He wasn't wheelchair-bound and he didn't even use a cane but he walked with kind of a semi-dead leg. I admired him really for his guts and attitude."

LeBow even left his mark on staffers who didn't spend much time with him.

"He's the guy who hired me. He was gone from there shortly into my tenure," Gary Cohen recalled. "My feeling is that Guy was a relic from a different era who was trying to breach himself into a more modern under-taking, and he had some good instincts and some that probably were not the best instincts, but he definitely was a motivating force there. There's no question."

Cohen's radio counterpart had a similar recollection.

"Guy was the first star and recognizable name that was hired to give Sports Phone some recognition. He had most recently been the Channel 7 sports anchor. Guy was a bit of a character. He was almost a caricature in some ways," Howie Rose conveyed.

"I learned a lot from Guy. I learned how to be, as I say, aggressive in trying to interview people and creative in thinking of people to interview and to use on the air, so I'll always appreciate Guy for that."

Eventually, LeBow's day-to-day duties began to fizzle out, opening the door for King Wally.

"As time evolved a couple of things happened. He rearranged his deal and instead of leaving after the last game, after a few weeks he started leaving at midnight, 11:30, 12 o'clock. He used to go out on the town and he was dating a couple of women at the time and all that kind of stuff. He was, at that time, already well into his sixties and he had this round face and this orange hair," Walczewski pointed out.

"He started leaving at midnight and I would finish up every shift by myself. That's how I started getting on the actual Sports Phone program. He was starting to do less and less over time in terms of actually going in the booth for updates, and I was doing more and more."

LeBow's son also worked at Sports Phone and explained the circumstances of his father's exit.

"They had a contract dispute... You know, Guy had built up the Sports Phone and music line and New York Report. They had a whole bunch of systems — and Chicago and New Jersey, and I think we had Detroit," Stephen LeBow clarified. "Although Fred Weiner and Phone Programs and the Air Time company had been very good in the beginning and all that, they had a contract dispute and so they parted ways."

But not before befriending The King and his court, however, a friendship that's lasted a lifetime.

"Guy, and me too, absolutely loved Mike Walczewski and [Mike's brother] Rick Walczewski, and the Walczewski family and the mom. You talk about anecdotes and all that. Their mom was a sweetheart and used to sometimes cook and bake for us," LeBow said.

"Mike and Ricky used to come into work with whatever Polish or Polish-American meal she made, kielbasa or dessert or whatever. She was great and we were like family. We worked hard but also played hard ... It was very good, and I went to Mike's wedding and I went to Ricky's wedding back in the day."

———

In Detroit, a pair with some on-air pedigree was brought in to get the ball rolling.

"I came in as the general manager and Kurt Schneider was my assistant. We both came from radio and had been established in the market for at least ten years," John Cwikla recalled. "They wanted us to assemble a team of broadcasters."

While cramming a heap of content into a single message unit at first proved difficult for some at Sports Phone, the Motor City mates had already faced tougher challenges in that regard.

"We had learned from doing our sportscasts on the radio to keep it short," Cwikla added. "Also on the network feeds, because we all free-lanced for AP Radio or ABC Radio, you had to keep your updates within 30 seconds. So, for Sports Phone, getting a minute was a luxury."

Each new office had its full-fledged staff of announcers, writers, managers, etc, although the folks in New York were still often responsible for getting some scores to the counterparts in these new locales, and vice versa.

"We'd have a conference [call], also they were responsible for a bunch of scores. They were responsible for all the Detroit scores and the games in Chicago," Samelson elaborated. "We got all the Chicago-area scores [from them]. Like if Northwestern was playing, they were responsible for that."

All these years later some still recall the number used to coordinate between locations, a line that was often kept open on busy NFL Sundays.

"There are things you never forget," Chuck Cooperstein revealed.

"I mean, look, I still remember the 800 line: 800-223-1040... The conference calls with Detroit and Chicago."

PHONE PSEUDONYMS

Not only did Sports Phone announcers have to tailor their rundowns for different regions when recording for out-of-town lines, in some cases they were asked to use fictitious names in place of their own.

"I started on New Orleans, some of those Southern ones. It was funny because Bob Grochowski is like, 'He can't be using the name Papa on the Southern ones,' so he came up with the name Scott Randolph," recalled Bob Papa.

"So I was Scott Randolph in New Orleans and Atlanta, and when I would get to pinch-hit on the New York channel — the big channel, the big feed, the primetime one — then I would use my regular name."

Cooperstein was Bo Tyler. Drew Esocoff, Drew Scott. In Atlanta, John Giannone was known as John Sanders. Howie Karpin? Nope, Johnny Lee!

Charlie Slowes often handled multiple lines back-to-back and found it hard to keep track of his multiple monikers.

"There was a time where you were doing a New York, an Atlanta, and a New Orleans [line] all in the same shift. I literally hit the button to start and I couldn't remember whether I was Peachtree Pete or Bourbon Street Bob," Slowes recounted. "I didn't know who the hell I was for Sports Phone for a minute."

Like many, Steve Cangialosi found the entire ruse absurd.

"Back then, New York was the precious piece of real estate. You don't get into that booth until you pay your dues. I remember in the early stages, it was so stupid. I was Alan Sanders's friend so they changed my name to Steve Sanders, like that's going to appeal to a Southern fan base. I don't know who had that idea," he explained.

"What makes it more ridiculous is that Alan Sanders had to change his name to something else, but I became Steve Sanders. Like everybody else, you walk in, you're low end of the totem pole. You're doing Atlanta and New Orleans and I guess somebody at some point decided, okay, this guy is acceptable enough where we can put him on the traditional 212-976-1313."

1-900-EVERYTHING

The year 1980 marked the dawn of a decade that would usher in a wave of significant technological advances, including a notable development in the telephone space, the 1-900 number. First introduced that fall, one of the original nationally available pay lines deployed by AT&T encouraged viewers watching a Presidential debate between incumbent Jimmy Carter and former Hollywood actor Ronald Reagan to choose from a pair of phone numbers, dialing the respective line tied to whichever candidate they felt had won the night. Each call resulted in a charge of 50 cents on their next phone bill, no matter the caller's location.

This interactive election activity was part of what AT&T referred to as the media-stimulus side of their Dial-It service, with the other half focused on information-style lines just like Sports Phone — whose parent company Phone Programs was contracted to produce the recorded content heard when ringing up many of these national exchanges.

"The birth of the 900 numbers opened the eyes of the owners of Phone Programs, the people at Air Time," recalled Farrell. "They were now convinced that they could be everything to everybody, and they were going to do every conceivable kind of 900 number that you could imagine."

On September 24, 1980, they jointly launched Dial-It National Sports along with the number 900-976-1313, a service that offered similar content to Sports Phone but was geared more towards a national audience. For the static price of half a buck plus tax, callers throughout the country could now get their score updates without incurring any fluctuating long-distance fees.

It was an instant hit, tallying over a million calls before New Year's Eve. Initially run by Phone Programs and the Sports Phone staff out of their Manhattan office, this national number with the familiar seven digits would later change ownership, a story detailed in the later chapters of this book.

"I remember the national version more than the New York version, because I grew up in Pennsylvania," Sweeny Murti reflected. "But I remember on different sports broadcasts it was the commercial with the cheerleaders, and I know a phone number because of this commercial. It was 900-976-1313."

It was around this same time that the original Sports Phone line out of New York saw its number change from 999-1313 to 976-1313. Those within the service's growing number of markets like Chicago, Detroit, and of course New York were still better served utilizing their regional services — as the cost of a local (or at least semi-local) call could still get them the updates they'd learn to count on in the latter half of the '70s.

LIVE AND DIRECT

Sports Phone eventually introduced an interactive line that substituted a live person on the other end of the phone instead of its traditional recordings, letting callers ask questions and even allowing for a version of real-time play-by-play in certain instances.

"They were starting something called Sports Phone Live, where you could actually call into a line and there was somebody there that you could talk to live who was watching all the games on the screens that they had in the office," Chris Carrino described.

"So you could call up and be like, 'What's going on in the Dodgers-Braves game?' and they will tell you, 'All right, it's bottom of the third. It's 4–0.' They would do like a play-by-play. You could just dictate what game. 'All right, now go look at the Colorado-Baylor game. Tell me what's going on there.'"

This line was manned by some of the service's announcers and provided an unparalleled experience for those willing to pay by-the-minute charges.

"The longer you stayed on the line the more money they were making. Back in the day before people had [home] satellites and things, in this little office in Elmont [Long Island] we had all these TVs. It wasn't anything like state-of-the-art where you had these big flat screens mounted on the wall. They were just all these little TVs all over the place, and they had a satellite that they would be able to dial up. We need to get this game or that game," Carrino added.

"It wasn't like you answered one phone and you just talked to one person. All of a sudden there can be like three or four people on the line with you and they're all asking you about different games, so it was a little crazy. It was like you're an air traffic controller. You've got all these people chiming in and you're trying to give scores, and they could hear each other so it almost became like a group chat."

Occasionally those runways got a little too crowded, and the air traffic controller had to scramble.

"You're calling into a kind of chat line, and it's like 30 gamblers all looking for scores at one time. It was kind of chaotic, but it was certainly entertaining for the people that worked at Sports Phone, maybe more so than the people that were calling," recalled Gordon Damer.

"You ever see the old talk show clip of a guy spinning plates on sticks? That's what it was kind of like. As soon as you got done getting one started, you had to get another one started. There were days where there were a couple of guys and it's manageable. A baseball night or an NBA night, it's not so bad, but an NFL Sunday that thing was jammed with people wanting to know every single game, all at the same time. They're all yelling and screaming. You gotta get them to shut up so people can hear the information. It was kind of a disaster but it worked."

By the fall of 1993 the *Mike and the Mad Dog* show had been airing in afternoons on WFAN for about four years, and Mike Francesa and Chris "Mad Dog" Russo had gained a rabid following among NYC-area sports fans. That notoriety went a long way when Russo mentioned on-air that he was a Sports Phone Live caller.

"That was the time when Mike and the Mad Dog were huge in New York radio, and I think Russo talked about [Sports Phone Live] one day and said that he had used it, that he would call, and that was like a huge deal," Carrino said. "All of a sudden that became very popular and people always wondered, are they going to talk to Chris Russo if he called in."

Switching from Sports Phone Live to 976-1313 and back could be a challenge for announcers.

"In the 900 line, I was looking to extend the time I was talking to people on the phone. In the booth, I had a limit to the time," Rich Coutinho explained. "I wanted to make sure I got all the stuff in, but I also wanted to make sure whatever market I was on, whether it was New York, Chicago, or Detroit, you had to tailor the reports [to the market]."

Sports Phone Stories

Luck of the Irish
(feat. Rich Coutinho)

Rich Coutinho was covering Sports Phone Live when a nervous gambler showed a keen interest in the Fighting Irish.

"One day, sitting at the live line, a guy was calling me and he wanted to know what was going on in the Notre Dame football game. As you're talking with this guy, you're letting him know what's going on because I'm seeing it on my TV screen. Little by little, he's telling me he bet a tremendous amount on Notre Dame. They were underdogs in that game and they were getting, I think, five points," Coutinho recalled.

"The game was fairly close and their [Notre Dame] opponent took a six-point lead late, and he was just miserable. As the game is winding down I said, 'Don't be so despondent.' He goes, 'Yeah, they're gonna punt the ball to Notre Dame and they're not gonna have enough time to do anything.' I said, 'There is a chance they don't want the punt to be blocked, and having a six-point lead, they may take a safety.' He said, 'You think that could really happen?' Well, it could and that's exactly what happened."

Coutinho's prediction came true, landing him some free booze courtesy of that grateful caller.

"We were talking a lot the whole time. I was telling him I was a bartender. He asked me what my favorite drink was and I said, 'Stoli's [Stolichnaya vodka] and orange juice is always what I love.' A week later, one of the guys at Sports Phone says, 'Rich, there was a package delivered to you this week.' It was a case of Stoli's from the guy. He was telling me how much he'd bet on the game and I was saying to myself, that's a mortgage down payment."

———

Sports Phone Stories

Hot Stove
(feat. Jim Cerny)

MLB's winter meetings are such a widely covered event these days that the league's own network broadcasts live from early in the morning until late at night for most of its duration, keeping fans enthralled with the latest free agent signings and trade rumors. On top of that, insiders and scribes from every imaginable outlet roam the hotel hallways seeking out the latest gossip, tweeting it out to the masses within seconds.

Long before there was such a thing as the internet or MLB Network, the annual gathering of baseball executives, agents, and others involved in the game took place with very little fanfare attached. Phone Programs saw an opportunity, and was able to keep fans connected with Sports Phone Live. Based on Howie Karpin's suggestion, the brass created the Winter Meetings Hotline beginning in 1983.

"Lon Rogoff and I, for several years in a row, represented Sports Phone. We would cover the winter meetings," Jim Cerny recalled. "WFAN had started, so Suzyn Waldman would be out there covering it, but nobody else was out there. And of course in those days no internet, so you weren't reading Joel Sherman or seeing his tweets every couple minutes."

Even with WFAN relaying updates on-air from time to time throughout the meetings, they couldn't provide real-time news in the fashion the live line could offer.

"We could provide instant access, here's what's going on. So we would work, I'm not exaggerating, 18-hour days down there and Lon would be doing the Sports Phone Live the whole time. I would be filing. I would tape reports for 976-2525, Sports Phone Extra," Cerny explained.

"You'd get an interview, say I get this GM, get some quotes, put it together. We're both constantly getting information. We worked our rear ends off but I was a kid, young guys in their twenties. It was great. You were right in the thick of things."

As talk of a possible signing or a trade broke, Cerny and Rogoff had it on Sports Phone almost instantly.

"I would come running back, I just talked to so and so in the lobby, and XYZ this, you know. Oh, he might be signing with the Angels or whatever," Cerny said. "So then Lon would go live. You've got all these people on Sports Phone Live like, 'What? What? What's going on?' Lon's like, 'Hold on, I think we have breaking news.'"

The live line charged callers by the minute, racking up a pretty penny for Phone Programs during events like the winter meetings.

"I'm telling you, 14, 18 hours a day. Some of these people were on for big chunks of that. 'Alrighty, Lon, I've got to go back to work but I'll call you back in 25 minutes.' It was nuts," Cerny marveled.

"We were a really good team together, and sometimes he'd want to get up and start working the room so I'd handle Sports Phone Live while he did that. Things like the winter meetings or a big boxing match or whatever the example might be, a big event, these people were hooked."

———

CHAPTER 3
TELEPHONE TRAILBLAZERS

Hundreds of Emmy awards and nominations. Inductees in an array of halls of fame spanning various states, sports, and areas of expertise. Prominent faces and voices of legendary franchises. Esteemed hosts, producers, and directors in the realms of radio and television. Notable editors and writers from a broad spectrum of publications.

One might assume these accolades belong to the distinguished alumni of a prestigious broadcasting and journalism school or perhaps the veterans of an influential media network. Think again. These are merely a selection of the many honors and achievements of the collective individuals behind Sports Phone and Phone Programs.

"At the time I don't think anyone realized it, but Sports Phone was a breeding ground for some of the most talented sports broadcasters and play-by-play announcers in America today," Pat O'Keefe remarked.

THE ORIGINAL EIGHT

Longtime Yonkers Raceway track announcer Bob Meyer was tasked with hiring the service's initial staff for its 1975 revival — a group that would include Howie Rose.

"Fred Weiner and Bruce Fogel, I think, were the guys who were the money men behind it and they hired 'Bullet' Bob Meyer, who had been Marv Albert's radio statistician, to put it together," Rose recalled.

Along with Rose, Guy LeBow, and Mike Farrell were a gifted quintet that rounded out the staff which got Sports Phone up and running again. Arguably the most recognizable voice in Sports Phone history, Mike Walczewski — aka King Wally — was initially the full-time producer on the weeknight crew, with LeBow creating the rundowns.

"I was one of the original eight on the restart. I remember all eight guys very well," he explained. "The daytime guys were Denis McNamara, who at that time was at WLIR on Long Island. Denis was the producer of the weekdays and the announcer was a guy by the name of Peter Newman."

Newman later produced more than 30 films featuring a who's who of Hollywood actors including Jeff Daniels, Harvey Keitel, William Hurt, Laura Linney, Gary Oldman, and Michael J. Fox.

"There were so few news services at that time that you could call the clubhouse after a game and say, 'I want to talk to some member of the Detroit Tigers and they'd get on the phone. We had a very primitive [setup]," Newman said, describing the work environment in the early going. "The entire setup was a booth with an old microphone, a soundproof booth, and we had a ticker. There were certainly no computers. [At times] I was the oldest guy who was in the room and I was 21. Most of the people were like 19 and 20."

McNamara's dreams were more on the music side, eventually becoming involved in International A&R for heavy hitters such as Van Morrison, Andrew Lloyd Webber, ABBA, and the Bee Gees.

"I was already at LIR doing part-time work. I started at Sports Phone and then I picked up some shifts," McNamara recalled. "I used to fill in [on-air] when Peter wasn't there. A bit of what I did was coach Peter because he hadn't been an announcer before that."

Later a pioneer himself in the world of rock n' roll, McNamara reflected on the crew that started a movement when it came to reporting on sports.

"[When talking about] the original group, my immediate thought was, 'Oh, we were like [The] Beatles.' It was a glorious time and I guess in some ways I may have overlooked the fact that I was a part of something so special," he suggested. "Doing as much as we could with such a small staff and achieving a lot. Now that you look back on it, it was such a moment in time."

Saturday and Sunday afternoons were often hectic, especially with a full college football and NFL slate on the menu.

"The weekend day crew, the daytime guy was Paul Gourvitz. He was the daytime weekend announcer," Walczewski said. "The daytime weekend producer, I think he went to Seton Hall, his name was Keith Parry. I think he ended up out of sports."

When things weren't so busy, Gourvitz was adept at filling airtime.

"Paul Gourvitz was the PA announcer, first at Island Garden [Arena] for the Nets and then he followed them to Nassau Coliseum, and also did PA for the Islanders. Paul was funny. I remember having gotten back to New York from out of town and calling Sports Phone. It was a Saturday afternoon. It was rainy," Rose recalled.

"It was early in the baseball season and I called Sports Phone to see what's going on and Paul goes, 'Paul Gourvitz for Sports Phone. It's raining out. There's nothing happening right now, but boy, what a great movie on Channel Five. Errol Flynn is in...' whatever. I forgot what movie it was. What a character!"

The weekend night duo featured Farrell as producer and Rose in the booth. The unofficial director of Sports Phone at the time, Meyer made it a cast of nine.

"I went up with [Bob Meyer] one time and sat in the booth [at Yonkers Raceway] and watched him do a couple of races and it was thrilling. It was just unbelievable because it's such a talent," McNamara recalled.

"I'm sure they just memorize things from the colors, and of course, you can't bet on a horse because it'll throw your whole announcing style off. It's that old Robert Klein routine, 'Run, you sonofabitch,' or whatever. It was just fascinating, and he was the man."

Sports Phone Stories

Money Tree
(feat. Howie Rose)

Darryl Sittler had a game for the ages in early 1976, notching a record-tying achievement that still stands at the time of publication. Howie Rose was in the Sports Phone office that night and managed to get a one-on-one with the Hall of Fame center.

"One of my most memorable nights was working in February of '76. Guy LeBow really taught us, especially Guy, how to be aggressive and line up interviews. So on this one night, Darryl Sittler of the Toronto Maple Leafs scored six goals in a game to tie the single-game NHL record and he also had four assists, so he had a 10-point night," Rose recalled.

"You can imagine how huge a story that was in Toronto. Well, I call Maple Leaf Gardens, got the switchboard, asked for the home locker room, please. Somebody picked up and I said 'Howie Rose, Sports Phone New York, would love to do a feature, a quick interview with Darryl Sittler, if we could,' and in pretty short order Darryl came to the phone."

Not only did he land the interview for Sports Phone, but Rose was able to cash in on the big night through some other big-name outlets.

"I don't know how long I talked to him for, but we were also allowed to and even encouraged to — after we did the interview obviously — to cut up the interview and use those cuts on Sports Phone. But we were also allowed, because they wanted our name out [there], we could sell it," Rose explained.

"We could cut those things up and sell it to UPI audio, AP. I made a little bit of money that night by selling that interview to other outlets, and sometimes it didn't only have to be a national network if you knew a station out of town. I don't remember who else I might have sold it to, but I made some money that night cashing in on the Darryl Sittler interview."

———

TRUE PIONEERS

It can be argued that Sports Phone and Phone Programs as a whole are at least partially responsible for many innovations still utilized to this day, not only in broadcasting but across the entire news, sports, and entertainment landscapes.

"It's like the [Six Degrees of] Kevin Bacon, that you seem to pop up with everything," Charlie DeNatale said. "Sports Phone has this connection. Today it pops up everywhere."

We've already mentioned several including minute-long updates, Sports Phone Live, the Quickie Quiz, real-time programming from major events like the Olympics, landing one-on-one exclusives through any means necessary (calling clubhouses, hotels, etc.), announcing rundowns in-venue as opposed to the booth, and more.

"All these people are yelling, 'Forget that guy. I don't care about that game! What about the other game?' People kind of arguing over each other. It was crazy. It was a brilliant idea," Chris Carrino said about the live line. "It was probably a harbinger of other things that came along. Obviously, technology has changed that now but it was pretty primitive and crazy."

The first and most obvious contribution to sports media, in general, was exposing the massive desire for live scores updated as often as current technology permits, which nowadays is instant.

"Back then the Associated Press wasn't even real time, per se," John Giannone opined. "We were as real time as you could get."

Before Sports Phone and its stunning call volumes demonstrated the breadth of public hunger, it wasn't very clear to anyone working in that space.

"There was a slow recognition of the degree to which sports were not just sports, but an amazing source of content and the passion growing for it. So for example, today 81 of the top 100 Nielsen-rated shows last year were NFL football, so that we would get to a time where a sport would not only be the most popular form of sports, but the most popular form of televised entertainment, that showed the depth of the passion that fans had and there was a market that was completely unexplored," explained agent Leigh Steinberg.

"You had consumers who were anxious for much more content than what they were getting, and sports played such a central role in their life that they were thirsting for a deeper level of content and immediacy. Sports Phone illustrated and was a precursor and an early recognizer of an unexploited market."

Those in the gambling industry also flocked to Sports Phone right away.

"They did a great job and it was very inventive. They were the Elon Musk of today," said Jim Feist, acclaimed handicapper who developed his own dial-up service discussed in detail later in this book.

It wasn't only scores that kept the public coming back to Sports Phone, but their mantra of delivering breaking news fast and first.

"Some of this predated the explosive growth of sports talk radio. The only information you got in real time was either a sportscast on TV at 11 o'clock or the quarter after the hour updates on WCBS or WINS. There were times when we were involved in crazy, chaotic situations like during the Yankee era of managers being hired and fired left and right. We would be there to report that out as soon as that happened," Farrell said.

"If it was a big, big story you could count on Sports Phone to at least have a headline on it. In 60 seconds you couldn't do a whole in-depth story, but you could give everybody the headline, you know,

Billy Martin fired for the 19th time or whatever it happened to be. That was a big component of what we did."

The professionals at Sports Phone also helped shape the market for team-specific content, creating separate hotlines for locals including the Knicks, Rangers, and Yankees — the latter voiced by revered radio man John Gordon, part of the club's broadcast crew in the early to mid-'80s.

"Long before the internet was available to everybody and teams could create their own websites and generate their own content, they kind of had an idea that they would like to be able to provide information and insight to their fans, but at the same time maintain control of it," Farrell explained.

"So if you had a Ranger hotline, you weren't going to go on there necessarily to rip the Rangers. In some instances, we were providing them directly for the teams and in some cases they were independent. There were all sorts of different models that were evolving, but the idea was you used the telephone as an information source which was still a relatively new concept, and I can find out about my team by dialing a number."

During the web's relative infancy, Steinberg helped create a pair of companies both inspired by Sports Phone.

"Sports Phone was a revelation that was years ahead of its time, and I actually used it as an inspiration for a later company I created which was Athlete Direct. Athlete Direct was in the very early phases, about [the year] 2000, of the internet. You still had to use AOL, but what Sports Phone had shown me is the inexhaustible desire for more information about teams and leagues and players," he said.

"We signed Ken Griffey Jr. and Michael Jordan and football quarterbacks, and they wrote weekly diaries and they talked about their charitable foundations. We designed an e-commerce to buy from it, but the genesis for that thinking came from a concept like Sports Phone, which filled a niche that wasn't being filled, but understand that you have to take yourself back into a time that seems so primitive, so embryonic that I don't know if a young person today could even conceptualize."

The real-life inspiration for the 1996 film *Jerry Maguire*, Steinberg and a partner later launched another online portal also based partially on the Sports Phone team hotline model.

"We created another business with Frank Cooney called Pro Sports xChange, and it operated on the premise that if you're a fan of a particular team it was hard to follow that team except with the line in your local paper. So you're living in Los Angeles, but you know what? You're a New York Yankee fan and you're desperate for all things Yankee. Batting average, steals, injuries, everything else."

"We went out and hired a series of writers from across the country so that every single team in baseball and football had a daily briefing. All of that stems from the embryonic days of Sports Phone where fans who had a special interest in sports, a team, a player, and a passion for knowing everything about that as quickly as possible."

Sports Phone Stories

Holy Cow! (Almost) Phil Rizzuto for Sports Phone
(feat. Stephen LeBow)

One of the most beloved characters in Yankees franchise history, Hall of Famer Phil Rizzuto suited up for 13 seasons, earning five All-Star nods and winning an AL MVP — missing 1943 to 1945 while serving in the Navy during World War II. Upon retirement, the diminutive shortstop went on to capture the hearts of new generations of Yankee fans as a longtime radio and TV broadcaster over the next 40 years.

Sports Phone announcer Guy LeBow was a friend of Rizzuto's and hoped to bring him on board with the rapidly growing service. Guy's son Stephen was also a Sports Phone announcer in the 1970s and recalls the company's efforts to court the lifelong Yankee.

"My father came up with the idea. I'm sure it initiated with him. Let's bring on some other people, either for a shift or a guest shot. We'll tape some things with them and put it on," Stephen LeBow recalled.

"So Phil Rizzuto came up, broadcasting for the Yankees, friend of the family, all this for many years. Phil comes down and they go out to lunch with heads of the phone company. Mind you, this is 40 years ago, but they go out, they have a nice lunch and they explained to him how everything works technologically and all that."

The Scooter seemed impressed at first, although he had to run it by his better half.

"They bring them to Phone Programs, to the studios on 919 Third Avenue. Nice studio, so on and so forth. They're sitting down in my father's office. My father's trying to feel Phil out so he says, 'So what do you think, Phil?' Phil is hemming and hawing a little bit," LeBow said.

"Tell me what you think."

"I got to think about it a little bit."

"Do you have any questions or what's on your mind?"

"I got to talk to Cora [Rizzuto's wife]. We got to talk it over."

"What else?"

"Guy, I gotta tell you something."

"What's that?"

Loquacious with a penchant for drifting off topic mid-inning to wish a friend well or dish on his favorite cannoli spot, the man who affectionally called boothmates "huckleberry" and often scurried to the press box elevator an inning or two early to beat postgame traffic had a major logistical concern.

"Now mind you, they used to get like 100,000 calls a day. So Phil says, 'Guy, I love the idea. It's great, providing all the sports information right away, timely basis and all that, but I don't know. How am I going to answer 40,000 calls at the same time?' Everybody was stunned," LeBow recounted with a hearty laugh.

"How do you answer that? So Guy said, 'No, no, no, Phil. You don't have to pick up the phone and answer so many thousands of calls at the same time.' He declined. He declined to talk it over with Cora and he declined because of that. He was afraid. He didn't know how he would be physically capable of answering all those phone calls."

———

REAL REPORTERS

Sports Phone reporters often faced resistance from conventional media members, mainly those representing a newspaper or radio station, as they were initially looked upon as interlopers who were interrupting the natural order of things. While traditional outlets were limited in terms of how quickly they could get information out to the masses, those roaming the locker room with a Sports Phone mic in hand could get their audio out to hundreds of thousands of people within mere minutes.

"You just didn't want to be known as a tape head, somebody who just stuck their microphone in, got sound bites, sent it back to the office, and called it a night. You wanted to show I'm a real reporter. I know what's going on. I have real questions to ask," Jim Cerny explained. "There were times when [a beat writer] asked a question but we all got the quote, and they'd be furious at you. Literally, there were times they would try and turn off my tape recorder."

This tension was palpable in many a scrum but would fade over time as the onsite Sports Phone personnel proved themselves worthy of a press credential.

"It was an adversarial relationship which to a point I understood, but it also meant a lot then when you gained relationships with some of these people because they respected you," Cerny added. "They were like, 'Oh, he knows what he's talking about. He's asking his questions. He's going to his own sources.' You build your own sources or people you're comfortable with in a locker room and they become your go-to guys."

You didn't necessarily have to be in-venue to eventually gain the respect of old-school media types, either.

"I think it's amazing that when you talk about Howie Rose and Al

Trautwig and Gary Cohen and [Steve] Cangialosi and [Bob] Papa and [John] Giannone, none of those people had to leave New York," Alan Sanders said. "They had street cred from Sports Phone and parlayed that into all those next levels."

Quickie Quiz

Q: Which acclaimed college basketball coach gave Rich Ackerman the inside scoop?

A: Lou Carnesecca

Ackerman: "It was a year St. John's did not make the tournament, but they went to the NIT and they were gonna play Ole Miss in the first round. We had set something up with [St. John's coach] Lou Carnesecca. I was a huge college basketball fan at the time, mostly because I was in college. The fact Louie gave us time, for me, it was a big emotional lift ... Not that he was the condescending type, but he treated [Sports Phone] as if we were legitimate, which we were, but I thought that gave me and us validation. How nice he was and how gracious he was with his time, but also he was very informative."

"He gave scouting reports. Ole Miss had a guy by the name of Gerald Glass. He explained everything and how they had to be careful of Glass, and he was the guy they had to shut down and things like that. Those things really stood out, because we just weren't guys who read wire copy. I think we were all obviously looking for a bigger thing and a break, but we had journalistic instincts. I thought that really helped us, and really paved the way and made us much more than a place that you just called for a score or two."

 # Sports Phone Stories

Courtside at the Garden
(feat. Howie Karpin, Jerry O'Neil, Andy Roth, Alan Sanders, Charlie Slowes, and Tommy Tighe)

Covering games and press conferences on-site for Sports Phone was a privilege that allowed its young reporters a chance to get up close and personal with some of the world's biggest and brightest. Coined the Mecca of Basketball, Madison Square Garden has always been considered extra special by players, fans, and media members alike.

Not only was Sports Phone credentialed for games at MSG, but for many years they were seated courtside.

"I said, 'Where am I sitting?' Because I went to the normal area where the radio guys were. I wasn't [listed] there. I wasn't in the upper hockey press box. I said 'Where the hell am I?' [The Knicks' public relations head] says, 'You're courtside, Tommy.' I said, 'Courtside?' Hey, great. I didn't know the situation, what courtside was," recalled Tommy Tighe.

"The other side was all sold, like the Spike Lee [seats]. What is he talking about? There's a table with three seats. I said, 'You're serious? This is preseason. You're serious?' He says, 'Yeah, I don't know about the playoffs, Tommy, but regular season you're here.' I said 41 freakin' games and five preseason games. I can take that. I'd go on Saturday nights when I didn't have to go. That's the best seat I'd ever had and will ever have."

Andy Roth once had a run-in with the "Round Mound of Rebound" in that seat.

"When I was at one 76ers game, Charles Barkley jumped over the press table and he knocked over my tape recorder," Roth described. "You can hear him say, 'You all right?' I had Barkley coming right at me. It was awesome."

Roth was a little more starstruck when he found himself a few feet away from one of his hardwood heroes in a prior season.

"This is my favorite story of all time. You know, huge Sixers fan, huge Doc [Julius Erving] fan. When I started the business in '79, I may have covered every game of his at the Meadowlands and at the Garden," Roth reminisced.

"One time I'm sitting courtside before the game. They're coming out for the warmups. He points to me, like to say hello. Another time at the Meadowlands he and I were the last two people in the locker room and he said to me, 'Hey, can you do me a favor? Can you watch my jersey while I shower?' and I said 'No problem, Doc.'"

Howie Karpin was on the floor for both halves of the NBA's dynamic duo in the 1980s.

"I remember seeing the Celtics with [Larry] Bird and I saw Lakers with Magic [Johnson]," Karpin said. "I sat up front."

Charlie Slowes recalls sitting in Sports Phone's premium seat during some of New York's lean years, back when head coach Hubie Brown would occasionally get into it with the fans.

"I remember coming to a game at the Garden when the Knicks were terrible around that time. That was like the Hubie Brown, Ray Williams, Micheal Ray Richardson Knicks. For us growing up in New York seeing only nine or ten thousand people in the Garden was a shock," Slowes explained.

"I remember how bad they were, and there was a foul, second quarter or whatever, and the Garden is really quiet. A guy's taking a free throw and a fan's yelling, 'Hubie, Hubie! Take him out! He sucks! Take him out,' and Hubie turns around and goes, 'Who would *you* put in?'"

Later a lead television analyst, Brown kept a sense of humor during those rough seasons.

"Hubie was the best," Karpin said. "I remember he wanted to throw a quarter to a guy, because the guy was ragging him the whole night, and he said he wanted to throw a quarter to him and tell him to take the subway and get out of here."

The location was so amazing that Jerry O'Neil pined to move back over to Sports Phone, after shifting to a business role with Phone Programs in '86.

"I went to work for [no relation] Floyd [O'Neil] and then I really wanted to get back into sports and continue to go as a stringer to the Garden and sit courtside at that time even though they sucked," O'Neil mentioned. "And I'd have to get lectured by Hubie Brown and all that, but yeah, I got back into it."

Of all the Sports Phone memories made from their courtside perch, Alan Sanders's was an all-timer.

"Before courtside seats at the Garden and every other arena were reserved for celebrities, our seat for Knicks games was maybe four or five seats to the left of the scorer's table by the visitor's bench. I lucked into covering [Michael] Jordan's first game as a Bull at the Garden. To this day, occasionally MSG will have the archive series. One of them is *Great Garden Debuts*, I think it's part of that series. You'd have to freeze frame it and you'd have to know me, it's not like clear clear, but I know it's me and that's enough. " Sanders conveyed.

"What I do remember — it might have been Rory Sparrow, I'd have to look it up — but in typical 1984 Knicks fashion, one of the Knicks guards threw a very ill-advised cross-court pass and Jordan intercepted it like five feet in front of me, because it was a really bad cross-court pass that never should have been. That was the play where I'd never heard a sound like it. It wasn't like an exhale cheer. It was like this enormous intake of 20,000 people just going, 'Uh, oh, here he comes.' Jordan's going in by himself. He did the behind-the-back rock the baby, whatever ridiculous move by himself, which Marv [Albert], I believe, called as one of the all-time Garden dunks. I love seeing that, because I remember he stole the ball literally right in front of me."

———

ON-THE-AIR SUPPLY

Before long it seemed like Sports Phone was everywhere, and terrestrial radio stations far and wide would often utilize the service's audio to play for their own listeners. The main client for these sound clips was the country's oldest all-news radio station, NYC-based WINS (1010 AM).

"It wasn't just in that building. Sports Phone was everything we did outside of that building. It was that delivery every night to WMCA, WCBS, and WNEW. Sometimes sitting at home listening to the radio, I'd hear the audio that I had cut up and prepared that was now airing over 1010 WINS," recalled sound editor Cedric Dew. "Different stations were using Sports Phone's audio as prominently as anything that was out there, and to have been a part of that was just absolutely amazing."

Postgame audio such as locker room interviews would be sent from field reporters and stringers to the Sports Phone office, where staffers including Ken Samelson would edit and package the cuts accordingly before hand-delivering them to the WINS offices near Grand Central Station. Other outlets were typically fed their sound over the phone, although some would also be serviced in person including WHN (later WFAN), WMCA, and WABC.

"We put them on carts and we'd also have to type out a sheet with all the incues and outcues. Cut number three is Davey Johnson talking about [Dwight] Gooden's performance, putting in the incue and the outcue on. For the home teams, it was easy. We'd have somebody come back from the game with a cassette and we just pop it in and cue it up," Samelson explained.

"When one of the New York teams [was] on the road you were at the mercy of whoever was covering it, and there were nights where it was tough to get tape. When Billy [Martin] was managing the Yankees, when they lost, sometimes you couldn't get anything on the road, or the stuff you got you couldn't use [due to vulgarity]."

With their backs against the wall, Samelson and others found ways to cover themselves with generic sound bites. This led to some interesting situations.

"There'd always be some evergreen stuff. [Mike Celentano] says you could always pop it in because it's a 162-game season, especially with baseball where you could have a general thing. If you had a road game where the stringer just didn't show up, or the tape he gave you was unusable," Samelson added.

"One night the guy that was working at WINS was Ira Mellman. He called back and just said, 'You guys, I know this wasn't from tonight's game,' and the exact phrase he used was, 'You guys are fucking with journalism.' Those were the exact words. I said, 'Look, Ira, I'm doing the best I can, man.'"

The first day this audio concierge service was offered by New York Sports Phone ended up being one of the more memorable in the city's storied baseball history. It also happened to land on a national holiday.

"It was July 4, 1983, the day of the [Yankees southpaw Dave] Righetti no-hitter. Mets were in Philadelphia that night, so we wanted to make an impression by having someone go to Philly to cover the Mets and bring the sound back to Manhattan so they would have studio sound from a road game," recalled Howie Karpin, who volunteered for the assignment at Veterans Stadium.

"There were no ISDN lines or anything like that. The Yankee game was [at Yankee Stadium] in the afternoon. I was taking a train to Philadelphia, so I'm following the game on the radio as best as possible and I'm missing this no-hitter. Steve Carlton pitched against the Mets that night and he took a no-hitter into the sixth or seventh that game. I brought the sound back and drove Ken [Samelson] to WINS and then I took him home."

The team at Detroit's Sports Phone office applied a similar tactic with a couple of their local stations.

"Because we were at all the games, we would get all the sound bites that we would collect and we would put them on a cassette or a tape, and then we delivered to the all-news stations, WWJ, WJR," John Cwikla described. "They would use our sound bites on the air, which gave them a prominence that they were at the games. It sounded like that reporter was at the game."

The Michigan-based outfit agreed to a notably different compensation structure, bartering sound for air time.

"It was not so much selling it for revenue, but I was selling it to promote the services that we were providing. They would air a quick 10-second, 'Get the latest scores on Sports Phone,'" Cwikla added. "We were trading for that service. That's what was kind of unique about it. We were not just promoting Sports Phone. We were promoting the weather line, the lottery line, the time line, and the horse racing line."

Radio stations didn't rely on Sports Phone only for audio clips. They sometimes used the service before giving updates on-air, something a broadcasting legend did at CBS with the help of his interns.

"So I graduated college in '87. I interned at CBS Radio after I graduated with Ed Ingles and Bill Schweitzer. They had tickers and everything, but there would be times in the evening when Schweitzer would be like, 'Hey, the ticker, I'm not sure this is up to date. Call Sports Phone,'" Jim Cerny remembered. "So I'd call Sports Phone and I'd update the scores and stuff for him. He might be watching the Mets and Yankees, but he needed the other scores, too."

Sportscasters in Detroit also dialed in often to get the latest before going live.

"You've got to remember, cable was just coming out. There weren't that many games on TV as there are now," Cwikla said. "So for the anchors on radio or TV to get their stuff before they went on the air, it was easier to just go on Sports Phone and get it."

 # Sports Phone Stories

AP Poll Hijinks
(feat. Bob Grochowski)

Before the internet was available, media members often used Sports Phone as a source for scores and news. This backfired one night when the NCAA basketball rankings were directly impacted by an unnamed announcer's on-air blunder.

"[He] was so enthusiastic and such a bright guy, but he didn't know anything about college basketball. So [he] had the wrong score on a Temple game and they were [ranked] number one. He said that Temple lost and he didn't know. It didn't register with him, so he kept reading the score on the system," recalled Bob Grochowski.

"I don't know who was on that night but they said, 'Hey, check your slate. You have the Temple score wrong.' He didn't know what it meant because he had no interest in college basketball, but then the next day it was reported that somebody didn't vote for Temple unanimously because they heard on Sports Phone that they lost."

The announcer was understandably bummed, so Bobby G. tried to lighten the mood.

"He felt very, very bad about the whole thing. I remember trying to make a joke with him," Grochowski said. "So I said, 'Jesus, you would think a Jewish guy would know the Temple score.' I know that he laughed about that because he felt so bad."

————

YOUR HOME FOR HOOPS

This sound-sharing game was ramped up exponentially when the NBA Hotline was conceived, as any radio station from around the country could access the cuts that were put on there. Sports Phone updated that line once in the afternoon and then again on the overnight shift, featuring commentary and clips from the schedule's two most noteworthy games.

"The thing I loved about the NBA Hotline was that it was about the performers, the people who were top performers for the night and you get to have like two athletes basically talking about their performance and what went into it," Dew recounted.

"We could summarize a game performance in 10-12 seconds. Athletes talk in clichés. The question is, what cliché is not going to be the same cliché that's going to be everywhere else? What are they gonna say a little bit different that gave us our signature sound bite for the night, that allowed us to be unique and make everybody else say 'Damn, why didn't we have that sound bite?'"

As on point as the Sports Phone staffers often were, they couldn't predict the future.

"We usually set up stringers for certain games, but we may have to change on the fly if a game that we didn't originally set up became the game of the night if somebody had 60 points or something like that," Karpin explained. "The announcer also had to do the scores every night on that line. He had to read the scores too besides the cuts, besides the two games they highlighted."

Over time the NBA Hotline morphed into a melodious orchestration between the stringers, the editor, and the moderator for the night, leading to some tight sound packages that were heard nationwide.

"Whether it was Michael Jordan or whether it was John Stockton or whoever, it would really shape how we had to put this thing together because we always wanted the best. I'd make a phone call to get the bite that we needed for the piece. You probably ended up getting maybe ten minutes worth of [audio], and you go in chop that baby down, and now you got two or three sound bites," Dew said.

"In between you and the moderator, you would decide what was the best sound bite and then now you got your two bites for the morning, and then you also did it for the midday. So you did it for your current update but you also did it for the next day."

Sports Phone Stories

Time Is On My Side
(feat. Cedric Dew)

Not everyone who made their bones at Sports Phone went into a traditional media role afterward. A whiz at audio and video editing, Cedric Dew has spent the decades since helping others.

"While I was working at Sports Phone I was also working [as a free-lancer] for national Pro-Am city leagues, which was sponsored by the NBA and in 26 cities. We were doing the Pro-Am all around the country, which at the time was a nonprofit organization," Dew explained.

"One of the ways we generated additional money was I started video-taping many of the games, and what I'd do is I'd edit a highlight reel, and those highlight reels started generating funds. We'd get sneaker endorse-ments. They could see the image of it and hear the real-life experience."

The endorsements ran the gamut, starting with ASICS and Rebook and eventually leading to a deal with Nike. Dew parlayed that freelance gig into other nonprofit endeavors, running his own tournaments for about a year before getting a job with a well-known New York City youth orga-nization.

"I went to Madison Square Boys & Girls Club and worked out of East Flatbush, where I was able to create an AAU traveling team as well as the Future Prospects — which was a sports program for kids. I created Flat-bush Gladiators, which was a spinoff of American Gladiators, for kids who wanted to engage in sports and fitness. I just did a whole host of sports programs," Dew recalled.

"I started moving up through the ranks, became program director and I found myself more running facilities after that. I did that for the next 11 years at Boys and Girls Club, got several promotions while I was there, then I came to the YMCA in 2002."

Still at the YMCA at the time of publication, Dew credits much of his success in these humanitarian roles to his time at 919 Third Avenue.

"Sports Phone made me a better listener. Sports Phone exposed me to people from different cultures. Sports Phone made me ten times more productive than most of my colleagues because we worked by a clock every second of every day we were in there," he said.

"I always believe that the greatest attribute you can acquire in business is how you utilize time. I can still hear a second hand ticking. At WNEW there was one ticking constantly in the last minute leading up to a newscast, and at Sports Phone it felt the same way."

Dew has made quite an impact on the YMCA organization over the past 21-plus years, ascending to vice president of transitional housing at the Jamaica branch and earning a litany of awards and accolades including being named a Black Man of Distinction for Queens and Brooklyn. Much of this work requires coordinating meetings and speaking to large groups, skills he first honed at Sports Phone.

"People don't understand how long a minute really is, and it was the time at Sports Phone and places like that where we got to look at time in a different way. We saw differently because every minute mattered. Whether you're doing an audio feed on the NBA Hotline or whether you're doing the 976 one-minute, you were constantly doing that while pacing yourself to time. And so, time in its smallest fragments in seconds and minutes," Dew said, expanding upon the concept.

"To me, time was the greatest value lesson that I took away [from Sports Phone]. I still today out-achieve many of my colleagues with that sense of time, and a sense of what it means. As someone who now is a public speaker, whether it's board meetings, leadership meetings, or whatever, I talk in sound bites. I understand how valuable a 12-second sound bite is, and so I talk that way because I know that for 12 seconds I can hold you. A 25-second sound bite, I can start losing people."

"All of our conversations at Sports Phone helped me talk through so much of my life as a young man."

———

LADIES FIRST

There was a time when newsrooms, recording booths, and anchor desks were largely dominated by a male presence. This proved especially true when it came to sports media in particular, where a woman breaking into the business was perceivably more difficult than going through Mean Joe Greene and the Steel Curtain or Mike Singletary and the '85 Bears.

When it came to Sports Phone and Phone Programs, there were several female staffers who not only snagged key roles in the organization but made indelible marks on the industry.

Likely the first woman on-air at Sports Phone and also the first at AP Radio years later, Shelley Adler has a tough time these days convincing her adult children that people used to get scores through New York Telephone. The concept itself seems unfathomable.

Fresh out of college and already working at radio stations like WNEW and WFAS, Adler was hired by Guy LeBow and covered mainly weekend shifts at Sports Phone.

"I really loved it. You start a career like that and it's just exciting because it's always different every day, and I got to do sports which is still a passion of mine and it was great. I don't remember finding it that challenging. It was very exciting," she said.

"Sometimes you made a mistake but there's nothing you can do about it because it's live, but I don't remember re-recording a lot. I remember it was fun being under that kind of pressure and having it come out perfectly, and getting that, 'Sports Phone, first and fast.' at the end."

Adler was well-versed in everything Sports Phone was covering, which eased any potential pressure.

"I knew sports so well that it was a natural thing for me. I would think it did help. Most people, I'm sure just like I did, ad-libbed it. You can't write it down," she explained. "You just look at the scores, and I think we were probably using the Western Union ticker tape … In fact, when I got my job at AP in 1983 we were still using the ticker, which is pretty amazing."

The Syracuse grad was then part of launching *CNN Headline News* during a brief spell working in television.

"I applied to do voiceover sports and edit tape, which I'd never done before. It wasn't that difficult," Adler recalled. "They teach you, you learn it. You like sports, so you do it."

Now with AP Radio for over 40 years, Adler credits Sports Phone with instilling some additional confidence when going live.

"I could be, but I can't guarantee it, the first female to go on network radio and do sports," she said.

THIS IS *SPORTSCENTER*

Linda Cohn was recruited by Mike Walczewski and Sports Phone after hearing the future *SportsCenter* anchor on WCBS NewsRadio 88, where the eminent Ed Ingles had given her some on-air opportunities.

"I remember [King] Wally. He's like, 'This is gonna be a fun place to work.' I actually remember being in his office talking with him about it, and he was explaining the concept. It was kind of cool because at that time there were no other women," Cohn recalled.

"That was part of my road. I didn't think about that aspect of it, but it just seemed to me like a fun place to work. I love sports and I love talking about it, even if it was just giving scores. I remember him showing me the little booths where you step in and you put on the headphones, how much time you had to deliver your report, and how you had to do it every 10 minutes. For them to come up with an idea to use phone booths, basically, because that's how big it was — the size of a phone booth. To somehow get the information out to the people in the way they did, I thought it was remarkable."

Traveling to Midtown from Astoria, Queens, the night shifts in those little booths went a long way in preparing Cohn for a bigger stage.

"It really did teach me the art of a deadline because you don't learn that in college. I knew a little bit about it from doing my little newscast at WALK Radio, but there's so much time in between those. In my other freelance jobs at WCBS-AM doing sports or doing whatever I was doing, I had more time to prepare," she explained.

"There is no question. Working at Sports Phone helped me in the urgency department. You just had less time to do what you had to do, and so I think that was a really big part of it. It was an absolute benefit."

Recording rundowns for 976-1313 also provided a geography lesson for the Long Island native.

"Here I'm a New York girl who grew up loving pro sports and had my favorite pro sports teams. I learned a lot about other places in the country," Cohn said. "Especially when you're working Saturday nights, these college football teams from these universities that I never knew existed. That was another thing, so Sports Phone was a bit of an education as well."

She also credits the environment at 919 Third Avenue with preparing her for a business that was once quite patriarchal in nature.

"I think because I was the only woman, just dealing with that. The atmosphere of wanting to fit in but also stand out. So wanting to fit in with the guys, wanting them to respect me and know that I was there just like them because I love sports so much, and if I could get paid for it that's remarkable. In the early stages of my career, I felt I had the right attitude. I feel like to this day, I'm not being cocky, I make people comfortable around me. By working in that atmosphere, you know there's not a lot of [people]. At one time during the night shift maybe there were like five other guys, six other guys, but I was the only woman," Cohn explained.

"I wanted them to know that I was just like them, and then they felt comfortable around me because they knew that I didn't have another agenda. It was really a very comforting situation, a comforting work-place, even though back then being the only woman and being in a male-dominated field. And so to have that early on, I think that was again one of the chapters that really prepared me … I could tell you about other situations, whether it's in clubhouses, locker rooms, or other workplaces where maybe I felt uncomfortable. I never felt uncomfortable at Sports Phone."

Now a hallmark of ESPN after 30-plus years on screen, Cohn has still been recognized from Sports Phone on occasion.

"When I lived on the East Coast, I've been out in LA for five years, but randomly when I've been at a game or something, Even as a fan, I did have some people [recognize me from Sports Phone]," she said.

"As many people that would say, 'I remember listening to you on WCBS-AM,' there would be a couple of people that would say, 'You were on Sports Phone, right?' You don't have a lot of time but with Sports Phone, you say who you are, so it has happened."

 Sports Phone Stories

House Rules
(feat. Shelley Adler, Linda Cohn, Pat Harris, Howie Karpin, John Martin, Alan Sanders, and Charlie Slowes)

Most work environments in the 1980s weren't known for being politically correct. This held especially true when it came to newsroom-type settings, so it's not surprising that the Sports Phone office had its share of moments that might be considered HR nightmares by today's standards.

One source of potential strife was the inappropriate content that often took center stage on the office televisions.

Alan Sanders: "Here's what I remember about it. Linda Cohn was a good sport, generally speaking. She knew her stuff. I think we were all maybe a little naive and not knowing what to do with a woman in our midst because it was still so unusual. I don't think there was anyone that was whatsoever against it or was anti-female. There was no phobia about it. It was just none of us quite knew how to act because we're used to being around each other.

"It's late. It's 11:30 at night and we're boys, and so anything goes. What I remember is that she went to the booth to do an update, and out of habit, someone tuned a couple of the little black-and-white TV monitors probably to [former pornographic actress] Robin Byrd. I honestly don't know who did it. I think someone did it, not out of any maliciousness whatsoever, but out of forgetfulness that we got to tone down the action when there's a lady present. Someone forgot themselves while she was in the booth, and I think absentmindedly must have just flipped a TV or two to Channel J. She came back from doing the update and she looked up at the TV, and she just kind of like rolled her eyes as if to say, 'Really?' I think

[Howie Karpin] was the one that thought it quickest to some way apologize or defuse the situation. I think it was [Howie] that said, 'House rules.'"

Howie Karpin: "The guys used to put on the porno shows from Manhattan Cable. One night Linda Cohn was working. There was a separate room for the TVs and all the wires and all that stuff, and that's where the writers sat that gathered the scores. So Linda was doing one of the updates. I was the night supervisor, and apparently she told somebody else, who came over to me and said that she felt a little insulted that the stuff was on TV and that she had to walk into the room and get her scores. She wanted to know if we could turn it off and I told the guy, good-naturedly, 'No, it stays on. House rules.' Looking back, I would get in trouble if I did it today. She took it good-naturedly and we've been friends ever since. I was in my twenties, maybe early thirties. In a lot of ways it was harmless, but I understand how people could be insulted."

Charlie Slowes: "Well, it's kind of like a locker room thing."

Linda Cohn: "It was a different time then. I love sports so much, and I wanted to be in the sports broadcasting business so much. I just accepted it. I didn't want to stand out in that way of standing up and saying, 'Shut that off.' Whatever, I didn't care. I just accepted it. Right or wrong, it was a different time. I thought it was stupid to have it up there because I would think that's pretty distracting."

"I remember there was a room with the TVs, and in that room was the wire with the paper to see what the latest scores were. That's how I knew they were watching the Playboy Channel because one of the screens was on it. I had to go in that room because that's where I got the latest scores, but I just went about my business. It really didn't bother me. I just was like, okay, whatever, I don't care. I'm not running this ship. You know, as long as everyone's doing their job. All I had to concentrate on was me, kicking ass doing my job and all that. But yeah, I don't know how they stayed focused with that on, to be honest."

Cohn wasn't the first female staffer who had to contend with question-able late-night cable content.

John Martin: "Shelley Adler was also working with us before Linda [Cohn]. Shelley was in the booth one night doing an update. I came out and I said 'Where's [Ugly] George?', the guy that would talk almost any [sic] out of her clothes. I said, 'Where's George?' Somebody said Shelley shut it off. I said, 'She did, huh?' and I reached up and turned it back on. I turned around and she was standing there. I didn't say anything to her but I had the same mindset, like it stays on, 'House rules.' Long after the fact, like what an asshole I was, shit."

Pat Harris: "I remember The Chief [Martin], I think it was Jane Charnin-[Aker] came out into the newsroom. The Chief always sat at that main desk there, and one of them goes, 'Oh, no. This goes off. I'm insulted. I'm not going to accept this," and The Chief looked at her and said, 'If you don't like it, go in the other room.'"

Shelley Adler: "I'm pretty sure I might have worked weekends and I don't remember a lot of people there, so I don't remember somebody watching [adult content]. I've had other jobs where they've had that on. You just have to ignore it."

———

HIS PRICES ARE INSANE

Now a director of CNBC's on-air promotion and scheduling, Lisa Wernick focused on the commercial side of things for Phone Programs — a role that included promo work for Sports Phone and several other hotlines.

"One of the things I will always remember is Jerry Carroll, Crazy Eddie," Wernick said. "He did a commercial for us. I think it was a Sports Phone commercial."

Certain hotline promos required traveling throughout the country to record, while others took place in the same booths as many of the Sports Phone rundowns. While sexism reared its ugly head on occasion, it never originated from her colleagues.

"We went into environments for some of the promos that we shot and you had to think on your feet. We went down to talk to a well-known country band, and they didn't want to listen to me because I was a woman, so I had to direct through the cameraman. So you learn how to work out solutions, and you learn how to work in any environment," Wernick explained.

"There was none of the stuff that you read about in today's papers, or at least if there was I was not privy to it. You did your job. It was fine. These guys were to me an exception because they were who they were. They were well known and they were country, and they just had an attitude. But in the office itself, I had no problems. Everyone worked together and everyone was terrific."

Because much of what they were doing was groundbreaking, Wernick got to work with some of the best in the business and gleaned a lot throughout this experience.

"I worked with so much talent, because as one of the promo producers [I was] someone who was creating not only the programs but the promotion for it," she said. "It was a great place to work and learn, and just creativity was top of the line because there was nothing to compare it to really."

CHINESE LOTTERY

Robbie Caploe would go on to become executive editor for some of the country's biggest publications, eventually working in digital media and the esports space. Fresh out of college in the mid-1980s, her first gig serendipitously led to a spot at Phone Programs and the rest is history.

"I worked [as assistant to the president] for a television syndication company called On The Air that was owned by Fred Weiner, Mark Goldman, and Bruce Fogel. They closed the business down and I was absorbed by Phone Programs, so I moved across the street and went into 919 Third Avenue," Caploe explained.

"When I went over to Phone Programs they started to train me as a producer. That's when I started to learn sort of what Sports Phone was, and Phone Programs was. I did not come from a sports background, nor was I a big sports aficionado, so they started having me work on the non-sports programming. It was Dial-A-Joke, the sex call hotline [and others]. We did a sex education show called *Speaking of Sex*. I hired the voiceover talent and writers to write the scripts, and then I was in the booth producing the sessions."

She even worked on a hotline that announced the lottery numbers... in Chinese.

"It was the kind of place that encouraged creativity, imagination, and an entrepreneurial bent. We would announce the lottery numbers whenever they came out, but we did it in not only English but in Chinese, too, so I had to go and find somebody who spoke Chinese," Caploe said.

"There was a lot of freedom and encouragement to be smart and look at the marketplace and figure out what the marketplace wanted, to go create something that they would want to participate and join, and that's pretty cool. Don't forget it was the go-go mid-'80s of Reagan, so there was a lot of emphasis put on whatever you could think of to make money."

Although she didn't work directly on the Sports Phone lines, Caploe spent plenty of time with those who did, even reporting to King Wally at one point. Like many of the other women who called Phone Programs home, she reflected on what was a positive overall experience.

"I knew all those guys really well. I knew Howie [Karpin], Bob Papa, Jerry O'Neil [Caploe's boyfriend at the time], Mike Celentano, and Charlie DeNatale. It was an extremely social place. We would go to the Old Stand, which was the bar across Third Avenue," she recalled.

"I never had the sense that any of the women were taken advantage of. There might have been sort of teasing, but I can honestly say nothing that ever made me feel uncomfortable ... Especially all the Sports Phone guys, they were rough and tumble."

PUT ME IN, COACH

Amy Lennard Goehner became a reporter for *Sports Illustrated*, a dream job that was her main focus once she chose a particular path.

"On a return visit during my Peace Corps Korea service, I was watching a Giants game with my Aunt Blossom. She pointed to then-announcer Phyllis George and said, 'You could do that.' It was my 'ah-ha' moment," she recalled.

"Then and there I decided I would combine my lifelong love of sports with a post-Peace Corps career in sports journalism. After four years overseas, when I got back to New York, I made my goal even more specific: to work at *Sports Illustrated*."

It's all well and good to have such a dream, but finding a spot in sports media can be close to impossible — especially for an aspiring female reporter in those days.

"I was working at the *Korea Herald* when I saw an ad in the *New York Times* under 'Sports,' and it turned out to be a secretarial job at Sports Phone. I was told the job was taken, but the person who answered the phone turned out to be fellow Colgate alum Drew Esocoff," Lennard Goehner said.

"He agreed to let me come by and introduced me to a higher-up at Phone Programs. The woman told me there was another job opening. It consisted of calling Sports Phone's list of stringers throughout the country to ask them to cover the local games. That was the extent of my job. The pay was about half of what I was making at the *Korea Herald*. 'I'll take it,' I told the woman, with no hesitation."

It was in this role where Lennard Goehner would gain invaluable experience, thanks in no small part to her Sports Phone colleagues.

"[Charlie] DeNatale, [Howie] Karpin, King Wally, Andy Roth, Cory Eisner, Mike 'Bingo' Weinstein, Kenny Samelson. All menschy guys. I knew sports, but I knew nothing about reporting," she explained. "Some of them were able to help me by letting me take one of those huge tape recorders home, and on slow nights watch the Yankees on TV and call in reports. They showed me how to send tape using alligator clips on the phone receiver."

Lennard Goehner took to it like a fish to water, soaking up the tricks of the trade. As soon as the opportunity knocked to cover something live, she seized the moment.

"Mike Farrell said he had no one to cover the tennis Tournament of

Champions in Forest Hills. Tennis was the one sport, in addition to maybe curling, that I knew very little about. 'Put me in, coach,' was my attitude. I got through the first day by asking other reporters lots of questions," she said.

"In one of the matches, Ivan Lendl was upset early and my Sports Phone colleagues had given my name to radio stations who were looking for press conference tape. I fumbled my way through it, but fed them that tape cause I knew how to use alligator clips! I made it through the whole week."

Another chance to work onsite would come months later when Lennard Goehner filled in at MSG for a Rangers game. She credits the aforementioned Sports Phone colleagues with teaching the basics of reporting, and with trusting her to get the job done when needed.

"Everyone I worked with at Sports Phone treated me with respect and never questioned my desire to become a sports reporter nor my knowledge of sports … I never felt [I had to work extra hard as a woman] at Sports Phone, nor *Sports Illustrated*. But at *SI*, I did have women friends and heard stories of others before me who struggled to climb the ladder to writer, editor, and above," she acknowledged.

"I was content being a reporter at *SI*, covering boxing and horse racing, and later being promoted to deputy chief of reporters by my mentor, who later hired me as head arts reporter at *Time*."

A lifetime of doing what she loved, sparked by answering a classified ad for a job that had already been filled.

"I think the guys that helped me at Sports Phone gave me the confidence I needed to prove to myself that I could be a reporter, even though I had zero experience before I went there," Lennard Goehner said. "I will forever be grateful to them for that. After all, how many people ever get their dream job?"

Sports Phone Stories

Marvelous Marvin
(feat. Amy Lennard Goehner)

Amy Lennard Goehner has covered plenty of different sports over the years, but her foray into boxing would prove fruitful down the line.

"Mike [Farrell] said a reporter from Sports Phone had been invited with some other New York press to visit Marvin Hagler's camp, and would I want to go. Hagler was training for his upcoming fight with Roberto Duran," Lennard Goehner recalled. "My love of sports had begun with watching the Friday Night Fights with my grandpa in Brooklyn. This time, my 'Put me in, coach' attitude was genuine."

The presser provided an opportunity to ask an offbeat question, one the Newark knockout artist nailed.

"The New York press was sitting in a room with Marvelous at the front. I had to sit right next to him, as I needed him to speak into my microphone for Sports Phone and most likely 1010 WINS news, whom we often fed our reports to. I was the only one with a tape recorder," she described.

"After the usual round of 'Marvin, what's your plan when Duran comes at you with those hands of stone?' questions, I asked a question that, full disclosure, my then-boyfriend had thought up — a question which I had never heard anyone ask a fighter. Clearly neither had Hagler."

"Marvin, despite the fame, the money, and everything that goes with being the middleweight champion of the world, do you actually enjoy stepping into that ring?"

"Marvin looked at me with a pensive expression and said, 'If they cut my head open, they will find one big boxing glove.' Oh, you could hear the scribble of pencils from the press corps, which Marvin must have noticed too, as he repeated that comment the next morning when he was interviewed on the *Today* show," Lennard Goehner added.

"More boxing reporting opportunities followed. After three or so years at Sports Phone, I had some reporting on my resume and wrangled an interview at *Sports Illustrated*. I wasn't hired right away but stayed in touch with the woman who would become my boss and mentor for 30 years. And one day in 1984 I wrote to her, this time writing, "It's not too early to think about the 1988 Seoul Olympics, and by the way, I speak Korean. Shortly after I began what turned into a 30-year career at Time Inc.'s *Sports Illustrated*, *Sports Illustrated for Kids*, and *Time*."

Those old boxing interviews came into play again recently.

"Most of the boxing tapes I saved from Sports Phone and *Sports Illustrated*, using my own little tape recorder, came in handy in 2021. Showtime did a boxing documentary called *The Kings,* and I ended up giving my tapes to the producers who were able to use them in the documentary about Hagler, Duran, Hearns, and Leonard," she explained. "They also interviewed me, and you can hear a few snippets of my voice in the doc talking about Hagler. An honor for me, as Hagler was one of two athletes who brought out the fan in me."

———

FAST TALKER

Now the *Guinness Book of World Records* Fastest Speaking woman, Fran Capo slowed the cadence down a bit and lent her voice to one of Phone Programs' most embraced holiday lines, getting to know much of the staff while doing so.

"I was a hired voice talent, so I didn't technically work at Phone Programs. I worked as an independent contractor, voice talent for them. I'd come in once a week and we'd cut five spots for the week. I believe it ran from Thanksgiving to Christmas," Capo recalled.

"I always joked since I was Candy Claus that I must have been Santa's illegitimate child since no one knew he had a kid … Kids would call in and hear the adventures of Candy Claus as the countdown to Christmas."

Sports Phone callers also heard about Candy Claus, and vice versa.

"We had me always saying don't forget to call Sports Phone, and that was the cross-reference. If you were on Sports Phone they would let you know about Candy Claus, and if you were on Candy Claus they'd let you know about Sports Phone," Capo explained. "They owned all of it so they would cross-promote."

The author and comedienne felt welcome each time she came to the booth.

"Everyone was great there, a supportive environment," Capo said. "Everyone wanted each other to succeed."

The feeling across the board was that Sports Phone and Phone Programs fostered a welcoming work environment for women, in an era when that was far from guaranteed.

"The ladies were phenomenal. You would say things that you

wouldn't even say today, but they were fun. All the women there were fun," recording engineer Joe Gauci said. "No one's standing out because everyone was on the same level. Happy to have lived it and I'm glad I still have the friends I still have today, for sure."

Those bonds were tightened by company-sponsored events.

"The owners were generous to us. Huge, exclusive Christmas parties at the Ritz. Yacht trips around the island of Manhattan. We had parties that promoted our friendships. They threw the most lavish parties twice a year, once at Christmas and once during the summer — going somewhere, doing something, but we all did it together, Sports Phone and Phone Programs," Gauci recalled.

"There was no expense held, none. We were all very close. We were lucky to have friends like that. No one was a real asshole."

OFF THE TOP ROPE

Part fiction, part sport, professional wrestling was a major part of the Phone Programs lineup early on and remained so for decades. As part of this programming, employees often worked directly with some of the wrestling world's biggest stars.

"I did some of the wrestling production work and it was hilarious because you would see Captain Lou Albano, who let me tell you was like a pretty fucking scary guy, but he was incredibly sweet. He would come over to my cubicle and ask me to validate his parking," Caploe recalled.

"Stone Cold Steve Austin used to come on up, too. Those guys were great in the booth. They were just natural entertainers. They were fantastic."

Many of these larger-than-life figures could often be spotted wandering the halls at the Midtown location, a surreal dichotomy to those who witnessed it.

"You have to picture, we had a recording studio in the middle of an office situation. At that time I think it was a quarter floor, but we had a recording studio around desks and secretaries and cigarettes and ashtrays," Gauci described.

"Everyone was smoking at their desk at the time. Then you walk past this door and you've got a little recording studio with a booth, a full booth. It was made very well."

Phone Programs also took their show on the road when needed, including monthly jaunts up the Taconic Parkway.

"In 1986-87 I took long once-monthly drives to Poughkeepsie with Joe Gauci [and others] to the Mid-Hudson Arena to interview WWF personalities, including 'Mean' Gene Okerlund for the WWF Hotline. Very popular at that time," Jerry O'Neil recalled.

"We would sit in an anteroom and wait for each wrestler to come in — Hulk [Hogan], Rowdy Roddy Piper, etcetera — and I'd sit with an index card with a question that Gene would pose on tape to each guy. It was, 'Give me 50 seconds on this,' and they were machines. Good actors!"

"It was huge because technically we were limited, society was limited technically still. It was The Analog Age," Gauci said. "[King] Wally came with us a lot. I was lucky to be a recording engineer, and I had to get a mobile reel-to-reel machine in a carry box in a rental car, go up to Poughkeepsie, interview, go have a major dinner, and then get back in the car and drive back. It was a really good time."

These road trips weren't limited to the arena.

"It was different because it was groundbreaking. It was new and it was creative. [Captain] Lou [Albano] was terrific to me. He was an extremely nice person, and that's where you first learn about personas versus people. He was terrific to work with," recalled Lisa Wernick, who served as producer for much of the WWF content.

"We worked with all the wrestlers. I remember going to some turkey farm somewhere for a Thanksgiving shoot and taping some of them on camera with the turkeys. It was unbelievable … Bruno Sammartino, another terrific guy to me. I remember recording with Bruno and Lou in Gleason's Gym. Bruno picked me up in one arm on his shoulder, picked up my associate in his other arm, and lifted us both over his head. That's a strong man."

Gauci once possessed a set of recordings, a jewel of the past, that would be worth plenty today.

"I had a reel of outtakes that would curl your toes. I lost it. I'd be a millionaire. I'd be very rich now," Gauci opined. "The outtakes, Freddie Blassie, Bobby the Brain Heenan, [Iron] Sheik. The things they would say to each other off mic, and I still had the thing rolling. I had gold, Jerry! Gold! But it's gone. That's all there is to it but it's a memory, and I'm glad to have this memory.

A key figure in Detroit's Sports Phone and Phone Programs operation, "Coach" Kurt Schneider was well-respected in wrestling circles for his work within the sport — which included variations of the company's wrestling hotlines. Schneider also wrote a weekly pro wrestling article in the Royal Oak, Michigan-based *Daily Tribune*, likely the first of its kind in a daily publication.

Sports Phone Stories

Blackjack Brown
(feat. Jim Cerny and Peter Schwartz)

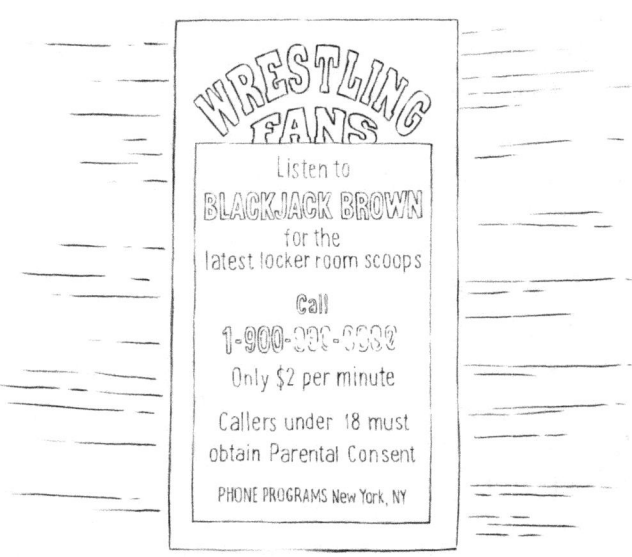

A pioneering pro wrestling writer and photographer who hosted a popular hotline out of Sports Phone's Elmont office, David "Blackjack" Brown left an impression on all who worked around him.

"They used to have this ridiculous cast of characters that would come in with Blackjack Brown and do the wrestling line," Peter Schwartz recalled.

One Sports Phone alum with vivid memories of Brown and his operation was Jim Cerny, who remembered the wrestling luminary fondly.

Cerny: "We had our booth set up, and of course, we had all the TVs lined up, desks to grab all the information, and then off to the side is a closet or whatever, where a fellow by the name of Blackjack Brown [worked] … He's a legend. Big wrestling guy, unbelievably well-connected. He would be the guy for the [New York] *Daily News* that would feed them results from one of the wrestling matches from the Coliseum or the Garden, anything local. The transactions and statistics section of the newspaper would have wrestling at Madison Square Garden, it would have all the results and then at the bottom, it would have 'by Blackjack Brown,' so I was familiar seeing the name before I met him. Blackjack was a character. He wore the blackjacks on his hands like he was some dude from Texas or whatever."

"Big guy, strong guy, but super nice, great guy. He knew how to keep those people on the line. They had several different lines. Some were recorded messages. But there was a live line, a wrestling live hotline, a 900 number, and Blackjack Brown could keep people on for hours. I have no idea what their bills must have been. It was a gold mine, what he was doing. He would sit back in his chair and just be talking to these dudes, and if there was a big match that night we would pay for it and Blackjack would have it on — and people might be watching it at home as well, but they wanted to hear Blackjack's take on it or talk with Blackjack about it because there's such a personality. I don't know what the numbers were, but I probably could argue that he was raking in more money on that than we were on Sports Phone. He was unbelievable, a piece of work but the greatest guy."

———

Sports Phone Stories

I Thought You Were Dead!
(feat. Joe Gauci and Mike Weinstein)

Women's professional wrestling quickly gained notoriety in the 1980s with the advent of GLOW, short for Gorgeous Ladies of Wrestling. As was the case with the WWF, Phone Programs covered the action for its related hotlines.

Joe Gauci and Mike Weinstein visited Los Angeles to get the ball rolling on the company's newest venture, just barely making it out of town by the skin of their teeth.

"There was a female wrestling show, *GLOW*. To start that off, they flew me and Michael Weinstein to LA to record these ladies over a couple of days. It's me and Michael Weinstein in LA with an expense account, so we had a very good time," Joe Gauci recalled.

"On the way back we were separated at the airport because my bag was left at the rental car place. He said, 'All right, I'll wait for you here in the terminal. Hurry up. We're going to miss our flight.' So I go get my bag, on the way back I'm in traffic on a bridge and we got hit with a 6.5 earthquake. My first one of my life. I'm from New York, we don't have earthquakes."

Weinstein sat nervously at Los Angeles International, unsure of Gauci's status.

"It was scary and exciting. It ended and no one got hurt. I got to the airport and Michael was like, 'I thought you were dead. Let's get on the plane.' We got on the plane, we took off, and they shut the airport [down] after that plane left," Gauci said.

"Our plane was the last one out of LAX that day because they had found cracks in the tarmac. When we got out, we toasted each other. We're going home, Michael, we're going home."

———

Quickie Quiz

Q: Which super-heavyweight wrestler and WWF broad-caster did Joe Bomrad mistake for a prank caller?

A: Gorilla Monsoon

Bomrad was a writer at Sports Phone, which meant he often had to answer phone calls from stringers and others throughout his shift. It wasn't uncommon to fall victim to prank calls as well, which is what he thought was happening one night when a famous wrestler rang.

Bomrad: "I got a phone call one time and it was like, 'Gorilla Monsoon with the WWF hotline.' I go, 'Whoa, buddy. I don't know how you got the number but that was pretty good. Tell me another one. People crank call us all the time.' He goes, 'No, it's really Gorilla Monsoon. I have the results.' I go 'All right, tell me one thing and then I'll know that it's okay.' I go, 'Where do you guys wrestle in Scranton, Pennsylvania?' He goes, 'Catholic Youth Center.' He's got the CYC [right] so I go, 'Oh, I'm so sorry, Mr. Monsoon.' Mr. Monsoon, I called him.

"I go, 'We get a lot of crank calls here. You guys are the best. We see you all the time.' They used to come to Scranton all the time besides Madison Square Garden. They'd go out and they'd booze. Andre the Giant would drink so much beer after but they're all buddies. They all knew each other. [Mr.] Fuji and all them, [Professor] Tanaka. They were just the best. Bruno Sammartino, we used to always see."

WITCHCRAFT

Whether featuring seasonal content like Capo playing Candy Claus or the latest updates from a bestselling musical act, Phone Programs seemed to have their hands in just about everything when it came to dial-up hotlines.

"We went and did a Halloween line with Laurie Cabot. She was the official witch of Salem, Massachusetts," Wernick said. "So Charlie [DeNatale] and I went up and interviewed Laurie and created a program around her."

Another spooky line was Tales of Terror, which offered bite-sized mysteries that were professionally produced.

"I was working with some of the most creative people I've ever worked with because you really only had audio. Back in the day when people [only] had radio then sure, it was something that they worked with a lot, but then television came and audio was secondary," Wernick said.

"But Tales of Terror was great. There were one, a minute and a half, two-minute horror stories. You absolutely had to create an entire environment of sound. We did have a sound effects library, but if you don't have the sound of a body hitting the ground you have to make one."

They each took turns becoming their distinctive version of a Foley artist, stretching the bounds of creativity to give the caller an authentic experience.

"[To simulate] peeling back people's faces we would use masking tape or duct tape, pulling the sound to create that. We had a terrific time," Wernick explained. "We had a great crew, and it was a forerunner because now you see how important in every sense of the word these murder mysteries are on television. It was a great learning ground."

"We had a sound effect library, per se, on reel-to-reel that they had accumulated over time but for the most part, we made all the sound effects. I needed basketball sneakers squeaking while they were dribbling for a Sports Phone ad. I had to go somewhere with a microphone and squeak my shoes, things like that," Gauci added.

"Breaking bones, we would get celery and break bones because we did a horror line, Tales of Terror. All the sound effects had to be done from scratch. Breaking heads, bleeding, stabbing. We would stab lettuce."

Even some working in the office became fans.

"[Gauci] was incredibly enterprising, like if you wanted to do something that took place in Paris he always had sound effects and records that would have like French recording and music. Joe did a shitload of work," Caploe recalled.

"We would jump into the booth if we needed a voice. Michael Weinstein was always doing this character called the Pesach Bunny. The Easter Bunny, it was like the Jewish version. We were just rolling on the floor all day. Lisa Wernick used to do Tales of Terror with Joe. It was a horror line. It was scary stuff. It was really good."

There were game-based hotlines such as one for *Family Feud*, where callers could dial in and play a slimmed-down version of the smash TV show. Those at the forefront of the music industry often got hotlines as well.

"To me, it was fan clubs on the phone and it was a very clever way for people to market to a different group of people, right? It was very easy for people to market that way," Wernick said. "I remember going to Philadelphia with a crew to see DJ Jazzy Jeff and The Fresh Prince."

Some artists also found their way to Third Avenue on occasion.

"Where again can you run into rappers and wrestlers?" Wernick asked.

Mike Weinstein worked with both groups, getting the inside scoop on the feuds and heel turns. A man of multiple hotlines, he befriended the Philly duo while capturing their recordings, lifting the veil on those supposed enemies in the ring.

"We loved Mike. I know he was doing all the wrestling, and it was hilarious because he would give us so much behind-the-scenes stuff," reminisced Will Smith's partner Jeffrey Townes [DJ Jazzy Jeff]. "I remember telling my nephew, and he was actually heartbroken, 'You know these guys go to dinner together, right?' and he's like 'Nah, no way the Iron Sheik goes to dinner with Hulk Hogan.' I'm like, 'No, they're all cool [with each other].' We definitely had a good time."

That one-of-a-kind environment both in the office and on the road allowed for the creation of imaginative content on a regular basis.

"Floyd O'Neil was the head of production. These people were down to earth, people wanting to have fun just as long as the job got done," Gauci explained.

Sports Phone Stories

Rock Royalty
(feat. Joe Gauci)

If a form of entertainment was in demand, chances were that Phone Programs was involved. As a recording engineer, Joe Gauci got to work with many of the greats.

"We did the Ozzy Osbourne Hotline. Ozzy came into [919] Third Avenue. I have his autographed *Wizard of Oz* album framed in my living room," Gauci recalled. "He came in, no problem. Three bodyguards, no problem. They stood outside the booth. He was incoherent but fine. We got the whole thing down."

Another oft-dialed line was dedicated to fans of The Who, the London rockers with over 100 million records sold worldwide.

"I worked with Pete Townshend, John Entwistle, and Roger Daltrey. They were doing the Meadowlands [Giants Stadium] for four nights," Gauci said. "They put me up at the Hilton. They gave me an all-access pass for the stadium, which I still have."

Gauci had actually moved on from Phone Programs by then, but by chance got the gig working for them as a freelancer since the regular staff engineer was swamped.

"I had to be on-call for four straight days. They'd call me at 2 a.m. plenty of times, because they wanted to talk, and I'd be in my hotel. Get in a cab, shoot on out there," he detailed. "Go talk to Roger. Go talk to Pete. Does John Entwistle have his Remy and coffee? Oh, no? Get him a bottle of Remy and coffee so we could talk to him. Go and do it."

A consummate pro, Gauci was ready for any technical difficulties that arose.

"I had to go with that reel-to-reel player. Matter of fact, on the fourth day they got me a DAT player, the very first DAT player I ever used, DAT recording," he explained. "Good thing I brought the reel-to-reel because the DAT didn't work. It was a rental from B&H [electronics store] and I turned on the reel-to-reel and I said 'Come on, let's go!' We had all these great hotlines."

The rock stars may not have fully grasped what these recording sessions were all about, but cash is king.

"They were all magical. They didn't understand the concept of this storytelling over the phone," Gauci said. "They were getting a lot of money so they didn't care, but they were like 'Whatever, you peon. Let's do this.'"

———

LIKE A SYMPHONY

The Phone Programs hotlines were generating so much action that you didn't necessarily need access to the call volume statistics to get a feel for how massive the numbers were.

"You knew that this was going nationwide. The computer room, which is the telephone room, was there [at 919 Third Avenue]. You heard the clicks. Each one of those is a phone call. Click, click, click, click, click," Gauci explained.

"They made me put hold music on it, and it was promos for Sports Phone and all that. I remember putting it into the telephone room with an electric cord. You can't use a battery because it's got to run 24/7, and I'm hearing clicks like a symphony and each one of those was a phone call. It happened 24/7 so I had a scope of what was going on."

The precise figures were available, of course, and offered management a clearer picture than even traditional media was privy to.

"A lot of times radio and television have always been dependent on rating services to estimate exactly how many people are watching a TV show or listening to a radio broadcast, but in this case, you know exactly how many people are consuming your information," Mike Farrell added. "You knew to the exact number how many people called and listened to that material and that was rather phenomenal."

 Sports Phone Stories

The Stringer Ball
(feat. Joe Bomrad, Gary Cohen, Bob Grochowski, Howie Karpin, and Alan Sanders)

In addition to its employees who manned the office and covered games in-venue, Sports Phone relied on a network of stringers spread throughout the country to phone in updates and provide sound bites. Found among their ranks were some of the most eccentric and entertaining folks ever to grace a press box, as well as a few rotten apples in the bunch.

"We could all do impersonations of any of the stringers because even if you were an announcer you would help out, especially on weekends when so many games were going on. All of us would help out answering the phones and we got to know the quirks and the ability to impersonate any of the stringers around the entire country," Alan Sanders explained.

"One of the writers [Jim Ritorto] came in one Saturday morning and Celly [Mike Celentano] was three-quarters hungover and everyone's half asleep. The writer, over breakfast in the newsroom, said, 'You know, Celly, I had this really weird dream last night. I kind of dreamed that I met [stringers] Skip Clayton and Sam Skinner and Greg Brinda, and some of the other guys that we deal with. Celly barely looks up and said, 'Where was that, Jim, at the Stringer Ball?'"

Based in the Bay Area, Skinner was one of the more memorable stringers.

"I was there the night Sam Skinner put Stevie Burtt on the phone with [Sports Phone announcer] Tom McQuade. Stevie Burtt went to Iona. He was with the Warriors back then," Bob Grochowski recalled.

"I remember the night that he also put Magic Johnson on the phone and Magic asked what the Michigan State basketball score was. I remember Howard Kellman, who I guess did a couple of Yankee games. He was from Brooklyn and he was so cheap. He would call, if you worked during the day, Howard would call on the 800 number and ask you to call his mother in Brooklyn for him."

Joe Bomrad picked up when Magic made his request, following up with a no-look pass to Howie Karpin.

"I think I answered the phone and it was Skinner and he goes, 'Magic wants to know the score of the Michigan State game,'" Bomrad said, explaining that he then gave the phone to Karpin, who ended up speaking to Johnson on the other end. "That was right in the heart of the Showtime [Lakers] stuff. They were at wherever Golden State played at the time."

Clayton was another dependable stringer, with a lengthy history in radio, who covered virtually anything and everything related to Philly sports.

"Skip Clayton in Philadelphia, I remember," Gary Cohen said. "There were people around the country who called in tape and who called in reports to be used in our segments."

A longtime sports broadcaster best recognized as the Red Sox public address announcer for every game over nine-plus seasons at Fenway Park, Carl Beane was also a Sports Phone stringer for many Boston-area events back in the day. The Massachusetts native with the infectious smile tragically passed away in May of '12 after suffering a heart attack while driving.

Another media mainstay that once provided content for Sports Phone was one-time Braves batboy Kevin Barnes, whose dispatches from the Atlanta area were utilized on 976-1313 and the supplemental lines. A statistician for multiple TV broadcasts including SNY whenever New York visits Truist Park, Barnes gained social media notoriety in recent years for his somewhat unique attire and appearance — which prompted tweets referring to him as a "time traveler."

Sports Phone's stringer roster also had its share of unsavory characters.

"[For] a couple of years I would go to the Rangers and Penguins playoff series at The Igloo [Civic Arena]. I loved The Igloo, and my brother was an occasional Pitt stringer. He would call in the Pitt basketball scores once in a while when he was in college, and so I would go out and stay at his dorm in those days. Not too often, but for a couple of Ranger playoff series, and I met [stringer] John Duffy," Grochowski recounted.

"Duffy was [later] arrested for child pornography. Oh, my god. It made my skin crawl. This is a guy I actually sat and ate dinners with in Pittsburgh, had conversations with him in Pittsburgh, talked about how my brother went to Pitt and John was like, 'Oh, I went to Duquesne.' and this and that."

Later a news anchor for Pittsburgh's ESPN Radio affiliate, Duffy was sentenced in January 2008 to four-plus years in federal prison.

Another Sports Phone stringer who ran afoul of the law was Mark Unger, a Detroit-based sports reporter who ended up with a much longer prison stretch than Duffy.

On October 23, 2004, Unger, his 37-year-old wife Florence, and their two sons, aged 12 and 9, were staying at the Watervale Resort near Frankfort, Michigan. It was here that Unger was accused of pushing Florence from the boathouse's rooftop deck. She fell 12 feet to a concrete landing and was then dragged into Lower Herring Lake where she drowned. The couple was reportedly in the middle of a divorce at the time.

Mark told police they were on the deck together until around 9:30

p.m., after which he returned to the cottage to check on the kids. According to his account, he returned to the deck to find his wife missing. He then went back to the cottage, fell asleep, and discovered his wife floating in the lake the following morning.

Just days after the incident, Unger was attempting to cover a game as if nothing had happened, leading to a now-bone-chilling phone call he made to Rich Ackerman, who had left Sports Phone and was working at WFAN.

"I just happened to answer the phone, and it was Mark Unger, and I don't think he was on the schedule for that Sunday. I'm not going verbatim here, but he said I was hoping to work the game this week, or something along the lines of hoping to work or get a pass. [He said] I could really use it. My wife died this week and I'm a person of interest in her murder situation," Ackerman recalled.

"I'm like, I think you have bigger issues than trying to get a pass for the game. He was a strange guy to begin with but you don't expect anything like that. When he said that, I was like, 'Holy shit!'"

It took almost seven months for authorities to arrest Unger, charging him with first-degree murder. On June 22, 2006, over two years later, a jury found the former Sports Phone stringer guilty of killing his wife and attempting to cover it up.

Housed at the Chippewa Correctional Facility in Kincheloe at the time of publication, Unger is serving a life sentence without the possibility of parole.

———

Quickie Quiz

Q: Which Sports Phone announcer was accused of breaking up a multitude of marriages?

A: Chuck Cooperstein

High phone bills and growing gambling debts may have caused some friction among frequent Sports Phone callers and their spouses. One of the service's most recognizable voices in the early '80s, Cooperstein got an earful from an angry wife at a nearby saloon.

Cooperstein: "One night we get done relatively early and we all go to Runyon's. The bartender behind the bar, he knows us, and he says to me at one point, 'God dammit, Chuck. You go too fast. I can't get my scores.' Of course, you listen for the scores and then we had that supplemental line, we had 976-2525. So earlier in the day or earlier that night, we would be moving games over there, and so we're obviously making Phone Programs quite a bit of money at that point but everybody was pissed. He's bitching and moaning, and I remember there's a woman who's sitting at the end of the bar and she's listening to all this. She then walks up and says, 'Hey, are you Chuck Cooperstein?' and I'm not knowing what [she wants]. Is she gonna pull a gun or, you know, what the hell? 'Yeah, I am.' So she says, 'Do you realize that you're responsible for 85 percent of all divorces in America?' I just cracked up. I don't deny it for a second. It was so funny."

CHAPTER 4
GETTING A JOB AT SPORTS PHONE

Broadcasting is an ultra-competitive business, with the number of applicants almost always exceeding available openings by a wide margin. This holds especially true when it comes to sports, as many dream of getting paid to sit behind a mic and talk about the action. Even for those ambitious neophytes looking to break into a role that isn't necessarily on-air such as a writer or producer, getting a foot in the door can be quite a challenge when so many others have the same idea in mind.

Today's relentless coverage and expanding platforms do offer more entry points than in the past, particularly compared to the 1970s, '80s, and early '90s.

During those years, many aspiring sportscasters of various backgrounds sought opportunities at Sports Phone, offering an unmatched chance to learn and advance in an industry where openings were scarce. The hours were long, the pay modest, and the pressure intense. Yet, for many, the experience gained and the doors opened made working at Sports Phone a blessing they wouldn't trade.

DAY ONE

The initial 1972 launch of Sports Phone didn't exactly work out the way ownership had planned, as we detailed in Chapter 1. They did, however, hire an upstart announcer in Mike Farrell — a New York University student at the time who would go on to fill many roles within the company.

"Somebody had called a couple of college radio stations and said we're looking for some sports guys. There was just a note hanging on the bulletin board at the [NYU] college radio station [that read] if you're interested in this thing call this number, so I just called the number. It was that simple."

This largely uncharted method of broadcasting over the phone allowed media hopefuls like Farrell to hone their craft without hitting the road.

"This came along at a point in time where it created windows of opportunities for a lot of young sportscasters, sports reporters, to find work in New York City — which was nearly impossible to do. You could send your resume to WCBS or WINS, or to the Mets or to the Yankees, and you'd get a polite rejection letter. Thanks, kid, but you're not what we're looking for or you need more experience. This was a way for young talent to get experience and not have to leave town," he explained.

"When I went to school back in the day and I had a journalism degree from NYU, you'd talk to the people who you worked with at the college radio station and from the college newspaper and there was always that mantra. Well, you gotta leave New York and go out and prove yourself in Sheboygan, you got to get experience ... But this was a way for young sports talent to stay in New York. You didn't have to pack up and leave town, and that for myself and a lot of other guys — and eventually gals — was an invaluable experience. It opened doors for you that would never have been opened before."

Farrell spent much of his early years at Sports Phone on-air, perfecting the speedy cadence and delivery required to do the job. Unlike later, when scores would come from several sources, he depended solely on what came over the wire along with the occasional television broadcast.

"I was one of the announcers. You went in, you read your scores, you read your commercial, you read your Aqueduct or Belmont or Saratoga race results. You jammed all that into less than 60 seconds. You got as much of that in as you could and 10, 15 minutes later you came back and did it again," he recalled. "You had to scramble around and get it yourself. They had the Western Union ticker that spit out ticker tape. You got scores that way. If it was a bowl game that was on you'd watch TV. You cobbled it together any way that you could."

His experiences at Sports Phone would prove invaluable, as they did for much of the cavalcade of talent that walked through its doors.

"Anybody who went into any kind of broadcasting at some point in time, somebody either gives you the signal or whispers in your ear, 'You've got one minute'. If you had that training, you knew exactly what one minute meant. It was an important part of my life, of the life of everybody who went on and had a sports journalistic career of any sort. It opened doors for you, opened windows for you, that you may never have been able to open without that Sports Phone experience," Farrell said.

"The introduction you had to teams, team officials, learning how to do your craft, learning how to be a reporter, learning how to act in a locker room, these were all the essential things that Sports Phone gave you and you got out of it whatever you put into it. A lot of people were able to get a lot out of it on the back end"

Farrell eventually trained many of the new announcers who came on board as part of the 1975 relaunch.

"One of the things that I was responsible for doing was basically training them how to do it. It's a little different than anything you had done before," he noted. "If you had worked on a college radio station or done play-by-play, this was different and it required discipline. You had to eventually learn how to count off those 58 seconds in your head. You really didn't even need the timer in front of you."

"BULLET" BOB MEYER

"I was a junior at Queens College. I had known Marv Albert because I had been the president of his fan club going back to 1967," Howie Rose recalled. "Marv had kept tabs on me because he would listen to my tapes when I would practice doing play-by-play and other things, and he knew that I was serious about wanting to be a broadcaster. Thankfully, he saw some potential in me so he recommended to Bob Meyer that I be considered."

"I walked into the office at the college radio station one day, WQMC. I saw a message to call Bob Meyer and I thought, could this be the same [Bob Meyer]? Well, turns out it was and he explained to me that they were putting Sports Phone together and they were looking for mostly young college-age kids with broadcasting aspirations, and would I be interested in coming in for an interview. I did and he hired me, and we were on our way. That was May of '75."

Quickly disseminating a slate of scores was only one of the skills Rose learned while at Sports Phone, as the recordings would sometimes include features when not many games were being played.

"It was a great training method to learn how to speak not only succinctly but understandably, in that short amount of time. Even if you were doing a commentary, you had to learn how to write copy for a certain amount of time," he said.

"If it was in the weekday afternoon, and you were just doing a commentary for that particular half hour or however long it ran, you better learn how to do a good, well-written, concise, succinct commentary in less than a minute and it was great training for that."

Peter Newman came out of Northwestern University without much broadcasting experience but a love and understanding of sports, qualities that Meyer likely saw when he opted to hire him, later coining a nickname for the future movie producer.

"I had sent in just an 8 x 10 of me interviewing a soccer referee in a stadium and Bob hired me," Newman explained. "One reason Bob Meyer called me 'Precision' [Peter Newman] was, I think I'm talking fairly fast to you now but I talked twice as fast when I was young and so I tried to get too much in. But, you know, we found a balance of sorts."

Now an associate arts professor at NYU, Newman appreciates what an idealistic group of youngsters were able to accomplish, often in an impromptu fashion.

"Sometimes I watch *NFL Red Zone* and I think yeah, that was not necessarily a direct descendant of Sports Phone but it was doing everything Sports Phone was trying to do but in a logical and organized or professional way," he opined. "I don't want to portray it as being this organized plan. We'd make things up. We'd be sitting there and we'd say, 'Wouldn't it be fun if we did this?' All of a sudden, it was something that became popular."

WHEN YOU COME TO A FORK IN THE ROAD, TAKE IT!

Tim Berra, son of the legendary Yogi Berra, etched his own legacy at the University of Massachusetts as a wide receiver for the Minutemen, setting single-season school records in receiving yards (922) and touchdowns (12) as a senior in 1973 and prompting the Baltimore Colts to select him in the 17th round the following year.

Berra played one season in the NFL, appearing in fourteen games over which he returned 16 punts for 114 yards and 13 kickoffs for 259 yards on special teams. He would later join the ranks at Sports Phone, working alongside Howie Rose and some of the original group.

HARDEST WORKING MAN IN GOTHAM

There was a time when Al Trautwig seemed to be in three places at once, covering everything New York sports and beyond. One of the most well-respected commentators in the city's history, Trautwig's love of sport began as a youngster, handling stick boy duties for the New York Islanders as well as serving as a ball boy for the then-ABA New York Nets.

A native of Nassau County, the multi-time Emmy Award winner worked for a litany of networks, covering the Knicks, Rangers, and Yankees along with the Olympic games, auto racing, cycling, tennis, gymnastics, and more.

This included pre- and postgame shows, play-by-play, and virtually any other role you can think of. The uber-talented Trautwig also spent time at Sports Phone, leaving a lasting impression on those around him.

Sports Phone Stories

You Don't Know What You Just Missed!
(feat. Pat Harris, Andy Roth, and Al Trautwig)

The TVs in the Sports Phone offices were often tuned to a big fight or an eventful game, with staffers crowding around to catch the action. The announcers responsible for recording the on-air updates weren't always so lucky, as they were in and out of the booths throughout their shift. Nor were those sent out on a coffee run at an inopportune time. Pat Harris found himself in both situations.

"I can even give you the date. I think it was December 23, 1979. We always had somebody go down to Smiler's [Deli] to get coffee," Harris recalled. "I was elected. I was only [at Sports Phone] for a little while. Pat, your turn. So everybody gives me the money and I go down."

The Bruins were visiting nearby Madison Square Garden that Sunday night, taking on the Rangers in what ended up being a tension-filled, physical contest throughout. With time running down, Rangers center Phil Esposito shot wide on a breakaway right before the horn sounded, ending any chance at a comeback and securing Boston's 4–3 victory.

What happened next would go down in NHL lore. As Harris was ordering coffees just a couple miles away and a dejected Esposito was skating off the ice, Bruins forward Al Secord landed a sucker punch on New York's Ulf Nilsson on the way to the locker room — sparking a chaotic scene at MSG. Both teams started brawling, during which a Rangers fan whacked Stan Jonathan in the head with a rolled-up program, causing him to bleed and yanking away his stick in the process.

Boston bruiser Terry O'Reilly climbed into the stands and charged the fan, after which most of his teammates followed suit, which began a second melee between the players and ticket holders. As Harris returned with some much-needed caffeine for the staff, his Sports Phone colleague and eventual broadcasting legend filled him in.

"The Rangers are playing the Bruins. I come back," Harris said. "It's the night when Terry O'Reilly and whoever else it was went into the stands. That's how I remember I worked with Al Trautwig because he came up to me and he said, 'You don't know what you just missed!'"

Less than three months earlier Harris had missed out on another wild battle, this time involving his favorite sport. Earnie Shavers and Larry Holmes met for the second time on September 28, squaring up for the WBC title. The two heavyweights put on quite a show in what ended up being one of the most talked-about fights from that era.

"I remember being on the Jersey [Sports Phone] side. It was the night of the Larry Holmes-Earnie Shavers fight, the one where they both got knocked down, and I was having trouble punching in [recording an update on the phone] everything I wanted. It's not that I couldn't do it but I wanted it to be perfect," Harris explained.

"I'm back there and Andy [Roth] is working with me that night. You know I love boxing and I'm saying to myself, I'm gonna miss that fight. I'm not gonna see any of the good stuff."

Known as Sports Phone's expert in the sweet science, Harris's premonition ended up being spot on.

"I had just gotten the report on and he yells, 'Holmes is down!' I said I gotta re-do this again. Then, it took me another four or five times to do it. I finally got this on. It should have been on sooner. It got on late because I'm trying to be perfect," he added.

"I finish that one and [Andy] goes, 'Shavers is down!' This whole time I was back in the Jersey booth for what felt like half an hour, almost missed the whole fight. Then I come back up to the front after I got it all on and he goes, 'Patty, is this a great fight!' I barely saw any of it. I just went by what he was yelling out."

———

APPLES AND ORANGES

Andy Roth would go on to cover professional basketball for numerous outlets including NBC and the Associated Press. Before that, he was just a kid looking for a score.

"I was a frequent caller. I grew up a huge Wilt Chamberlain fan. 1973 NBA semifinals. Lakers-Bulls, Game Seven. I'm calling Sports Phone every 15 minutes for the score, and the Lakers were trailing most of the game," Roth recalled. "As it got towards the end, I forget who the announcer was, but I'm praying he says the Lakers score first. This way I knew they won, and they ended up winning the game. So yeah, I was a frequent contributor."

Less than six years later Roth would find himself in the booth as a member of the Sports Phone team.

"I was still at Brooklyn College on the station, WBCR, working part-time in Waldbaum's in the produce department, weighing fruits and vegetables and such. My roommate, who was also on the radio station at the time, was working in the field at a job. He got *Broadcasting and Cable Magazine* and there was an ad for a desk assistant at Sports Phone. I put together the tape, sent it in, got interviewed, did a demo tape on a cart in one of the booths, and a few days later I found out I got the job," Roth said.

"I was just trying to take in as much as possible. I hadn't worked much with tape, and I had to work with the reel-to-reel and the cart machines. When I got trained to be an announcer, it went pretty smoothly. I don't know how long it took, probably less than a year. I was promoted from the desk assistant to an announcer. It was like working in a college radio station but getting paid. Just the atmosphere was like a fraternity house, but you got to watch games and get paid for it."

Sports Phone Stories

Boys Will Be Boys
(feat. Rich Coutinho)

Some of the debates that took place at the Sports Phone office would get very heated. Former employee Tom McQuade would debate Andy Roth on who was a better point guard, Mark Jackson or Rod Strickland. One day the argument got out of hand, resulting in a messy office wall.

"Tom was a huge basketball fan and he was a big Mark Jackson fan. He loved Mark Jackson, and Andy Roth loved Rod Strickland," Coutinho recalled. "The Knicks are playing on the [Christmas] holiday and we all brought stuff into the office. Pastries, a cake, someone brought baked ziti. It was around Christmastime and the Knicks were playing the [Chicago] Bulls."

Tensions rose as the game reached its final moments.

"Mark Jackson was having a ridiculously good game and Tom was rooting hard for it. At the end of the game, Jackson makes a turnover right into Scottie Pippen's hands, and Pippen hits a turn-around, like a 40-footer at the buzzer to beat the Knicks. Tom is so fuckin' mad, and Tom wasn't a big Knick fan, but he was a big Mark Jackson fan. Andy Roth is in the office. He goes, 'Rod Strickland wouldn't have thrown the ball away.' They went on that Rod Strickland-Mark Jackson debate," Coutinho said.

"Tom turns around and goes, 'Shut up, Andy, and I don't want to hear anything else about it. I'm so pissed at this game.' There was a rum cake on the desk, and he threw it up against the wall. It stunk up the room because it was rum. I was like, 'You threw a rum cake. If my grandfather was alive, he'd kill you right now.' The stench was so bad. I was going to try and clean up the room a little bit and Tom goes, 'Nobody touch that. That has to be left there.'"

———

Quickie Quiz

Q: Which Sports Phone staffers narrowly avoided dangerous airborne fibers?

A: Bob Grochowski and Howie Karpin

Bobby G: "[I remember] the Friday night that [office manager] Paulette Jordan forgot to tell me and Howie Karpin that they were emptying the building of asbestos and the [building security] guy came to the door. I guess he was just making sure that nobody was working. He came and knocked on the door like 11 o'clock at night. I answered the door and he had that [Hazmat suit] outfit on and the guy was screaming at me like, 'What the hell are you doing in here? You're supposed to be out!'"

Grochowski and Karpin left the building right away, but the night shift wasn't over.

"For whatever reason there weren't a lot of late games that night, because we did the last two tapes off the payphones on the corner across from 919 Third Avenue."

HEY... I KNOW YOU!

Like many in the industry, Steve Torre began his journey working at a college radio station. It was at C.W. Post (part of Long Island University) where he learned about a part-time opening at Sports Phone, a name he was already familiar with.

"I graduated high school in '82 so I remember that was really the only outlet to get up-to-the-minute scores. You didn't have ESPN, it was well before the internet, and social media wasn't anywhere close to the radar, so that was the immediate way to get scores. So for a guy like me and all my friends growing up, and we were avid sports fans of all sports, that was the way you got the immediate information," Torre reminisced.

"When I used to hear the actual announcers, whether it was Chuck Cooperstein or Charlie Slowes or some of the others, in my head those guys were like celebrities because they were a big deal. I remember they had the Lou Piniella commercial when he was on the Yankees, and he's running down the runway to go to the payphone and he screams out, 'Hey, they won!' because he called Sports Phone. ... Then when I was in college, I found out about an opportunity to be part of it and I jumped at the opportunity. I couldn't wait, because I was well aware of what they were doing and how much of an impact it had."

Torre eventually became sports director at WINS Radio in New York City and later the program director for Mad Dog Sports Radio on SiriusXM, but his first significant experience came via Sports Phone.

"They used to send you to the games all the time and you'd make contacts at Yankee games, Knicks, St. John's Alumni Hall, Nets at the Meadowlands, Seton Hall at the Meadowlands, all the local venues. For a kid who was in college trying to break in, that was like, 'Wow, are you kidding me? I'm going to get paid for this?' Meeting all those people and not only the guys you work with, but people on the outside to make contacts. It was an incredible training ground," Torre fondly recalled.

"I knew right away, no bullshit when I walked in there, whether it was working for Howie Karpin or Andy [Roth], it was a professional outlet. I remember having a lot of fun and I remember people took it seriously. I remember feeling after a very little amount of time how comfortable I was, just with the people I worked with and the training that I got. I couldn't have asked for a better first gig to earn a paycheck."

Tucked away in a relatively small recording booth and not exactly broadcasting over the airwaves, it was often surprising when rookies like Torre first realized their reach.

"I remember being out to dinner once and the waiter or waitress overheard us talking. Just in conversation, somebody had mentioned my full name and the waiter said, 'Wait, Steve Torre from Sports Phone?' I was like, holy shit, I couldn't believe it," Torre said.

"He goes, 'Yeah, I dial into that all the time to get my scores. I've heard of you.' Then it kind of hit me like, I'm probably reaching more people than I actually thought. Remember, Phone Programs had [Sports Phone lines] in Boston, Pittsburgh, New Orleans, and Atlanta. You were getting exposure at that young age on a professional level."

Trying to explain that to a new generation of broadcasting hopefuls can be a tall task.

"Here at Sirius sometimes the management and some of the talent get on Zoom calls with a lot of the interns. They're all aspiring sportscasters, or talk show hosts, or hosting their own podcast, and a lot of times you have to kind of go over how you got your big break and how it started," Torre explained.

"For some of them, you see the reaction on their face and [they] say,

'Wait a minute, you used to get sports scores by dialing up a phone?' They can't comprehend that."

Quickie Quiz

Q: What unconventional programming did Steve Torre have to deal with during his second stint at SP?

A: A porn line.

Torre: "I had to input some tape, back in the day there was a reel-to-reel thing. There was like a porn thing that we had to input that was always like – Jesus, this is what I got in the business for? I gotta listen to this 59-second tape of a guy having fun with his cold turkey? Happy Thanksgiving? You know, that kind of stuff. I remember sitting there. I was worried about the Pirates-Reds in a matinee and here I am listening back to this, which was not what I signed up for, but it was part of the gig."

ROOMIE REFERRAL

Torre had moved on to traditional radio by the time he learned that Sports Phone was branching out, a development he passed on to an old college friend.

"My roommate was Steve Torre at college. He was unbelievably talented. He got a job at 1010 WINS and told me they were looking to expand at Sports Phone," recalled Brian Kilmeade. "They had opened up Detroit and Chicago... So I went down there and I got a job, and I thought it was awesome."

Like many others that ended up on the recording end of 976-1313, Kilmeade was once a customer.

"Everybody was [aware of Sports Phone]. I mean, George Steinbrenner was doing the ads on TV," Kilmeade explained. "Before sports radio, if you wanted to know the score of the game wherever you were you would call."

A television and radio host for Fox News since 1997, Kilmeade's original ambitions involved working in sports, a fact that helped quash any potential tension at home when the monthly phone bill arrived.

"I didn't get in any trouble [for calling Sports Phone often] because everybody knew I wanted to be in sports and I convinced my parents," he recalled.

Kilmeade's years at Sports Phone would prepare him for future roles as a sports anchor, sideline reporter, and play-by-play announcer for some of the early UFC events in the 1990s — as well as his current job.

"I was making $12,000 a year. I was able to write on my taxes that I was a broadcaster as an occupation. I had to waiter on the side to make money, but I loved every second," Kilmeade said. "Getting to go into locker rooms, covering Mets and Yankees games, Old-Timers' Day. It was unbelievable."

"I always managed [like] I was on camera while I was [in the Sports Phone recording booth]. You look down, you look up, and if you can do that, it is your fundamental. A lot of people say go to a small market and learn. But if you do sports, if you want competency, you start at something like that. I don't think it's any coincidence that so many successful people like Al Trautwig, Steve [Torre], Steve Cangialosi, and Howie [Karpin] ended up very successful, because you check your ego at the door. Eight hours, forty hours a week, countless sportscasts. You talk about how many hours it takes to be successful at anything, that's a boot camp."

His time in the Sports Phone booth also taught the importance of keeping the listener or viewer in mind.

"You don't do Sports Phone unless you want to do this for a living and you have so much respect for the games and the players, so when you go on and do your 59 seconds you owe it to them to get it right. Then you think about the customer. I still think about that to this day. That person that's going to spend whatever it costs for that phone call… Don't screw it up, and that sense of always being live has always helped me."

THE SECOND TIME AROUND

A longtime sports talk host on SiriusXM spanning multiple stations including MLB Network Radio, Jim Memolo worked two stints at Sports Phone in the 1980s — a path initially set forth by Andy Roth.

"I was finishing up my time at Brooklyn College and I worked at the college radio station there. Andy Roth was there and he started working at Sports Phone, and that opened the door for a handful of us to get a job there," Memolo recalled.

"At the time we may have all had some aspirations of some sort to be in sports media without really knowing what that was going to be. So opportunity lands to do any kind of sports broadcasting, regardless of pay, you jump at it. That's what I did."

Memolo even contributed to the call volume totals while at Sports Phone, often using the service on his days off.

"I'm sure most of us used Sports Phone at one time or another when we were off and wanted to get an update on something, beyond potentially having a bet on a game. I know I did," he said. "I wasn't always calling Sports Phone to find out how my bet was going. I didn't do that much [betting] back then. Using myself as an example, I certainly would check in on a score for one of the teams I was rooting for. No doubt about it."

In addition to getting Kilmeade in the door at Sports Phone, Steve Torre was also an instrumental part of Memolo's current gig on satellite radio.

"The first time [at Sports Phone] was a couple of years and it got to the point where it was comfortable. Looking back on what we were getting paid, it seemed like a pittance. As a kid, I was 21 or 22 years old, I wasn't having any problem making ends meet at that stage of my life, but then eventually I got an opportunity to work on a terrestrial radio station and so I jumped into that," he explained.

"I was between radio jobs and I went back to Sports Phone back in '85. It was a necessary move at the time to try to find a paycheck, but it turned out to be a great point in my life because there was a second wave of people working there that I never would have met like Steve Torre at SiriusXM. I met Steve when I came back in '85 and I've spent the last eight or so years doing shows on Mad Dog Sports Radio. I don't do that much on that channel anymore on SiriusXM, but I met Steve and knew Steve."

His time at Sports Phone helped lay the groundwork for that radio career.

"It was the most valuable training ground I ever had. It was not just about being concise. It was not just about editing to be able to fit as much information in a 57-second broadcast as you possibly could," Memolo elaborated.

"Ad-libbing, thinking on the fly, to the point where I did updates at WFAN in the late '80s and at some stations in Chicago, which is where I'm now based, and writing out an actual two-minute radio script or

90-second radio script seemed impossible to me. I was so used to just winging it and ad-libbing it from my Sports Phone days. There's no doubt it was valuable training for me in terms of doing sports talk shows."

His days there also taught Memolo how to say cool under pressure, adapting on the fly while on live radio.

"I've been doing sports talk radio shows for over 30 consecutive years. My reputation is I'm pretty unflappable when something goes wrong," he said. "I don't lose it, and I never lose it with people necessarily. I could probably trace that back to the Sports Phone days. If there were no Sports Phone, I don't know how many of us wind up staying in this business."

In addition to on-air reports from the booth, Sports Phone gave Memolo experience breaking big stories from in the field.

Sports Phone Stories

Deal at the Doral
(feat. Jim Memolo)

Careening toward a second economic recession in as many years, a large majority of Americans were feeling the financial crunch with many looking to sports for an escape. When the Major League Baseball Players Association voted to strike, with free agent compensation being the main issue on the table, struggling fans were rightfully furious. The walkout officially began on June 12, 1981, and would eventually result in 713 scheduled games axed from the slate.

The dog days of summer were in full swing one late July night when ownership (represented by negotiator Ray Grebey) and the players association (along with rep Marvin Miller) finally came to an agreement in the wee hours. Jim Memolo was wrapping up a long stretch in the booth when rumors began to swirl about a potential resolution. Luckily, the two sides were meeting not far from Sports Phone's midtown digs.

"Because baseball was on strike, we had nothing to report except North American Soccer League scores back in '81. We were doing updates once an hour. It also was an example of how there's been a shift in the timing with all the sports. Now you have the NBA and Stanley Cup Finals going into late June. You have NFL preseason, covering everything from August and beyond. But in '81 when the baseball players strike happened, there was nothing going on, nothing except the North American Soccer League," Memolo recalled.

We all had to educate ourselves in terms of labor terms or legal terms. None of us got into Sports Phone to talk about the National Labor Relations Board, but that was a big part of the strike."

Memolo was working overtime on Thursday, July 30, and it looked like there was no hope in sight as far as MLB was concerned.

"I agreed to do a day shift, and at that point, none of us anticipated that the strike was ending anytime soon. Anyway, as luck would have it, I wound up doing the day shift on New York Sports Phone, and as the day progressed it looked like there was something moving forward. We started scrambling all the personnel, so I wound up also doing the night shift on New York Sports Phone. So now I had done the day shift, I was doing the night shift, and we get to the end of the night shift and now we're hearing rumblings that they're closing in on a possible deal," he explained.

What happened next was a matter of good location and even better timing, allowing Sports Phone to break a possible strike resolution to its callers well before dawn.

"The hotel they were at [the Doral Inn] was three or four blocks away from the Sports Phone office. The shift supervisor sent me over there with a tape recorder. I got to the hotel. I get in the elevator, and as it turns out all the negotiators are in the elevator and they're all kind of laughing. I think to myself, you know, I think this thing is over and they're all headed up to do a press conference," Memolo described.

"I remember I called in to Sports Phone and said, I think the strike's over.' Couch it any way you want. There are reports that there may be a resolution today but let's not confirm it, and sure enough they resolve the strike that morning. I stuck around. I don't remember when we did the last live update. Looking back, it felt like it was the middle of the night."

A settlement on a new basic agreement was announced at 6 a.m. Friday, but a weary Memolo's work was far from complete.

"I wound up doing a 24-hour shift. I did the day shift on New York Sports Phone, the night shift on New York Sports Phone, and then I stuck around the hotel and got all the sound and the tape and brought it back and edited it. I remember I got out of the office at 10 a.m., Friday morning, so now I had done 24 hours," he said. "By the way, I was supposed to go to the Jersey Shore that night with a bunch of friends of mine, which is exactly what I did, and then I came back and did the Saturday afternoon shift the next day … I'm not putting my hand up to do any 24-hour shifts now in my life, but I did it back then."

———

WINDY CITY CONNECTIONS

A mainstay on the Chicago sports broadcasting scene, David Schuster landed a gig at his city's Sports Phone office right out of Southern Illinois University Carbondale in 1978 and worked there until that location was shut down over a decade later.

"I think I turned out the lights," Schuster recalled.

Despite having other opportunities available upon graduating, the Chicago native just wanted to come home — even if that meant a dearth of radio openings.

"[Veteran radio reporter] George Ofman was my roommate and a sports director in college, and he started at Sports Phone. I had job offers around the Midwest and the South… There was no chance I was going to do that out of college. I just wanted to come back to Chicago," Schuster explained.

"I came up to Chicago and there was nothing. There were no jobs in radio back then but there was Sports Phone, and George said why don't you come in and talk to the guy who was in charge at the time. His name was Dick Gonski. Dick was the color commentator on Bulls basketball, like in the mid-to-late '70s. He said, 'I'll give you five or ten minutes just to see who you are.' Well, that turned into about a three-hour conversation and I guess he liked me so he found some part-time work for me. I then graduated to full-time work and I was the nighttime voice for basically all those years."

 Sports Phone Stories

Disco Demolition Night
(feat. David Schuster)

Known for unorthodox innovations and credited with many contributions still present in today's game, former White Sox owner Bill Veeck was also at the helm for one of the most unfortunate events in baseball history.

As the 1970s wound down, interest in disco music saw a sharp, sudden drop-off — a movement that would be permanently rubber-stamped by a raucous night on Chicago's South Side. In collaboration with Veeck's son Mike, the club's promotions director at the time, WLUP's Steve Dahl would blow up a bunch of disco records at Comiskey Park in between games of a doubleheader against Detroit on July 12, 1979. Fans who brought the soon-to-be-vanquished vinyl could gain admission for just 98 cents, a tie-in with the station's 97.9 frequency.

Veeck and others sorely underestimated the number of people that would show up for the twi-nighter, with at least 2 1/2 times the expected crowd swarming Comiskey, many storming the field after a crate of records was detonated, ignoring pleas to return to their seats.

What started as a seemingly innocent idea concluded in a full-blown riot, with a severely damaged field forcing Chicago to forfeit the nightcap. David Schuster was still fairly new at Sports Phone when he trekked to the ballpark for what should have been a routine evening.

"It was a twi-night doubleheader against the Tigers that started like four o'clock Chicago time, and it was just an innocuous throwaway doubleheader because the Sox stunk. They weren't drawing flies, but Steve Dahl, who was a shock jock in Chicago, had this promotion of blowing up disco records, and he blew them up in between games at about 6:30, 7 o'clock. He told all his fans to come out," Schuster recalled.

"Now normally, games like that would have drawn 4, 5, 6,000 people. But there were 55,000 people that jammed in there for that Disco Demolition. [There was] destruction and people climbing over the wall, and there were bonfires in the outfield, bonfires in the upper deck. The place was trashed and they had to call off the second game. Here I am, right out of college covering that game, then all of a sudden this major story happened."

By circumstance, Schuster ended up in a correspondent's role for some of the nation's biggest media outlets that night — sowing the seeds of a longtime on-air run in the Windy City.

"I was like the only radio person that was there. The phone in the press box started ringing, and I was the only one up there so I answered it, and all of a sudden I became a correspondent for I think it was Westwood One, and NBC, and AP, and UPI," he explained.

"To this day, I have to thank Steve Dahl because I made a name for myself covering that stupid twi-night doubleheader, covering a major story because the second game was forfeited by the White Sox. That actually led me to my radio career because I started whoring myself out, for lack of a better term, to a lot of people. That was really a memorable thing."

———

Schuster would later work at a pair of Chi-Town sports radio institutions — 670 The Score (WSCR) and ESPN 1000 — as would fellow broadcaster Fred Huebner, who got his start at their local Sports Phone a year prior also thanks to a Bulls connection.

"Sports Phone started and I had just finished broadcasting school. It was the Midwestern School of Broadcasting, long since gone. I found out who the GM was so I could send a resume," Huebner recounted. "Turns out it was Dick Gonski. My father had previously hired Dick as a color commentator, along with play-by-play guy Andy Musser to do TV broadcasts of Chicago Bulls basketball. That got me an interview and got me started."

Huebner spent over a decade at Sports Phone, formative years that sharpened his on-air skillset.

"I was able to develop my broadcast skills, work in the field with other TV and radio professionals, and gain confidence in my abilities. What Sports Phone did for me and so many others was allow us would-be-broadcasters a place to grow and develop our skills," he said.

"So when other opportunities came along we were more than prepared for them. It also allowed people in the business to hear us and understand our abilities, so that they knew of us when openings came about."

Sports Phone Stories

Bo Knows Sports Phone
(feat. John Cwikla and Charlie DeNatale)

Charlie DeNatale was new in town, helping to get a fledgling Sports Phone operation off the ground when an offhand joke was taken as fact, leading to some trouble.

"In 1979, Mike Farrell calls me in his office and asks me if I would move to Detroit to help run the Detroit Sports Phone office, as they were just getting started. Being among new co-workers, I humorously joked with a colleague that the University of Michigan traded head football coach Bo Schembechler to Ohio State straight up for coach Woody Hayes," DeNatale explained.

"Apparently the colleague thought I was serious, so he called the Chicago Sports Phone office, and the next thing you know Sports Phone Chicago was breaking this story which was obviously false. Mike Farrell was not too pleased, to say the least."

Soon after, Phone Programs hired John Cwikla to serve as Detroit's general manager, a role the radio vet accepted under one condition — that he also be able to cover the local teams as he'd been for a decade prior. In doing so he secured a bond with the very coach DeNatale had fibbed about, a Michigan legend, all to Sports Phone's benefit.

"One thing I do remember is covering Michigan and Bo Schembechler, and back in those days they didn't have the exclusive rights for radio or coaching shows like they do now. But after the game, they would do the typical postgame press conferences and then everybody would get their quotes from Bo and file [their stories]," Cwikla recalled.

"I would stick around, and I got to build a friendship with Bo. I'd say, 'Hey, Bo, can I get you afterward for a few minutes, just for a quick two to five-minute interview?' Nowadays you'd have to pay for that. You have to go through an agent to get that, but he would stick around and he got to build a relationship and friendship with me. That meant a lot. The PR staff at Michigan knew me and they liked me a lot too, so they thought it was kind of cool. I didn't get content that was breaking any big stories, but it was unique in that I got sound that I could use at Sports Phone."

———

BRUNO, CAPTAIN LOU, AND IRON MIKE

An established hockey announcer, writer, and editor since the early 1990s, Jim Cerny's path to Sports Phone had a lot to do with being in the right place at the right time. It helped that the place happened to be the country's most famous boxing gym.

"I was working at Gleason's Gym in Brooklyn doing public relations work for them. You had [Mike] Tyson come in. It was mainly trying to get publicity for when we had big moments like that. Tyson's there for a day or something, Buddy McGirt's training there, whatever the case was. But we had some commercials, people would rent the place out and do commercials there, and Phone Programs came in. Along with Sports Phone they had all these other programs and one of them was a highly successful wrestling line, Captain Lou Albano's Wrestling Hotline," Cerny recalled.

"There's Captain Lou, Bruno Sammartino, and they're doing a commercial for the number. So I'm watching it, I'm taking pictures, I'm trying to get them some publicity or whatever, and am talking to the rep, whoever kind of shepherded Albano and Sammartino that day. I'm like, 'Oh, this is really cool.' She said 'Yeah, we do this, this and this, and Sports Phone,' and I'm like, 'Sports Phone? I'm a sports broadcaster.'"

It turned out Sports Phone was hiring at the time and Cerny was able to snag an appointment. The lifelong Jets fan was already familiar with the service, something that likely helped during the interview process.

"When I was in high school, I was that guy that was calling Sports Phone. I remember before the NFL draft was this big primetime event, being in high school and calling. Jets got a top pick this year. I'm fired up being I played football in high school. Me and my football teammates, we were all fired up. There I am on the phone calling Sports Phone. 'Oh, they haven't picked yet. They haven't picked yet,' then it's me slamming the payphone down at our high school because they had drafted Johnny 'Lam' Jones and just the anger. I'm like, 'You gotta be kidding me,'" Cerny explained.

"It cycled back to me years later [on-air at Sports Phone], where people would tell me stories. 'You know, I was so pissed at you, Cerny, because you delivered this trade news or this score,' or whatever the case was, even though I had nothing to do with the outcome. I was the voice that delivered it, but I remember having that feeling because I had it as this high school kid."

LORD OF THE FLIES

A veteran of the New York airwaves, Gordon Damer has been with ESPN-NY since its inception and has also appeared on other major networks. Before becoming a regular radio voice around the tri-state, the St. John's alum lucked out with an adjunct professor who just so happened to be a broadcasting legend in those parts.

Utter the name Ed Ingles in media circles and you're likely to hear unanimous praise in return, or at the very least a story about paying it forward.

"St. John's had a radio station, but it was a radio station unless you were in the parking lot you were not going to [get the signal]. So I had a little bit of experience. When I went to St. John's, I didn't know what I wanted to do. I was kind of rudderless," Damer recalled.

"I took a sports broadcasting class, which was taught by Ed Ingles who used to be a sports director [at WCBS 880] and he was looking for interns. At that point, his interns had to be in the city at 5 a.m., which was not appealing to most college students."

Setting an early alarm time didn't stop Damer, who began to see a potential calling.

"I got the internship there. I started working for him, writing scripts for him. Eventually, I got to be on the air," he said. "He had actually suggested, 'Sports Phone is always looking for people. Why don't you send something there?' That's how I got the introduction to Sports Phone and I [eventually] got the job."

Damer joined Cerny, Don La Greca, and others at Sports Phone's Elmont location in late 1993, having called the service plenty of times before but not knowing they were recording right in his backyard.

"Absolutely [I was a caller]. I remember there were commercials on TV about Sports Phone so I guess I knew about it from there. I absolutely knew what it was before I applied there," Damer acknowledged. "I think when I applied there, I didn't even realize that it was in New York. It was like one of those things that you just know exists, but you don't really know where it exists or how it exists."

When he showed up to be interviewed by Pete Walker, there was no mistaking the Sports Phone offices.

"This is before the internet, it's before anything where you can get the information on a regular [basis]. I want to say it was even before DirecTV. We had the giant satellites that you would be like, 'Oh, I want to get this [game]' and the satellite would be moving on the roof of the building," Damer described. "I remember that's how I knew when I went for my interview, I knew that I was at the right place because they had these giant satellite dishes ."

The experience of repeatedly cramming a large slate of games into a one-minute clip prepared Damer for the future, a lesson he imparts to his students today like Ingles once did for him.

"I always liken it to *Conan the Barbarian* with Arnold Schwarzenegger, where they capture Conan as a little kid and they put him on the wheel, and then all of a sudden the next scene is years have passed and he's still on the wheel, and he's Arnold Schwarzenegger. It's kind of a similar experience. I don't know if I ever became Arnold Schwarzenegger, but it definitely forced you to get better," Damer explained.

"I teach a class at Montclair State University about broadcasting and performance and I tell them, 'The two main things you have to have is preparation and reps.' Prep and reps are the main things, and in terms of reps — Sports Phone, you could not have created in a lab a better test to get better in a short period of time. Doing it every two minutes, doing it every five minutes. You just had to get better."

In many ways, that repetition could be likened to mastering a musical instrument.

"If you want to learn to play piano or learn to play guitar, you can't do it once this day and then skip a couple of days. You were doing it every single day. I always tell students to just talk into their phone for five minutes a day, almost imagine like a TikTok video for five minutes a day and you'll eventually get better. The proof is in the pudding, right? The amount of people that came through that company and went on to have really big careers, I don't think it's an accident that that's kind of how they got better at it at a very early stage."

Looking back, Damer appreciates being a small part of the history at Sports Phone, one bred out of a combination of competitiveness and brotherhood.

"It was almost like getting dropped into a fraternity where it was almost a little bit *Lord of the Flies* kind of thing," he said. "There's a thing with guys where you want to show that you're the best, especially at that age — 19, 20, 21, just out of school. There's definitely an 'I'm gonna show you' kind of thing to it when you have guys all in that age and you're all together in that group."

BOLOGNA SANDWICHES

La Greca's name and voice may now be entrenched in the New York sports scene, but the content he worked with initially was a far cry from scores and trade rumors.

"I started at Phone Programs in the spring of '90. I was putting in the Samantha Fox line, lottery, all the porn lines and stuff like that, those big cassette cases, hook them into the television machines. There was like Spanish porn, fetish porn. There was the Dial-A-Joke," he recalled.

"I remember Fred Weiner, who was the owner of the company, he comes in and he's like [co-creator] David Lynch just signed the contract with us for [cult classic TV drama] *Twin Peaks*. So at the end of every episode, somebody is going to call in with a recap of the episode and you have to load it in, and if anything goes wrong David Lynch himself is going to call. I was crazy and working all kinds of wacky hours and, then in May of '92 is when I finally got the chance to go down [to Elmont] and work at Sports Phone."

La Greca certainly wasn't getting rich in his new gig, but he was finally working in sports and having a great time doing it.

"You know, [I was making] no money. I spent most of the money that I made on frickin' tolls. I was living in New Jersey so I'd have to George Washington Bridge, Cross Bronx, Throgs Neck, Cross Island," he remembered.

"I remember buying a pack of bologna and a loaf of Italian bread and that would be like three sandwiches for the week, but I loved it. It was friggin' no money, but we all got to sit there and tell stories about how we wanted to make it. So happy for the guys that made it."

He also got paid to cover games in-venue, invaluable access for someone trying to get a foothold.

"The other thing with Sports Phone too, obviously before 9/11, all the passes would be tacked up against the wall, so you'd have the Devils pass. I used to go to Nets and Devil games all the time," La Greca said.

"Fifteen bucks [per game] doesn't sound a lot but you go to two or three games [it adds up]. When I got made supervisor at Sports Phone in '94 my starting salary was $19,500 and bennies, so that was wasn't a lot of money but the benefits were nice to get. It was costing me at the time like ten bucks in tolls just to go there, not counting the gas and the wear and tear on the car, but the experience was just too good — doing interviews and getting to know people. One of my favorite things to do was go into the out-of-town room so you get to meet the Brett Hulls and Grant Fuhrs, the Gretzkys, and all that."

Quickie Quiz

Q: Which Conn Smythe Trophy winner chose to interview in his birthday suit?

A: Claude Lemieux

As a member of the media, dealing with professional athletes isn't always a walk in the park. Every once in a while a player will make things difficult or awkward after a game, something Don La Greca became all too familiar with as a Sports Phone reporter.

La Greca: "[I remember] a Devil game where it's me and Steve Goldstein, and me and him go down and get sound [after the game]. Claude Lemieux had a big game for New Jersey. The Devils locker room at the Meadowlands, there was the dressing room and then there was another room that had a couch and a table. We talked to the PR director, I forget who it was at the time. I said, 'We need to talk to Claude. He had a big game.' He was like, 'Well, Claude doesn't want to come out.' and he's like, bring them. Have them come in here. So we walk in and there he is, laying completely naked on the couch, He had us sit on the table in front of the couch and interview him while he was naked. It was almost like, I want to see how badly you want the sound."

 Sports Phone Stories

Fuck This Place
(feat. Don La Greca)

An elite scorer over a 19-year career, Brett Hull's frustration with his St. Louis Blues boiled over one night after a lopsided defeat at Meadowlands Arena. Don La Greca was covering the game for Sports Phone and snagged some solid audio.

"It's Devils-Blues. Devils beat the crap out of them so I'm like, I'm gonna go into the Blues room and see Brett Hull. We go over there, and I've got my Marantz [recorder] and my microphone, and Brett Hull is sitting in the corner with two or three writers around him," La Greca recalled.

"So I stand over there and he's in the middle of just mother fucking the organization. Fuck this place. So tired of this place. We don't deserve to win, and he's just going on and everybody's just standing there with their mouths open and just letting him talk, and I got all the sound."

A radio reporter late to the room didn't realize what was going on and asked the Hall of Famer about the next day's game, mid-tirade.

"In comes [another radio reporter]. He stands next to me, interrupts him, and says, 'Brett, so you got the Islanders tomorrow at the Coliseum. What do you think?' "He needed a preview," La Greca said.

"Brett Hull looks at him and goes, 'Fuckin' what do you think's gonna happen? We're gonna get killed because we suck.' Brett didn't stop. He didn't want to stop. Everybody's looking like, oh my god, this is just such great stuff and now you're gonna kill the momentum, but Brett wasn't having it."

The expletive-laden rant made for great content, landing La Greca some extra spending money.

"That was the first time I was able to make some extra money. This radio station in St. Louis called me wanting the sound because it was a really big deal and I guess they didn't have any audio of it," La Greca explained. "Because all they had was, I guess the beat reporters were just writing down what he was saying. There was no Twitter at that time, no video. There was no camera there and it was just very, very funny."

Experiences like this have stuck with La Greca throughout his career.

"I can't believe that I'm like 24 years old or whatever. I still tell everybody it was like going out-of-market but staying in New York," he explained. "The experience I got at Sports Phone would be like going to work in some radio station in North Dakota. We get to stay local but get to be around players and news."

———

Co-host of ESPN's *The Michael Kay Show*, radio host of the New York Rangers pre- and postgame shows as well as their backup play-by-play announcer among other gigs, La Greca has traversed a well-earned journey that may have never even begun if not for his time at Sports Phone.

"Nothing that's happened in my career would have ever happened if not for that place. I was just some kid from Jersey and my only connection was a guy that I went to school with, Tim Reid, who worked at K-ROCK and he was able to get me the internship there in '90. K-ROCK deejay Maria Milito hooked me up with her then-husband Pete Walker. [Later] working at Sports Phone was when Andy Roth, who was friends with Steve Malzberg, recommended me to Steve about doing stuff at Shadow [Metro Broadcast Services]," La Greca explained.

"If not for Steve Malzberg none of this would have happened because Steve's like, 'Listen, I'd ask you to send me a tape and I'd send it to WINS. I'm telling you WINS will reject it. I'm not going to do that. I'm just going to put you on the air. You do updates and I'm telling you, they're gonna love you. But if I send them a tape, they'll just reject it. That's just the way they are.' So he just threw me on a weekend, a Saturday or Sunday afternoon on WINS, and they were like, 'He's valid.' [WFAN Program Director Mark] Chernoff heard it and that's when they started doing live overnights, and then that's how I got into the FAN. So the connection I always tell people on networking is if I don't work at Sports Phone I don't meet Andy Roth. If I don't meet Steve Malzberg none of this happens. None of it happens."

 # Sports Phone Stories

Slumber Party
(as told by Don La Greca)

Don La Greca began his Sports Phone career in 1992 at the service's Elmont, Long Island office.

"The first assignment I have is the 24 hours of Le Mans. So the boss calls me into his office and says, 'Listen, 24 Hours of Le Mans is going on. We worked out a deal, we got a hotline for it.' He goes, 'I'm going to need you to come in at five o'clock in the morning on Saturday. I'm gonna give you the keys to the place, I'm gonna give you the alarm codes and a guy is going to call every hour with updates and I need you to put it on the system, but nobody's gonna be there. The shift doesn't start 'til 10 o'clock. The guys, when they come in, they can finish up.' So I was like okay, and I had just started training. I just met [Sports Phone anchor] Doug Thompson and I really didn't know many other people."

"So I go in there and it's dark and the sun's coming up. So the phone rings, I put it into the cart and I'm like, 'Oh, this will be cool. I'll go into the New York booth and do it.' I thought that was a cool thing. New York [booth], that's where the supervisor goes, so I'm gonna go into the New York booth. It's like 5:15 in the morning and I go to open the door to the New York booth and I hear, 'Oh my God, oh my God, oh my God!' so I close the door. It was clearly Doug Thompson's voice."

"On the bottom floor, you went into a hallway and there was the New York booth, there was the Detroit booth, Chicago, all the sports were there. They're like little closets, little tiny studios. So I recognize Doug's voice. I'm like, 'Oh, God. Doug must be sleeping here,' because that was the shift I eventually had. You worked Friday night until the last game [was over], then your shift on Saturday at 10 in the morning. Because he lived outside Princeton, [New Jersey], he slept there."

"I felt so bad. I'm like, 'Oh my God, I must have woken up Doug.' I go into one of the other booths, load it, come back out and I'm waiting for the guy to call. All of a sudden, I hear a door open. I'm assuming Doug's gonna come out. It's not Doug, it's Steve Rugh [another Sports Phone anchor], and Steve Rugh is wearing a nightgown and a sleeping hat and he's wandering."

"I had never met Steve, had no idea who this guy was. I'm like, Doug and Steve Rugh in the room together. Did I walk in on something? I didn't know any of these guys. For a good couple of hours, I'm thinking I walked in on those guys, like, having sex or something. Eventually, I got that Doug was in the New York booth and Steve was sleeping in the Chicago booth because I didn't realize everybody was sleeping there."

———

NEW YAWK

The play-by-play announcer for New York Mets' TV broadcasts since 2006, Gary Cohen was a Sports Phone caller in the 1970s.

"I had called. I was not really a gambler but I was a fan," he said. "There were very few ways of getting scores other than listening to the all-news stations at 12 after the hour and 15 after the hour, but if you wanted scores faster there was no other place to go but Sports Phone," he said.

Cohen was later introduced to working at the service by a friend at Columbia University in late '77 and ended up on several different lines.

"When I was there we had New York Sports Phone, New Jersey Sports Phone, and something called New York Report, and then there was also like a music phone thing," the longtime broadcaster recalled. "So a lot of us would do reports on some of those other services, too."

Part of the Gary, Keith [Hernandez], and Ron [Darling] trio considered by many one of the best booths in the game, Cohen credits the gig with helping him overcome a thick New York accent.

"There is no question that it helped me in terms of enunciation and in terms of accuracy, and just being able to talk rapidly but clearly because we were trying to fit 30 scores in 58 seconds. It sounds like an impossibility and some days it felt like it," said the Queens native.

"It really forced you to concentrate and enunciate and get it all in, because if you made a mistake you had to wait for that minute to go by to recycle, and you had to start all over again. First of all, it meant that your report was going to be late. It also meant it cut down the time that you had to then update the scores for the next go-round. It was a real, high-pressured kind of a thing and I think it definitely paid dividends down the road. It was crazy. It felt like madness in the moment, but it was incredibly satisfying."

As was the case with most of the young Sports Phone crew, Cohen's fandom was often on display.

"Gary Cohen was a huge Jets fan and he worked weekends, and he would jump on the desk when the Jets scored. With hair down to his shoulders," recalled Mike Walczewski. "He was crazy nuts, in a good way. But cool, calm, professional Gary Cohen that you see now, he was younger and more energetic."

A member of the Mets Hall of Fame, Cohen is not surprised by the high success rate of those who started at Sports Phone.

"I think at the time there weren't a lot of outlets for people who were aspiring sportscasters. The cable TV explosion in sports really had not happened yet. ESPN hadn't even happened yet when I was there," Cohen explained.

"So if you wanted to be a sportscaster this was an entrée, and I think for a lot of us this was the way to get our foot in the door. I think for people who were serious about being sportscasters, it was a great training ground and it doesn't shock me that a lot of people have gone on to bigger and better things."

HARD NEWS

Peter Schwartz can be heard on WFAN, CBS Sports Radio, and plenty of other places — serving as a host, anchor, play-by-play man, or public address announcer depending on the day. Before becoming an audible jack-of-all-trades, the Long Islander helped contribute to Phone Programs' coffers regularly.

"As a kid growing up I used to call Sports Phone all the time, especially when my teams were playing on the West Coast. Obviously, my parents never let me stay up to watch the games on school nights, so the first thing I would do when I'd wake up in the morning was pick up the phone. Like when the Yankees would be in Seattle, I would call up and listen for the score," he recalled.

"I did it a few times and my parents would get the phone bill and say, 'What is this number?' I'd be like, 'I was calling Sports Phone to get the Yankees score.' At first, they were a little upset about it but then they understood that I needed to know what the Yankees did, because back then it was the quickest way to find out. They were a little more lenient once I explained why I was doing that, but it wasn't like I was calling five times a day."

Schwartz was about 400 miles away, a second-semester senior preparing to go on-air at Buffalo State University, when his eagle-eyed mom spotted something in the local paper that would change the young broadcaster's life.

"Somehow my mother got the number of the radio station, and she called me about half an hour before my show. Because she knew I was looking for a job, she was going through the classified ads in *Newsday*, and she called and said, 'That thing you used to call as a kid, Sports Phone, they're looking for announcers,'" he explained.

"So April of '89 I come home on spring break and I go into the city in the old office on Third Avenue. I went and I interviewed with Ken Martin. He had me take a sports test. He had me go into a studio and do a demo recording. I had mailed in a cassette tape to him after I had faxed in the resume, but he had me do a demo in the studio. After I took the test and did the demo he offered me the part-time job right then and there. There was no waiting."

There was still the little matter of finishing up college in Buffalo, but Martin and Sports Phone proved accommodating, holding the job for Schwartz until after his May graduation. He worked a few shifts in Manhattan before the Sports Phone operation was moved to

Elmont, not ideal for many but perfect timing for the East Meadow resident.

The workflow at Sports Phone was night and day when compared to what Schwartz had experienced in Buffalo.

"It was certainly an adjustment. Even in college radio, you go into a studio, you turn the microphone on and once that red light comes on you're live. There's no going back. It took me a little while to get used to it, actually recording the updates. There was a different process to go through to getting the reports on air," Schwartz described.

"I thought it took me a pretty quick amount of time to get the hang of it, especially the 60-second updates and working the Saturday nights with a million college football and college basketball scores and getting them all in."

Schwartz worked at Sports Phone for about four and a half years, a span over which some moments of great consequence occurred.

The first that came to Schwartz's mind was an inspirational one for sure, being at Yankee Stadium for Sports Phone on September 4, 1993, when Jim Abbott no-hit a stacked Cleveland Indians lineup that included Kenny Lofton, Carlos Baerga, Albert Belle, Jim Thome, and Manny Ramirez.

Abbott had defied the odds his entire life, born with a birth defect where his right arm ended at the wrist. Simply reaching the big leagues is a monumental achievement for anyone, let alone ascending to those heights with a perceived limitation like the one Abbott contended with from the beginning.

Yet on an overcast Saturday afternoon in the Bronx, the kid from Flint, Michigan, drafted eighth overall by the California Angels in '88, took that dream to another level.

"That was a pretty good thrill, being there to cover that. I think this about Sports Phone in general, my general feeling of working there," Schwartz said. "It was a great way for me to get experience doing updates and doing the reports, but also getting a chance to get out in the field. There were a number of games that I had a chance to cover that will always stand out."

Other memories were tragic, such as manning the booth Christmas night 1989 when Yankees legend Billy Martin was killed in a single-car accident near his farm in upstate New York. Another was being in the Sports Phone newsroom on November 7, 1991, when a shattering development came out of the NBA.

Sports Phone Stories

Magic Shocks the Sports World
(feat. Cedric Dew, Howie Karpin, and Peter Schwartz)

On November 7, 1991, Los Angeles Lakers guard Magic Johnson announced on live TV that he had tested positive for HIV, also announcing that he was retiring from basketball as a result. A trio of Sports Phoners were on shift that day and recalled the stunning moments both leading up to and following the eventual Hall of Famer's press conference.

"We all didn't know what was going on. We found out that Magic Johnson was going to retire and he was going to make the announcement at a press conference. At that point there's no social media, so you don't know what's going on with him retiring," recalled Peter Schwartz.

"I remember [Howie Karpin] saying in the newsroom, 'This could be AIDS... Maybe this is AIDS,' and sure enough, that's what it was. I don't remember what I had for breakfast this morning, but I remember we were in the newsroom and we were trying to figure out what was going on, how we were gonna roll on sound and things like that."

As they scrambled to prepare updated recordings for Sports Phone's callers, the enormity of the moment started to set in.

"We were all in there together and I remember the shock that we felt in that moment, kind of how we started reflecting on the lives that these guys were living. It made me realize that oftentimes we were both adults and children in the room," Cedric Dew remembered.

"We looked up to these athletes like heroes, that when they failed, we ultimately held them accountable for failure. I think society has gotten better at that. But to me, that was an important one."

The shape and form the announcement was made in was rare for that era, especially considering the tragic nature of the news behind it.

"There came a point when athletes, particularly Black athletes, started trying to control their own narrative. Magic basically, in his moment, controlled his own narrative," Dew opined.

"We started seeing more athletes after that controlling how their announcements would happen. Whether it be a tragedy, whether it be trades, whether it be other things, you saw them controlling their narrative more, whereas before that the broadcasters controlled the narrative. I got to watch society change through the eyes of sports. I got a chance to watch a level of equality, a level of empathy, begin to happen in a way that I never would have imagined it would have happened, while at the same time doing a craft that I will do the rest of my life."

———

Quickie Quiz

Q: Which Sports Phone announcer witnessed stakeouts while working the night shift?

A: Peter Schwartz

Schwartz: "This was not really more of a singular moment because it happened a lot, but because of where we were at Elmont, we were across the street from the stables at Belmont Park. Anybody familiar with that area knows that at certain times of the night, over-night, it could be a scene for crime. The police officers always used to come in on a Saturday night and they used to go hang out in one of the wrestling or horo-scope studios, and with binoculars, they would look out the window across the street and see certain things going on. There were a couple of times I remember hearing, 'Okay, let's move!' and they would leave the studio, go across the street and take care of a situation that was going on."

CHOP SHOP

A member of the Sports Broadcasting Hall of Fame, Drew Esocoff has directed NFL primetime games for almost a quarter-century. One of his first jobs in the industry was at Sports Phone in the early '80s, a time when the New Jersey native burned the candle at both ends.

"Charlie DeNatale interviewed me. He had me do a test tape and I got hired shortly thereafter," Esocoff recalled, noting that he called the service all the time before landing the role. "I was actually working both at Sports Phone and a radio station in Jersey, where I'd get home from Sports Phone at 2:30 a.m. and have to be at the station at 5:30 a.m."

Before winning 19 Emmy Awards, Esocoff had dreams of being behind the mic.

"We all had the same goals. We want to be the next Marv Albert. Anybody who claims they didn't want that while they were working there is lying," he said.

"So you went in, you tried to do a good job, have a little humor, have a lot of enthusiasm, and provide an accurate report in whatever it was — 59 and a half seconds — and have a good time while you were doing it. There was nothing overly gimmicky about it, except you got frustrated if you fucked up."

Esocoff has fond memories of his Sports Phone days.

"You would call some guy in Detroit to get the Midwest scores, and then you had your slate and you kept erasing the score and putting in the new score but it was fun, man," he said. "It was a hoot working there. The pay sucked and the hours sucked, but you were 24, 25 years old. Who cared?"

Well, most of them are fond.

"My fondest memory of Sports Phone is parking over on 57th Street, when you couldn't park til 6 p.m. but you had to be at work at six," Esocoff sarcastically quipped. "So you'd leave your car there for seven or eight minutes, and I guess I didn't pay enough parking tickets. [My car was towed] and it ended up at some chop shop or garage up in the Bronx."

TOO CLOSE FOR COMFORT

Fans of the NBA's Dallas Mavericks have been tuning in to hear Chuck Cooperstein's voice since the mid-2000s. Long before relocating to Texas, the New York native gained some valuable experience at 919 Third Avenue.

"I actually knew about Sports Phone growing up, but there was a classified that I think my dad saw in the *New York Times* and that's how I found out about the job," he recalled.

Like many newbies, Cooperstein started on an out-of-town line before working his way up to primetime.

"[I started] on Buffalo, probably my first three or four months, and then back and forth to New Jersey," he said. "Probably about seven or eight months into it I started to get to do New York."

Also like many of those just dipping their toes in, learning to handle the chaos of football Sunday proved challenging at first.

"What I most remember was the frustration of NFL Sunday and doing basically one minute on, one minute off. If you screwed up the tape, you were screwed, and when we first started doing that I could not get it down," Cooperstein explained.

"It was one thing to do college football. I think we were doing every five minutes then or something like that. With the NFL we were doing every two minutes. It was like, 'You gotta be kidding!' This is absolutely exhausting and frustrating, and it took me a while to figure that damn thing out before I could actually feel comfortable doing it."

The close quarters didn't help either, with several announcers shuffling in and out of the booth.

"You're in there the whole time. It's like, my God," Cooperstein exclaimed. "That room was small enough. That closet was small enough that yes, you were truly in the loony bin at that point. That was just crazy, just nuts."

Luckily Sports Phone provided opportunities to get outside once in a while, often to the area's most well-known venues.

"Obviously in New York, there's so much to cover. I covered the Jets. I covered the Generals in the USFL and I covered the Major Indoor Soccer League Arrows. I covered St. John's basketball the last year [at Sports Phone]. I got to cover an occasional Knick game and all the college basketball at The Garden," Cooperstein recalled.

"It was incredible. I tell people all the time. It's one of the greatest experiences of my life. It set in motion so many things for whatever followed for me."

Sports Phone was responsible for kicking off a series of broadcasting trends, one which Cooperstein noted is still a common practice today.

"You just think about ultimately the talent that ran through there and then think we were doing one-minute sportscasts. We were doing all of this in a minute and yet so many of us have gone on to do so many other different things," he said.

"And then ironically enough, where in the past we would listen to WCBS and Ed [Ingles] and Bill Schweitzer, and they would be doing three-minute sportscasts. Well, how long are sportscasts now? If they're on at all, they're maybe at the most 90 seconds."

"But two, two and a half is like, that's like going along and reading *War and Peace*, you know? That's forever… But isn't it amazing how it's all come back around to one minute and what can you give people in 60 seconds?"

 Sports Phone Stories

I'm Real and I'm Fantastic!
(feat. Chuck Cooperstein)

Sportswriter Jim Dent has certainly experienced a wide range of ups and downs, penning a *New York Times* bestseller and seeing his work used in the creation of two movies. He also had his share of legal troubles, spending time in prison on account of double-digit DWI convictions and even ditching a sentencing hearing and fleeing to Mexico at one point.

When Mavs radio man Chuck Cooperstein left Sports Phone for Texas, he had an encounter with Dent almost immediately.

"My first day in Dallas was in August of 1984, and on Monday night we had what they used to call the Cowboy Hour. It was the *Tom Landry Show* from 6-6:15, and then Tex Schramm had his own show from 6:15 to 7. After that we had what we call the football writers roundtable, the three beat writers from the *Morning News*, the *Dallas Times Herald*, and the *Fort Worth Star-Telegram* would come in with Brad Sham and they would talk about the Cowboys for an hour. And then it was a guy Steve Perkins from *Dallas Cowboys Weekly*, who very famously wrote the book *Next Year's Champions* because the Cowboys could never win," Cooperstein recalled.

"So from *The Times Herald* is a guy named Jim Dent, who later went on to be a pretty famous author and wrote *12 Mighty Orphans* and *The Junction Boys,* which got turned into movies. Ran into trouble. Jail and escaped bond, ran down to Mexico, did all kinds of crap. Anyway, back then he walks in the door. I introduce myself and he stops dead in his tracks, eyes bug-eyed, and says 'No, cannot be! Absolutely impossible. There is no way that there is a real person named Chuck Cooperstein.'"

It turned out Dent liked to place more than just the occasional wager, and that he was a regular caller to Sports Phone.

"Oh, [he called] all the time. He was he was an inveterate gambler," Cooperstein explained. "So I introduced myself and he hears the voice, and he puts two and two together."

———

JUNK MAIL

Jim Berman's career in television management has spanned well over 30 years, most recently as president and general manager of NBC and Fox affiliate Dakota News Now. The former New Yorker attended high school on Manhattan's Upper East Side before enrolling in Rutgers University, where his on-air demo would help secure a job with Sports Phone.

"It was one of the greatest thrills of my young life. They were looking for a couple of people. I sent in my tape. I was at WRSU. I was a college junior at that point at Rutgers and I was doing play-by-play. To me growing up, Sports Phone was the ultimate," Berman said.

"Oh my God, I am going to be working with King Wally. I'm going to be working with Howie Karpin. I'm going to be working with Charlie DeNatale, all these names that I knew, Mike Farrell. I was just floored."

After working primarily on the Buffalo and Rochester lines, the bosses at Sports Phone suggested that Berman cover the New Jersey line — not from the booth in midtown but from the Rutgers radio station.

"So I wound up having press releases from the various New Jersey colleges sent to me so that I could do it during the day when we were looking for content on a weekday. I could say "Here's the New Jersey college report, William Paterson took on Glassboro State over the weekend" and whatever. I was able to do that and so I got elevated to being the Jersey guy," he recalled.

"Whenever I was on the road for Rutgers basketball and Sports Phone needed to have an update of some kind, I would make sure that I did that. Even if I wasn't on the road, because I was always involved with something like the postgame show, I would make sure that I did an update."

Those press releases arrived in droves, with many Garden State colleges pining for coverage on Sports Phone. While this offered Berman plenty of content for the New Jersey line, it later became a paper problem for an unwitting student.

"I had all the New Jersey colleges sending me stuff to my P.O. box at Rutgers, and so it was jam-packed with press releases because all these colleges want the coverage. They were so excited and so this was a big deal. This was the only way they were gonna get coverage because they weren't gonna get coverage on WNBC. Marv Albert's not going to give them the coverage, so I was their guy," he explained.

"It was funny because then I of course graduated, but I wind up going back to Rutgers a couple of years later and I always thought about those Sports Phone press releases. So I went over to my old P.O. box and I took a look through the window, and it was jammed still with press releases. So whoever took over my box, some Rutgers student who probably had no idea what Glassboro State football was even about, is getting inundated with these press releases. That poor person, I have no idea how many years that went on."

Although he'd later move out of sports broadcasting, Berman learned lessons at Sports Phone that translated to his current career.

"It was really my first job and it taught me discipline and focus and timeliness, and making sure you were on top of things. It was one of the greatest prep opportunities that I could have possibly asked for, not to mention that the people that I worked with were just some of the most amazingly wonderful people," he said.

"I will tell you very, very sincerely that it was one of the hardest decisions that I had to make. I graduated and I have the opportunity now to start my professional career in the TV management side of the business, but it was really hard to leave Sports Phone because I loved it. I loved every minute of it, every day that I came in was just so much fun and I missed it desperately."

Quickie Quiz

Q: Which Sports Phone announcer was asked to give an impromptu rundown while tipping a few back?

A: Jim Berman

Berman: "As soon as I left Sports Phone, I would go out to bars and I would meet different people. Near the end [of my tenure] I was on the New York system, so people sort of knew my name. When I would go out to bars I'd hear, 'Wait a minute, your voice is very familiar.' I'd be like, 'Yeah, I did Sports Phone for a little bit.' 'This guy was on Sports Phone. You've got to do your Sports Phone shtick.' So any bar I would go into, everybody would gather around me to see if I could just go into my 58-second [rundown]. Quick, read the scores, even though I had no scores in front of me. Just whatever would pop into my head and see if I could do it without breathing, and then finish up with, 'Stay with us!' Everybody in the bar would take a shot and drink, and they'd go crazy. It was hilarious ... It speaks to the power of what Sports Phone meant in the '80s."

 Sports Phone Stories

You Fucking Moron!
(feat. Jim Berman)

On the morning of January 3, 1982, the Giants were in San Francisco, preparing for a playoff showdown with Joe Montana and the favored 49ers later that afternoon. Back east the anticipation was building, and callers to New York Sports Phone were pining for the latest updates from Candlestick Park.

Jim Berman was on duty at 919 Third Avenue when someone he thought was stringer Sam Skinner called in to recap a pregame interview with Niners' All-Pro cornerback Ronnie Lott.

"So what happened was that there was always some tape to cut and stuff like that, and so someone said, 'Skinner's on the phone, pick up line two and set up a voicer and get his comments.' Bingo [Mike Weinstein], he did the perfect Skinner [imitation]," Berman recalled.

"'Hey, this is Skinner. Okay, now we're going to talk about the 49er-Giant game.' I don't remember exactly what he said but he's going on and on and on, and I'm hearing laughter in the background as I'm recording this. I just think, there's always laughter going on at Sports Phone, and it goes on and on and on. Finally, it's like, '... and Ronnie Lott was quoted as saying, Jim Berman, you fucking moron!' I was like, 'What?!?'"

The staff erupted in laughter, and the Hall of Famer had a new moniker in Berman's brain from there on out.

"Everybody was roaring. I mean, they were just roaring ... I realized I was clearly part of the team because they wanted to do that to me. It actually made me feel good, but I never forgot it. It was so funny, so I will always remember that," Berman reminisced.

"All these years later, whenever Ronnie Lott's name comes up I immediately think of that moment, so that's what Ronnie Lott means to me ... To me, Ronnie Lott's name is 'Ronnie Lott Jim Berman You Fucking Moron.' It's all one name."

———

NBA TO FDNY

Not everyone working at Sports Phone had dreams of moving forward in the industry. For Tony Matteo, it was the perfect job for a young man who lived, ate, and breathed sports.

"I had a friend named Mike Lopiparo, who was a news writer for 1010 WINS. He knew I was a sports fanatic and a sponge for sports information. He originally got me a job at 1010 WINS being a production assistant, and then when I guess he heard of a job at Sports Phone opening up he got me the job there," recalled Matteo, who worked at both the Manhattan and Elmont locations.

"My motivation for the job was not really professional, as most of these guys used it as a stepping stone. To be completely honest, I never took the media business very seriously. I was just a sports junkie and the opportunity to work there, even though it wasn't great pay at that time, my living conditions afforded me to have a job at that point where I didn't need to make that much money. I just jumped at the chance because I was a fanatical Sports Phone caller as a kid."

Matteo wasn't behind the microphone as much as some of his colleagues, but he did quite a bit behind the scenes.

"I was rarely on air. I basically was a production assistant, so I used to take in the live feeds from the stringers and the reporters and I would put them on cart and reel-to-reel and prepare them for the updates — basically seven-second sound bites for the updates and stuff like that. I was also the overnight producer," he explained.

"Most of the guys went home after the last West Coast game ended and the tapes ended for the night, and then I would stay there through the evening and prepare any kind of late news that came in, and prepare any kind of sound that came in after the West Coast games for the next day."

He was also responsible for Sports Phone's NBA Hotline, one that was aggregated and broadcast by news outlets across the country.

"We did something called the NBA Tonight so Phone Programs, if I remember correctly, had a contract where I would get in the raw NBA footage. I would highlight two games from the night and have a sound bite each from those two games, and national radio stations and such would lift that off of our broadcast," Matteo said.

"So I would end the night with an NBA report, with two seven- to eight-second sound bites nationally. They [NBA clips] were coming from individual stringers from different cities."

On one of the rare nights Matteo was on the main line, he decided to slip in a score that wasn't on the Sports Phone slate.

"One night when my local roller hockey team won the championship in Brooklyn I told my buddies, 'If you call at 11:30 tonight for one recording I'm going to mention that we won the roller hockey championship, and then I'm going to erase it right away because I'm going to get fired,'" Matteo reminisced.

"So basically, at the end of one of my tapes I was like 'and the final scores: the Rangers 2, the Islanders 1, and in Fort Hamilton roller hockey, the Panthers won the B championship by defeating Farrell's Blues 4-3.' Click. They called [and heard it], and I was able to get it off the air before any of the bosses heard it."

Matteo was still at Sports Phone in July of 1994 when he joined the New York City Fire Department, and even continued to work there part-time for a while afterward. With a little over seven years on the job, the Brooklyn native later found himself at Ground Zero shortly after the North Tower of the World Trade Center collapsed during the 9/11 terror attacks.

"I was working that day in Coney Island and we got called when the second plane hit, and we actually were driving through the streets of Brooklyn to the Battery Tunnel to try and get through, but we could not get through the tunnel at that point. There was nobody getting through. So we're basically staged on the Brooklyn side of the Battery Tunnel, and kind of watched the towers go down from there, right in front of us," he described.

"And I would say within about an hour after the second one came down we were mobilized and we went over the Brooklyn Bridge, and I spent the rest of the day and night there, and then many, many days there over the succeeding months. Basically, from September till the following spring."

Promoted to lieutenant two years later and then to captain in 2013, Matteo remembers a former Sports Phone teammate checking in on him not long after that tragic day in '01.

"So after 9/11, I was married and I had bought a house in Staten Island, and I do remember Don [La Greca] tracking me down somehow, giving me a call. This was in the days when I guess the White Pages still existed, before the internet, and he was able to track me down. He called me one day at home to make sure everything was okay, so I appreciate that."

Although he opted for a helmet and rescue gear over headphones and a recorder, Matteo's time at Sports Phone instilled a level of confidence.

"I was a Brooklyn guy. I knew I had a very outer-borough accent. I knew my communication skills were kind of limited. All these guys went at it knowing that if I'm going to work in the media, I'm probably going to have to relocate somewhere else in a small town and work my way back, and I never had the resolve for something like that," he explained.

"But it did give me the confidence that I could do it because I knew

I retained sports information like a sponge and I would go toe-to-toe with anybody there. I knew my stuff as well or better than most, but it kind of gave me the confidence that I could do what I could do within the business, and I was able to basically succeed."

It also impressed some of his FDNY colleagues, especially those who liked to wager.

"In my years with the fire department, I would mention to some guys that I worked at Sports Phone and their eyes would light up. They couldn't [believe it]. There was one guy, who was a retired chief. He's moved to Florida since but he was a big gambler, and he was a big Sports Phone junkie," Matteo said.

"So when I mentioned to him that I worked at Sports Phone he couldn't believe it. It was like I told him that I was on the set of a national television show. He's like, 'You worked at Sports Phone? I don't believe it. I used to call it every day!'"

 # Sports Phone Stories

Captain Cutup
(feat. Don La Greca and Tony Matteo)

A common theme throughout Sports Phone's storied history, Tony Matteo was no stranger to shenanigans during his shifts. One that comes to the FDNY veteran's mind ironically involves an in-office fire, one that he happened to spark himself.

"We had an Islanders calendar hanging up in the office and I decided one night, in my eminent wisdom, to light it on fire and the smoke detectors went off. The building had an automatic fire alarm system," explained the die-hard Rangers fan.

"So the Elmont volunteer fire department actually came across the street and started questioning what happened. The manager at the time was quaking in his boots that the fire department was there. I just came up with this story that a piece of rubbish had burned and we put it out but, yeah, it was because I lit an Islanders calendar on fire."

The legendary Jiggs McDonald was an NHL play-by-play man for more than 40 years, eclipsing 3,000 games behind the mic and winning the prestigious Foster Hewitt Memorial Award. Stan Fischler once called McDonald "the hockey play-by-play man's play-by-play man." High praise, indeed.

To Matteo, McDonald was simply the voice of a team he despised — making the Ontario native an ideal target for his next Sports Phone prank.

"Not the most professional thing to do, but sometimes we had some downtime. There was a media book that gave us the phone numbers and addresses of all the local people who worked in media. So we had a three-way, we had a conference call phone. I would always initiate it. I would find two guys who worked in media, and I would dial them at the same time and see if they figured out that they hadn't called each other. We would put it on mute and put it on speaker and sit back and laugh as these guys try to figure out who called who," Matteo recalled.

"But Jiggs McDonald, I hated him because I was a Ranger fan, and just from him being the Islanders announcer I took him as basically a homer and a Ranger hater even if that wasn't true. I just couldn't stand him. So I got Jiggs McDonald's address via that book. At that time, when you watched television, you could send items to people's houses C.O.D, cash on delivery. I just started sending obscure items on television to his house, C.O.D."

Matteo doesn't recall participating in the following piece of mischief, which Don La Greca recounted for us.

"Apparently, the phone number to the scorer's table at the Boston Garden, which you'd have to call sometimes to get a score or whatever, ended up being the same number of the penalty box for hockey games," La Greca explained.

"So Matteo would always call up if like [Rangers right wing Tie] Domi took a stupid penalty or something. It'd never work out, but he'd call and be like, 'Give me Domi. I want to ball him out for committing that penalty.'"

Quickie Quiz

Q: Which lucky Sports Phoner witnessed golf history live?
A: Drew Esocoff

One of the more memorable shots at historic Westchester Country Club took place in June 1982, when long-time pro golfer Bob Gilder made an extraordinary double-eagle on the 18th hole.

Esocoff: "I didn't get out too many [times for Sports Phone] but they sent me to the Westchester Open Classic one year at Westchester Country Club. I was standing behind the green when Bob Gilder had the double-eagle, when he jarred his second shot on the par-five. That was fun."

CHAPTER 5
THE WFUV AND WNYU FAMILY TREE

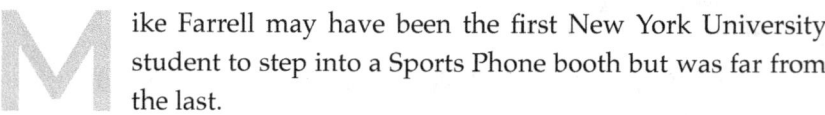ike Farrell may have been the first New York University student to step into a Sports Phone booth but was far from the last.

"NYU became known as a feeder line. It never hurts to have a connection," noted Farrell.

BORN TO RUN

One of the gang hired by Bob Meyer for Sports Phone's 1975 reboot, Denis McNamara had been a journalism major at NYU who already had experience, interning as a newsroom desk assistant at both WNEW and WPIX-TV. When WNYU went from AM to 89.1 FM, he served as general manager, working alongside Farrell at their alma mater's radio station.

"Mike was a great guy and he said, 'Look, those guys up there are hiring. You may want to give it a try,'" McNamara recalled. "Somehow in that maze of stuff, I had gotten married and moved up to 52nd and Second. I got an apartment there with my wife and I needed to start making more money. That's around the time that I went to Sports Phone and applied for the job with Bullet Bob."

Immersed in sports scores throughout the week, McNamara was now deejaying at WLIR on the weekends, a job he landed with some help from radio icon Scott Muni. In an ironic twist of fate, the Long Islander was able to keep tabs on his radio performance figures during shifts at 919 Third Avenue.

"I used to come in and look up my weekend ratings because [Phone Programs/Air Time] was an advertising company, and there was a woman there that always gave me the books to look at and see how my ratings were doing," he explained.

"They were in the New York books, and there was a Long Island book. I was doing Saturdays and Sundays, so I could look and see what the ratings were. She taught me how to read them. I learned a lot about what I was going to get into professionally when I was [at Sports Phone]."

McNamara was grateful for the opportunity but biding his time, with an end goal of working solely in music radio. As it stood, the other weekend disc jockey at LIR was none other than the widely influential Murray the K, known as the "Fifth Beatle" due to his close ties with the band.

"I had developed a reputation in New York because of working at [W]NEW but also because at NYU we developed a series of concerts from The Bottom Line [in Greenwich Village]," McNamara explained. "I worked on the Bruce Springsteen broadcast, the famous one and all of that. I was being groomed to be music director at LIR, and so it was just coming in time."

Springsteen's star was about to rise on the heels of the *Born to Run* album, and McNamara was on his way as well, eventually leaving Sports Phone to become WLIR's music director.

"I never thought as a kid I'd be working with Billy Joel or U2 or the [Rolling] Stones and stuff like that. so it's always been a thrill because I loved their music," McNamara reminisced.

"I turned LIR into the most listened to Class A radio station in America for a period of time, and for a 3000-watt station that was quite an achievement … I never take it for granted that we were in the back-yard of the biggest radio market in the world, but we were a huge music force."

"We played records before anyone else, and they went national and they became hits. In England, they called us the gateway to America, and I was very proud of that because I was always a British music fan. Overall, a lot of people came through that little station and went on to become major successes, just like at Sports Phone."

A member of the Long Island Music and Entertainment Hall of Fame, McNamara's tenure at Sports Phone proved valuable in the biz.

"I always was fascinated that people did listen to us. Whether it was the audiences at NYU or Sports Phone or LIR, because they were the people that helped you so much and gave you feedback to be better," he elaborated. "They'd call and grumble about something and you'd say, 'Yeah, maybe we should fix that. Make it better.'"

No matter if it was covering Bono or Bert Blyleven, some attributes learned transcended industries.

"Thinking of Kenny Albert calling as a kid on the phone. I think the Alberts have been just fabulous in broadcasting stuff and that makes me feel good. It's like when David Bowie told me he listened to LIR, I was thrilled by it," McNamara pointed out.

"Because you don't know who you're influencing when you're doing some of these things, and it's just amazing. You can't think about it [in the moment]. You just do what you do at the time and we were so into what we were doing, and that sometimes gets lost with people working in all fields, especially in communications. We were really into sports. You had to be into it, and those were important qualities."

The NYU roots ran deep in Sports Phone's family tree, including Kenny Albert's one-time roomie Rich Ackerman.

TEENAGE DREAM

Ackerman's on-air initiation at Sports Phone took place while he was still in his teens, not long removed from the now-seasoned broadcaster's days as a patron.

"[I was] not only a caller but I played the [Quickie] Quiz as much as I possibly could, 212-355-7474," he said. "I don't know where the hell I pulled that number from but I just remembered it."

Later a student at NYU, Ackerman needed work to offset the costly living expenses of the area.

"CJ Papa was working there. When you start college all of a sudden, especially if you're living in downtown Manhattan, Greenwich Village, things get a little expensive and so I had been looking for a job," Ackerman recalled. "Then CJ had told me they were looking for a writer and he said, 'Are you interested?' and I said sure. He recommended me and the rest was history."

What started as a way to help pay the bills quickly turned into a life-shaping gig.

"I was 19 and I did a shift on New York. Probably spring of '88 I was on the air, so I definitely did a shift on New York Sports Phone before I turned 20. I remember that it was a big deal to me," Ackerman said.

"But we had expanded to Boston that summer, so there were more shifts available at that point. So I was probably working Boston Sports Phone more, but I didn't care where I was working. Whether I was writing, whether I was on the air, it was all good to me."

He quickly realized how invaluable the opportunity was.

"It was a dial-up service but it was still on the air. It felt every bit like you were on the radio or TV. Back then there weren't too many outlets. There weren't iPhones, there weren't social media [services] where you could post your own stuff or anything like that. You're left to your own devices," Ackerman explained.

"It was hard to get TV equipment or studio time to practice that so really, the only thing you could do was, for me in college, the campus radio station, a tape recorder. But this was practical on-air work so it was very big. It gave you some name recognition. It gave you experience doing it."

While the on-air shifts helped prepare Ackerman for his future career, representing Sports Phone at games was when he was especially able to hone his craft — chopping it up with some elite athletes.

"If I could work two shifts a week during college and cover a couple of games, it was paradise. Not only was I making money and I was just gaining experience, but I was practically living at Madison Square Garden and interviewing guys. I still remember the first time I covered an NBA game, and I remember we had to get tape for the NBA Hotline. You had to go up to certain guys or certain teams to get preview sound for the next game," he described.

"I remember being intimidated by Clyde Drexler and Steve Johnson because I had read such stories about how they were coach killers and how things were not going well in Portland. Now that was previous to the coaching situation that they had at that time, but I went up to both of them and they couldn't have been nicer. I'm like, wow, this is great.

These guys are such good guys to deal with. I remember going up to Charles Barkley too, talking about an intimidating presence, and he couldn't have been friendlier."

Players weren't always as friendly, and those uncomfortable run-ins also proved important going forward.

"To show up in front of a locker and, whether the guys were cooperative or not as cooperative — as Keith Hernandez was difficult after games, you kind of felt as if you were earning your stripes doing that type of stuff," Ackerman said.

Quickie Quiz

Q: Which big football game did Rich Ackerman get to update on Sports Phone?

A: The 1989 Fiesta Bowl

Ackerman: "I worked New Year's Day in '89 when Notre Dame played West Virginia for the national championship, and I loved Notre Dame that year. I had all these things off the top of my head, you know, these lines ready [to use on-air]. That was a pretty big game for Notre Dame because back then they had gone a while since their previous national championship, and they had been through a lot with the Gerry Faust years and getting crushed by Miami. To see it all come to fruition in the third season under Lou Holtz, that was pretty important and a big event that day."

Sports Phone Stories

Wheel of Miss-Fortune
(feat. Rich Ackerman)

The Sports Phone crew played a practical joke on one of their own, which had him believing that an unlikely co-worker dated Wheel of Fortune hostess Vanna White before she became famous.

"Tom McQuade, the mastermind of it all, was a very good practical joker. I don't even know how he came up with it," recalled Rich Ackerman. "Whether he had talked about it before or whether it was spur of the moment, he told me that Vanna White dated one of our colleagues, Ken Martin, and I didn't believe it. He was so insistent about it that you start to think, well, maybe it's possible."

When Ackerman questioned the tryst's legitimacy, further proof was offered.

"Kenny, at that point in time, could have stood to lose a few pounds. [They] said he used to run track, which I think he did at one point in his life. They showed me a picture of what he looked like back then and so I was like, I guess it makes sense," he explained. "He was lean [in the picture]. The relationship predated her stardom on *Wheel of Fortune*, so I start to think anything's possible, right?"

The ruse continued for a few months.

"It went for quite a while, but I'd look at Ken and I'd just shake my head like, 'Nah, it can't be,' but it happened. I was just so perplexed by it. Part of me knew the reality, but the other part of me wanted to believe that this fairy tale was actually the case," Ackerman said. "You want to think something good about one of your friends and colleagues like wow, this is pretty wild."

Falling for the prank (and possibly a few others) earned Ackerman a moniker tied to Nicholas Colasanto's character in the sitcom *Cheers*.

"I guess that's why I got the nickname Coach," he said. "You could kind of tell me anything."

––––––

IT'S LIKE PULLING TEETH

Just as CJ Papa referred his Sigma Phi Epsilon fraternity brother Ackerman to the gig, future sports agent Alan Sanders was the one who first encouraged him to give it a shot. No relation to fellow Sports Phone alum Bob, CJ started on several out-of-town lines before working his way up to New York.

"I remember doing New Orleans, Seattle, Minnesota, and Pittsburgh," Papa recalled. "You had to prove yourself there before you got a chance to do the New York Sports Phone, which I eventually did. Because I remember I used to tell my dad, call the Sports Phone so you can hear me."

Some of the out-of-town lines were slightly less pressurized, as their recordings could run longer than one minute. One common theme across all was the frustration over those West Coast matchups that moved at a snail's pace.

"We always hated the Seattle games, because in the Kingdome the games ran long. You always had to wait for that game to end and you waited and waited for someone to go, 'Game's over' and then you could do your final report, which had to be perfect. Otherwise, you had to keep redoing it," Papa added.

"We were college kids so staying up is not an issue, but back then the Mariners used to play the longest games. A Yankee-Mariner game took forever to play. Can't this thing end? Even though you were excited you were working, still you wanted the game to end."

Late nights or not, getting the job at Sports Phone provided CJ definitive clarity on which career he wanted to pursue — a path that came *this* close to involving drills and novocaine.

"Sports Phone showed me that I didn't want to be a dentist. My neighbor across the street where I grew up was like, 'Go to dental school and you come to work for me'. I ended up marrying a dentist. My mother always wanted a doctor in the family. I had to go to medical school," Papa explained, noting that a career in dentistry seemed to be in the cards.

"I started doing [Sports Phone] and I was taking journalism courses. When you got your feet wet, this is what I want to do. I want to be around sports. I want to be a reporter. Whatever that turned out to be, I don't know, but at the time you're like this is what I want to do."

The long nights in the booth and the trappings that came along with them provided clarity.

"It was either one of two things. If you didn't like working nights, it showed you that you didn't want to be a sports reporter," Papa opined.

"If you didn't mind the hours, didn't mind the frenetic pace, [didn't mind] eating Chinese food out of a [carton] and having indigestion because you're eating on the run, and you still smiled at the end of the night then you knew this business was for you. Sports Phone did that. There's no doubt."

With all due respect to the dental field, Papa appears to have made the right choice, leaning on those experiences at Sports Phone still to this day.

"I do an hour show on SiriusXM Radio so the clock is timed. I can always lean back on the fact that I did that when I was 20 years old. Now getting a minute's worth of stuff in, I don't want to say it's easy but it's comfortable because you look back and go, 'Wow, I did 40 scores in a minute and 20 seconds.' I can get four stories in for a one-minute update, which is really 57 seconds," he said.

"It laid the groundwork for your brain to be able to think, read, and look at the time clock — which is what you need to do when you're in radio. It helped in TV because I don't remember many times where I had a problem, where someone was counting me out of a break or counting me to a break, and I'm talking and they're telling you stuff. You process that because you've done that."

MARV AND KEITH

Well before Sanders was in a position to recommend CJ for a job, he was a Sports Phone caller with hopes of one day being on the other end of that phone line.

"I had grown up with it. I remember Chief [John Martin], Cory [Eisner], and Charlie [DeNatale] as the people that I heard the most when I would call Sports Phone in my teens in the late '70s and early '80s. And I thought if I can get a job like that, how awesome is that? I knew what Sports Phone was and I knew how culturally relevant in that moment it happened to be in New York because we had the ubiquitous commercials on TV," Sanders recalled.

"Look, we all know it was the dark ages of technology. Nobody had computers. There's no internet. There are no cell phones. There's 976-1313. In that unique moment, we were kind of like a unique game in town. Getting that job, I was over the moon. I thought it was the greatest thing."

Working at NYU's radio station and trying to land an internship, Sanders decided to aim high and target one of the biggest names in town.

"All you needed to do at that time, was look in the phone book and find out the phone numbers of the local stations. I left a message on Marv Albert's voicemail at WNBC when he was still doing the six and the 11 [o'clock news] there, and to my astonishment he called me back less than 15 minutes later and was willing to talk to me on the phone," Sanders marveled.

"Unfortunately, WNBC did not do internships at that time but he gave me some advice on what to do and where to go. I realized in that moment that wow, all you got to do is reach out to people and try to figure your way through all the red tape and morass, and it's not maybe as hard as it might seem."

He eventually secured an internship with another notable broadcaster, one that would lead him right to 919 Third Avenue.

"I had an internship at CNN with Keith Olbermann. He had left RKO Radio and was in his first TV job at CNN as a sportscaster. I went over to his apartment once and he showed me his insane baseball card collection because he knew I was a collector, too," Sanders said.

"Keith introduced me to King Wally and it was Wally who hired me in '83. Like everybody else there I had ambitions of being on the air. I'm just not sure I was as confident in my abilities as some of the other guys were, but in any case, I loved being on the air."

Although he didn't end up pursuing a career behind the mic like many of his colleagues, Sanders still credits Sports Phone for his success as an agent.

"It had an enormous impact on me because at a minimum, while it may not in the end result have driven me to pursue broadcasting on the air, it kept my passion for sports in and of itself and it taught me how to meet people and be less shy. [It taught me to] be more comfortable in myself because we all created a very comfortable atmosphere for each other, in a workplace that was pretty tight and pretty crowded and you'd have to get along with people," he said.

"In terms of what Sports Phone meant to me, for instance, Howie Rose and I would sit next to each other any time I covered a Mets game. Howie and I would have fun sitting around and talking. It's just the people that we met along the way and the places that we got to go in terms of inside the locker room. For a six-dollar-an-hour gig, you wouldn't think that you would get to do some of the crazy stuff that we got to do."

Quickie Quiz

Q: Which Sports Phone announcer's friend showed him off to his future wife?

A: Alan Sanders

Being on Sports Phone meant bragging rights back in the day, even for friends of the on-air talent.

Sanders: "It was funny, all our friends were Sports Phone users too. I had one of my best friends who wanted to show his girlfriend at the time, who became his wife, that I was actually one of the Sports Phone announcers. He handed her the phone to hear my voice and she didn't understand that it was a recording, and the way he told the story was she kept saying, 'No, Alan, you can stop. It's me.' It was a big deal for people of our age to be able to say I worked for Sports Phone. No one knew it was [paying] six bucks an hour or anything like that."

 Sports Phone Stories

The Magic Number
(feat. Alan Sanders)

Alan Sanders grew up rooting for the Mets, getting to experience first-hand a major milestone in their 1986 championship run as a member of the Sports Phone crew.

"I remember the summer of '86. It was basically a countdown to when the Mets were going to clinch. There was never a question that they were going to win the division," he recalled.

"In August, we had to put in our September [game coverage] requests. I tried to calculate the most likely day that the Mets would clinch, and so I put in September 17 … September 17 was a [Wednesday] and the Mets' magic number over the Phillies was one. They had a three-game series at the Vet [Veteran's Stadium] on Friday, Saturday, and Sunday."

Rather than miss a possible clincher on the road, Sanders and squad headed down the turnpike.

"So the magic number is one going into Philadelphia and my brother and I and a couple of friends drove down because we figured if we can't see them clinch at Shea we might as well drive down there," Sanders added. "Of course, they got their asses kicked on Friday night. I worked at Sports Phone on Saturday and Sunday, and they got their asses kicked on Saturday and Sunday and only came back with the ability to clinch [at home] because they had gotten swept at the Vet."

The Phillies had helped postpone the inevitable, setting up a dream scenario for the future sports agent.

"So I ended up in the insanity of that locker room when they clinched against the Cubs," he happily recounted. "And now I'm 23, and basically I've reached the pinnacle. I've been in a champagne-soaked locker room. It's unforgettable, and the luck that had to be involved."

Sanders's swan song for Sports Phone may not have been as memorable, but it wasn't anything to sneeze at either.

"I would say the last thing I did for Sports Phone was cover the Mets-Dodgers playoff series in '88. I had already graduated from law school. I'd already taken and passed the bar, and I got the job at the agency right after the '88 postseason," he said. "It wasn't quite as insane in '88, but somehow or another I also chose the right date in '88. I don't know why. I don't remember how and when that happened."

———

IS MY LUCK UP?

Sanders introduced classmate Steve Cangialosi to King Wally, helping him score a spot at Sports Phone. The young broadcaster arrived confident but quickly realized he was among a distinguished circle.

"I know this sounds like I'm overdramatizing it but not everybody can walk into that setting, be comfortable in that office, and do the job well. Back then for a young kid like me, and I was 19, when I walked into that place for the first time you think you've got it all figured out. You know as much about sports as anybody," Cangialosi explained.

"Then you walk into that setting with people who are all your colleagues and they're also New Yorkers, but they come from different sections of New York. They've been watching all the same things that you have throughout your whole childhood, and you realize that they're just as smart if not smarter than you've been all of this time. It raises your level of sports acumen."

Working in a city where sports was king, Cangialosi felt the Sports Phone crew could go toe to toe with any other outlet.

"Looking back on it now, I'll bet you that some of the most intelligent sports conversations and discourse happened in that small office on Third Avenue as they did anywhere else in the city, including the best newspaper sports rooms," he said.

"Most of the people that we worked with not only had a clue, we had strong opinions that were rooted in the right things. I think you see less and less of that today."

Those convos pushed Cangialosi to be better.

"I was a huge hockey fan growing up and suddenly I walk into that room and I realize that guy [who works there] knows more about the Calgary Flames than I ever will and that pissed me off," he explained.

"It makes me want to know more about the Calgary Flames than that guy the next time I see him. There was that internal spirit that I think we had in the room that made what we did a great New York thing."

One particular playoff game during the Mets' 1986 championship run helped Cangialosi realize Sports Phone's impact, and it's probably not the one that first comes to mind for most.

"You go back to 1986 and the Mets win the World Series. I thought in retrospect we always talk more about the wrong Game Six that year. We talk about the ball going through [Bill] Buckner's legs and the Mets surviving and ultimately winning it all the next game," he reminisced.

"The best Game Six was the one in Houston. I happened to be in the chair that day for New York Sports Phone, the day the Mets are going to clinch the National League pennant."

Because that was a daytime matchup, many nervous Mets fans stuck at work relied on 976-1313 to know what was taking place inside the Astrodome.

"It's one of the last, great New York sporting events that we witnessed that happened on a weekday afternoon. The game just keeps going and going and going and it goes 16 innings and it lasts four hours and 42 minutes with ridiculous highs and lows for the Mets fan, knowing that [Cy Young Award winner] Mike Scott is sitting there for a Game 7, waiting in the wings," Cangialosi recalled.

"The Mets aren't going to win that game if it gets to Game 7. The roller coaster ride of that game with Billy Hatcher hitting the home run in the 14th inning to extend it and I'm sitting there, just in the moment, and I'm the guy updating the New York Sports Phone with every score change, every half inning change, or, at least every ten minutes."

While he certainly grasped the magnitude of the game itself, at the time Cangialosi didn't realize how much of the city was depending on him with each passing inning.

"It wasn't until days later that I remembered how big of a deal it was that I was on New York Sports Phone because so many people, little did I know at the time, had me as the eyes and ears for that game. We're talking 37 years ago," he acknowledged.

"How many people were in the office, not allowed to have a radio or TV broadcasting? What they did have was a phone and they had this 'idiot' telling them everything that was going on in probably what was, at the moment, the most important thing in their lives. There are gonna be those occasions where you might not be Howard Cosell, but you are the avenue to the most important piece of information for the New York sports fan more so than you ever thought you were."

Three decades later, Cangialosi's name still rang bells from his time on the New York line.

"When I lived in the West Village in New York, one of my friends owned an Italian restaurant. Some people, occasionally, would walk in there that are a little bit shady, if you know what I mean. One night, I'm sitting in there eating a late dinner at the bar by myself after work. These three guys, you kinda know right away these are guys you don't get cute with," he said.

"They heard me talking sports with the owner of the place. They go, 'What do you do?' 'I'm a sports announcer.' They go, 'What's your name?' I go, 'I'm Cangialosi.' One guy looks at the other and he goes, 'Thirteen-thirteen.'"

What's this guy talking about? Herman Munster at 1313 Mockingbird Lane? Cangialosi was confused.

"I go, 'What the fuck does that mean? Thirteen-thirteen, what the fuck is he saying? Is my luck up?' It's an unlucky number. It took me a second to piece together what he was talking about, 9-7-6-1-3-1-3. He remembered me from Sports Phone," he clarified. "With one mention of my last name, probably 30 years after the fact, this guy's making a connection to Sports Phone. It's part of the lore of the city. I don't think that's gonna go away for a long time."

 # Sports Phone Stories

Pardon My French Open
(as told by Ken Samelson feat. Steve Cangialosi)

Steve Cangialosi was covering a shift when an irate woman called the office to complain that the French Open tennis scores were not being reported on Sports Phone. The future play-by-play veteran ended up victim to the telephone equivalent of a hot mic.

Ken Samelson was there that day and recounted the story.

"The French Open was going on and it was a very busy day, so they didn't put it on the main line. Some lady calls the office, and usually you didn't have to answer it. It was the general line, and this lady calls and Cangialosi picks up and she starts bitching,

'Why is the French Open not on?' and he tries to explain to her that it's on 976-2525 [the supplemental line that was used for scores and news that didn't fit on 976-1313], you can get it [there], and she's arguing with him that that's more important than some afternoon Brewers-Tigers game. She was really annoying him, and he couldn't get her off the phone."

"Finally he does, and as he's hanging it up he goes, 'This stupid bitch' or whatever. About five minutes later, the phone rings again. I pick it up and she goes, 'Who's this?' I go, 'This is Ken.'"

"'Oh, so your name's Ken. So you think I'm a bitch, huh?' She says, 'I'm gonna get you fired.' I'm like, 'No, I didn't talk to you.' I went to Steve and I said 'Look, if she calls I'm not taking the rap for this.' I don't think she called back."

———

THE FORDHAM PIPELINE

Another set of college call letters with a storied history behind them is WFUV, Fordham University's Bronx-based radio station that first went live across the New York City area in 1947. Since then, the student-run outfit has been designated a professional station, as well as part of a small group in the Big Apple that broadcasts National Public Radio.

Over the years Fordham's sports department and WFUV have churned out several broadcasting notables including longtime Dodgers announcer and Baseball Hall of Famer Vin Scully, one of the station's founders. More than a handful of these would-be anchors, announcers, and sportswriters completed some invaluable reps both on-air and in the field as Sports Phone employees — an opportunity many credit to another WFUV alum, veteran New York Knicks public address announcer Mike Walczewski.

The PA voice for the Knicks since 1989, and New York Liberty since '97, as well as a multitude of college basketball contests at Madison Square Garden, King Wally got his start at Fordham — also spending some time behind the mic for their men's basketball games after graduating.

Before his booming voice would echo through one of the world's most famous arenas, Walczewski was a key piece in Sports Phone's 1975 resurrection, initially working full-time from their Manhattan office while simultaneously handling a full slate of classes uptown in the Bronx.

As representative of Sports Phone as the digits 976-1313, his on-air alias originated from a throwaway remark made during a school meeting.

"I was elected sports director for my junior year. We had like a 30-person sports department. It was a little bit unwieldy and you've got to remember, WFUV at that point had five-day-a-week sportscasts on their news program. We were broadcasting four different Fordham sports. You needed a play-by-play announcer and a color person. We were doing features," he explained.

"So there was a guy on staff there by the name of Len Klatt. He was a year ahead of me. He was a comedy writer in Hollywood afterward and he had this acerbic wit. So I walk into my first meeting and there are 30 people sitting in classroom seats. I walk in and he goes, kind of caustically and sarcastically, 'Oh, look. Here comes King Wally.'"

The royal sobriquet didn't stick at the time, but it came in handy shortly after.

"So fast forward to Sports Phone. Nobody at Fordham really called me King Wally but that was the seed of it. Before I even started, Fred Weiner said you've got to give yourself a hook, a moniker," Walczewski said.

"He was big into that, so I picked King Wally. I said that's because a few people at Fordham would call me that, but it wasn't really. Everybody just called me Wally. So I started and I just said, 'King Wally for Sports Phone' and it stuck. That's how it started. The seed was planted by Len Klatt."

Walczewski was often heard on the New York Sports Phone line Monday through Friday and typically voiced the daily Quickie Quiz question, a popular segment with a caller base that quickly became familiar with The King.

"It was cool hearing King Wally. I felt like he was a friend and we were chatting on the phone because that's what you did back in the day. You talked to your friends on the telephone," recalled high school basketball coach Steve Finamore, who first called Sports Phone as a 12-year-old growing up in Brooklyn.

"He talked so fast, too. Sometimes I would hang up at the end and call back because I missed what inning or what quarter the game was in. That's crazy to think he's now the PA announcer at the Garden."

Walczewski replaced the exemplary John F. X. Condon, who had been the voice of MSG for 42 seasons.

"When you think about it, between John Condon and then me, that's 76 years it's been the two of us," he said, marveling at how the time has flown by.

Way back before the Garden came calling, King Wally recommended his younger brother for a Sports Phone gig, one that ended up lasting about five years.

"When I turned 16, Guy LeBow needed a gofer-boy, so, most likely based on a recommendation from my brother "The King," I came in for an interview and got the job," Rick Walczewski recalled. "Mostly to answer the Quickie Quiz and get Guy food from Smiler's."

Despite being part of so many iconic moments including the 1998 NBA All-Star Game with Michael Jordan and Kobe Bryant on the court, or Game 7 of the '94 Eastern Conference Finals when Patrick Ewing nailed the winning shot against rival Indiana, many to this day still associate the elder Walczewski with the telephone.

As Finamore fondly recalled, "976-1313, I never forgot the number. I never forgot 'This is King Wally for Sports Phone.'"

Others who worked for Walczewski at Sports Phone also never forgot his voice.

"I went to a preseason game with Joe Masi and it was Joe [a former Sports Phone announcer] that recognized [his voice]. He goes, 'That's Wally' and I'm like, 'Holy crap. It *is* Wally," recalled Ken Samelson.

"We're watching the game and he's bellowing out 'Pat-rick Ewing!'

I said, 'You know what, Joe? I remember when I used to have to sit and listen to Wally yell at me all day. Now I can sit here and listen to him yell at me all night!'"

GOOD TIMES

Charlie Slowes has been the Washington Nationals' radio play-by-play man since 2006, previously working at an array of outlets including ESPN, NBC Sports, CBS Sports Radio, and Westwood One, among others. Before all of that, however, the Bronx and Yonkers native did his thing for Sports Phone.

"Everybody knew [King] Wally so there was certainly a connection to when you wanted to see if you could work there. The lure was experience, to make connections, and they had credentials to cover games. That was huge," Slowes said.

"If you were just going to the office and doing the reports, that would be one thing, but then you got out in the real world of covering games around professionals so that certainly helped for context and getting to know people in the business. It didn't hurt."

The veteran baseball voice succinctly summed up the Sports Phone experience as he saw it.

"It was a team effort and we all loved sports, so we were all into games," Slowes said. "I would say we went there, we talked about sports, we watched games, and we laughed."

 Sports Phone Stories

I Fought The Law (And The Law Lost)
(feat. Ken Samelson and Charlie Slowes)

The staff at Sports Phone were typically supportive of each other, even if that meant risking a perjury charge. Charlie Slowes headed to Bronx traffic court one day, with colleague Ken Samelson in tow for support.

"Place is a zoo. His case gets called in and he [Charlie] says, 'Yeah, Kenny was with me,' and I had no idea I was gonna have to testify under oath. I'm like, holy crap," Samelson recalled.

"I'm *lying* here and it's really funny. What happened was, the cop or whoever was running things says, 'You were with Charlie on February whatever,' and I said, 'Yes, I was.' 'Repeat, you were with Charlie?' So I think, oh my God, they're gonna get me."

What happened next was a stroke of luck for the duo.

"He flings the ticket at me and he goes, 'Read the year on the ticket.' Apparently what happened was the cop wrote the wrong year because it was February, so he was writing whatever it was the year before," Samelson explained. "So he says, 'I'm throwing this whole case out.' I'm like, 'Oh, thank God.' As we're getting up to leave he [the judge] says, 'If the cop hadn't done that, you would have lost.'"

Samelson and Slowes headed to the Sports Phone office for their evening shifts, but not before another run-in with the law would take place.

"So Charlie's all happy and he's driving [us] to work and we're in the right lane about to turn onto 57th Street. He sees a phone booth on the other end of Sutton Place," Samelson said. "Now, we are in the far right lane. He says, 'Oh my God, I'm supposed to call the union office [Sports Phone employees were unsuccessfully attempting to unionize at the time].' He forgot he had this court date. So we're in the far right lane, and he makes a left turn through three lanes of traffic to get to the phone booth, right in front of a cop car."

Slowes rolls down the window. Here we go again after Samelson had already lied under oath that day...

Cop: "Sir, what kind of turn was that?"

Slowes: "Not a very good one."

Cop: "What's going on?"

Slowes: "My friend here is really sick. I have to call his doctor."

Cop: "Next time, unless your friend has a knife sticking out of him, don't do that."

"So Charlie, he didn't get a ticket. I think I said, 'Charlie, when we're on our way to the office, you're going to stop and buy a lottery ticket because you've already won two things today that you had no business winning.' He beat two raps in 45 minutes."

———

Quickie Quiz

Q: Which Sports Phone announcer impersonated Howie Karpin?

A: Ken Samelson

Samelson: "What happened was, it was a really busy Saturday and [King] Wally wanted to call to update the supplemental line. He wanted to talk to Howie Karpin, so I think [Howie] was out getting lunch or moving [his] car, whatever it was, so Wally says, 'Oh, I'll call back,' but he called back and [Howie] still wasn't there. He called again. I answered and he goes, 'Howie?' and I went, 'Eh, what's up,' and I just took the scores down as [Howie]."

LIGHTS OUT

A senior director and executive producer at ESPN for over a quarter-century, John "Chief" Martin auditioned at Sports Phone in 1977 in front of broadcasting pioneer Guy LeBow, a meeting made possible by Walczewski. Martin started on a separate 976 line, one that was critical during the infamous New York City blackout in July of that year.

"So I got hired part-time and they had just fired up another program, *New York Report*, which was kind of like a feature-y news and information thing," Martin recalled.

"So I did that, and essentially, overnights, and I was just popping in some prerecorded stuff and loading it into the system and that's pretty much what I had to do until the night of the blackout. We became a go-to for people looking for information that didn't have transistor radios or whatever. So that helped grow that program, *New York Report*, and I was the voice that night."

Martin eventually replaced Howie Rose (who had moved on to terrestrial radio) on the Sports Phone roster, working regular nighttime shifts Monday through Friday. He had other memorable moments before going to work for RKO as Charlie Steiner's producer in 1981, perhaps none more than the night he learned NBA superstar Bob McAdoo was shipping up to Boston...

Sports Phone Stories

Fast and First
(feat. John Martin)

In its early days, Sports Phone was headquartered in a 47-floor skyscraper that was built around one of New York City's most historic saloons, P. J. Clarke's. In business since 1884, the storied establishment hosted many famous patrons from the worlds of sports, politics, and entertainment over the years. Frank Sinatra was a regular, and for a period had his own table. Mick Jagger was known to drop in, as did Nat King Cole. Former first lady Jackie Kennedy Onassis patronized the pub, as did TV's Dick Clark.

P. J. Clarke's also became a go-to for Sports Phone employees after they were done with their shifts.

While Sports Phone was relied on for providing the latest scores and other updates, there were times when the service was also the first to break big news. Such was the case on a bitterly cold February night in 1979 when the hometown Knicks swapped their high-scoring forward Bob McAdoo to Boston for a trio of first-round draft picks and backup center Tom Barker.

One of the NBA's elite offensive players, McAdoo was averaging 26.6 points per game at the time of the trade, third in the league. This was no small deal, nor was Sports Phone having the news first ahead of the so-called traditional media members who covered the two clubs.

"It was a Saturday night, the Knicks played the Celtics at the [Madison Square] Garden. So we finished up after whatever the last game was, and I forget who was with me, but I stopped at P. J. Clarke's downstairs because I knew all the bartenders. One of the bartenders was an Irish guy who had emigrated to the States around the same time as my parents and knew my parents," John Martin recalled.

The Fordham alum began to wind down, assuming his work for the night was done. What happened in the next few minutes would shift Martin right back into reporter mode.

"We're downstairs hanging out and [Celtics owner] John Y. Brown walks in with [pioneering sportscaster] Phyllis George, his wife. So one of the bartenders is like, 'Mr. Brown, teach us something pithy,' and John Y. Brown looks at him and says, 'I just traded for the NBA championship tonight,'" Martin said.

"It was obvious he'd already had a few so the guy behind the bar said, 'Oh, then you want to talk to this gentleman right here.'"

So Martin turned to Brown and said…

"Mr. Brown, you traded for the NBA championship?"

Brown said: "Yes, sir."

Martin continued: "You did a deal with the Knicks?"

Suddenly coy, Brown replied: "I'm not saying."

Based on Brown's boisterous comment to the bartender, however, Martin had him figured out.

"'Well, if you think you traded for the NBA championship,' I said, 'then you got [Bob] McAdoo?' He kind of like looked at me and he reached into his pocket and he pulled out this crumpled paper napkin and he was holding it and he says, 'Well, it's all right here.' I said, 'Well, show it to me,' and he says, 'Can't do that.' So, he and George head for the back dining room," Martin explained.

He may not have seen the contents of the napkin, but Martin opted to take a chance.

"Again, I forget who was with us and I said, 'You know, what the hell. Let's take a shot, and I went back upstairs and I recorded the end night [tape]," he said.

John Martin for Sports Phone. We're back with the morning update. Sports Phone has learned that the Knicks have swung a possible block-buster deal with the Boston Celtics, sending Bob McAdoo to Boston. Details still to be resolved, but we'll have more on this developing story.

"It was something like that, right? I did the scores and people said you're doing that [just on what happened at the bar]," Martin recounted. "I said, 'Hey, the worst we could be is wrong. I said, 'If he's fucking not bull-shitting, who else is on the fucking Knicks that could help bring them a championship? So McAdoo was the only guy, right?"

So there it was, news of a major trade between two charter franchises first reaching the public not through a major newspaper or over the airwaves, but at the other end of a dial tone. Not everyone was happy about this, including the Knicks beat reporter for the *New York Times*.

"The Times comes [out] at whatever the hell time, like 4 a.m., and Sam Goldaper had a story, Knicks trading McAdoo, right? So the next time I was at the Garden was Tuesday night. I went to the next game and I walked into the press room," Martin described.

"I had never said anything more to Sam Goldaper other than hi because the print media and us, they looked down their nose at us. I didn't even think Sam Goldaper knew who I was, what I did."

Not only did Goldaper know who Martin was, but he also had a few choice words for the Sports Phone announcer. "I walk in the press room and he jumps out of his chair."

"No fucking way you knew that. No fucking way you knew that," Goldaper exclaimed, to which Martin replied, "Why, Sam?"

"There's no way you knew that. You were guessing?," asked Goldaper.

"Sam, we all have our sources, right?"

"Bullshit!"

"Okay, but I did see the napkin."

"And he stopped. I didn't say if I saw what was on the napkin. I said, 'Sam, I saw the napkin," Martin noted. "I don't think he had that in his story, that they scratched it out on a napkin."

McAdoo only lasted until the end of that season with Boston before being jettisoned to Detroit, an underwhelming campaign in which the Celtics finished 29-53. Although the Hall of Famer's impact wasn't quite what Brown had boasted that winter night in a New York bar, Martin's late-night recording certainly had a lasting effect on how the print media viewed Sports Phone and its band of reporters.

"I realized it certainly wasn't Exhibit A of any type of journalistic process or confirmation, but it was process of elimination," Martin said. "And then when the story came out everything about the napkin, every-thing, it all came to fruition."

———

Quickie Quiz

Q: Who scored his share of free drinks on account of Sports Phone's notoriety?

A: John Martin

In Sports Phone's Midtown Manhattan days, trips to nearby watering holes were common after a long shift, especially to local spots where the staff was known to the bartenders and could count on more than a few buybacks. John Martin stumbled on similar generosity in one of the outer boroughs, thanks to some sud-slinging callers from Queens. "Chief" was no freeloader though, leaving his share of tips.

Martin: "Besides P. J. Clarke's, when I would go out by my home in Jackson Heights where I grew up. [By] then I was living out in Douglaston, Little Neck, and I'd go into places there and see somebody I knew and they might say to the bartender, 'You know who this guy is?' They'd say, 'His name is John and you were listening to him the whole night. How many times you dial Sports Phone tonight?' And a lot of times you'd get, 'No shit? That's you?' Yeah, that's me. I didn't have to go in my pocket pretty much the rest of the night, or ensuing times when I might pop into the place. So [my wife] Maryanne used to joke. She said, 'You think it's a big deal you're drinking for nothing, but you're leaving them 10s and 20s, right? So you're fucking paying money.' I can't just nod and say thanks, right? I mean, c'mon."

GIANTS AT THE GARDEN

Widely known as the New York Giants' play-by-play man since the mid-90s, a younger Bob Papa also came highly recommended by King Wally — starting at Sports Phone in the spring of 1984.

"It was unbelievable, to be a student in college, and to [have] millions of people hearing you," Papa said. "And then the opportunity to go cover games, which is where you make all your connections in the business. It's an experience that can't be replicated in today's world."

Those connections went a long way for Papa, who had the chance to work alongside some of the biggest names in broadcasting while donning a Sports Phone credential.

"Marv Albert, Jim Karvellas, Bob Wolff covering Knick games in that old press box. People got to know you and they became guests on the show at Fordham, and then they asked to hear your tapes and then they started looking at you differently," he explained. "This business is about relationships and if you're good on the air and getting experience, there's no teacher that's going to teach you how to do this."

Sports Phone Stories

Home Blown
(feat. Bob Papa)

On August 2, 1985, the Yankees hosted the Chicago White Sox in a nationally televised game. Tied at three in the seventh, the Yankees had runners on first and second with no outs when Rickey Henderson singled to left-center field. The runner at second, Bobby Meacham, assumed centerfielder Luis Salazar was going to catch the ball, so he went back to tag up. The runner on first, Dale Berra, correctly assumed the ball would drop in and was already at second base when Meacham retreated.

He then stumbled on his way to third with Berra, who was watching the play instead of the lead runner, hot on his heels. Meacham was then waved home by third base coach Gene Michael, while Berra was given the stop sign, one he completely ignored. Cutoff man Ozzie Guillen fired the ball to Carlton Fisk behind the plate. The Hall of Famer tagged both bumbling runners out to complete a bizarre double play.

Manager Billy Martin was heated, yanking Berra from the game. Sports Phone's Bob Papa was in the clubhouse afterward and witnessed one of Martin's trademark tirades.

"One of my great baseball memories is the night that the Yankees got two guys thrown out at home plate. Billy Martin was the manager. I think it was Bobby Meacham and Dale Berra," Papa recalled. "I remember having to go to the locker room, they had that old picnic table, and Billy Martin was going absolutely bonkers."

The sometimes combative and often intimidating Martin also had a softer side to him, one the football Giants play-by-play man got to experience first-hand.

"I also remember Billy Martin kind of befriending me, because he just randomly asked me, 'You look kind of young.' I told him my background, about how my dad used to as a kid play stickball in the Yankee Stadium player's parking lot when the Yankees were away, and how as a kid he played baseball [almost] every Saturday and Sunday in Macombs Dam Park, how all the Yankees lived in the Grand Concourse Hotel and would come down for their games," Papa explained.

"They would stop at the park and actually umpire, or play a little bit, or take an at-bat. This is unheard of in today's world, and Billy Martin remembered those games. He remembered those kids. He didn't remember my father specifically, but he always kind of treated me differently after that. I remember him saying to me, 'Oh, well, you're a real Yankee.' I hadn't worked for the team or anything, but that was kind of cool."

––––––––

JACK FROM J.C.

YES Network commentator and former *New York Times* national baseball correspondent Jack Curry learned about an opening at Sports Phone through his on-air partner at school.

"Bob Papa and I were good friends and radio partners at Fordham's WFUV," Curry said. "He was working at Sports Phone and he told me about openings there. I interviewed and got the part-time gig."

Growing up in nearby Jersey City, Curry was once a frequent caller himself.

"To be a 13-year-old who called Sports Phone and then to be a guy who was giving the scores seven years later, I've always thought that was very cool. I answered phones and took some scores from reporters. I also did some of the recordings in which you had to read all of the scores in 60 seconds," Curry reflected.

"I was never asked to do the New York Sports Phone audio because that was the top assignment, but I did some other cities. There was one time when I had to read some horse racing results and I failed miserably. I didn't read them quickly enough and had to redo the taping. I was mortified. Since we had to update the results in another 10 minutes, it wasn't like we had a lot of time to redo them."

While there for less than a year before graduating in May of 1986, Curry's limited reps at Sports Phone still proved important down the road.

"Even though I was only at Sports Phone for a short period of time and was a very small part of their history, that group of people showed me how passionate they were about sports and how much they cared about getting things right," he noted. "So, yes, having that experience definitely had an impact on me as I moved forward in my career."

HAWKEYE PIERCE

Bob Papa helped another friend land a job at Sports Phone in the fall of 1993, a brief stint that has had an enduring impact on Chris Carrino.

"I worked with the Giants radio network, I interned when I was a senior in college, and then right out of college I was still working with the Giants," Carrino recalled. "I also started doing stuff with the Nets and I worked with Bob Papa in both places. Bob knew Pete [Walker] who was the guy who ran things [at Sports Phone] for a while."

Long before his days on the Fordham campus, Carrino was quite familiar with the seven digits that delivered the scores.

"It was never a gambling thing for me. When I was a kid, sports were the most important thing in my life from when I was eight years old," Carrino explained.

"So if I was out with my parents somewhere for dinner and I came home and wanted to know the score, I missed the Ranger game, I was calling 976-1313 to find out the score. I was always utilizing Sports Phone back in the day, no doubt about it."

Carrino's dad was also a customer, a fact that helped mask things when the monthly phone bill came.

"I didn't abuse it," he said. "I didn't get in trouble that much that way, and maybe my father would call too a little bit so I could always hide behind that."

The radio voice of the Brooklyn Nets since 2002, Carrino likened Sports Phone to the old US Army field hospital units in the way they operated.

"It was a great training ground, because you have that all the time in your broadcasting career where you've got to do a recording, and you've got to fit it in a certain amount of time. Sports Phone was a bit like a MASH unit. You're just trying to give people what they need, not getting too elaborate," he emphasized.

"We're not doing fancy surgeries. We're just getting you the scores until can you get to watch the highlights or the news or get to a game when it's going on. We were just a MASH unit, patch you up and move you on."

Advice from a legendary New York sportscaster helped Carrino out under the pressure of Sports Phone's demands, wise words that he pays forward to this day.

"Marty Glickman was my broadcast coach at Fordham, and Marty used to say consider the listener. That's always my mantra. It still is today. And he would say even when you're doing updates, make sure that you're presenting it in a way that the person can understand it," Carrino recounted.

"If you're racing through it, you're not separating between games, can that person listening comprehend what you're saying? That training was always in my mind when I was doing an update for Sports Phone."

No matter where you're broadcasting or who might be listening, the message remains constant.

"I've always said, even when I talk to young people today about broadcasting. I don't care what the platform is. You may think it's not a large audience, you may think it's not significant," Carrino said. "But it's always a training ground, you always should be doing the best possible job that you can and using that experience to help you get better, and all the other stuff will work out the way it is."

Growing up in the area helped Carrino settle in, as he believes it did for his fellow FUV broadcasting brethren.

"It was all a bunch of New York kids trying to be broadcasters and the thing that people have in common here in this area, me, Michael Kay, Bob Papa, John Giannone, not only were we Fordham guys but we're from New York," he observed.

"We had that sensibility and we grew up in this area. We know what it's like to be a sports fan in this area, and we've gravitated towards those teams and this market and they've gravitated toward us."

Quickie Quiz

Q: Which Sports Phone alum revealed a secret about Bob Papa's NFL loyalties?

A: Don La Greca

Bob Papa's been a household name to New York Giants fans for decades, serving as the team's play-by-play voice since the mid-1990s. Before becoming synonymous with Big Blue, Papa apparently backed division-rival Dallas.

La Greca: "I remember Kevin Rogers telling me a story about it. He's like, 'Bob Papa's a Cowboys fan.' I'm like, no way, he's a Giant guy. Kevin goes, 'Papa used to have this thing back at Third Avenue. There was some sort of long hallway and Kevin told me that Papa, to pump himself up, used to run and dive headfirst and slide down the hallway.'"

Sports Phone Stories

Touch 'em All, Joe!
(feat. Chris Carrino)

Chris Carrino will never forget the specific year and season he worked at Sports Phone, as it coincided with one of baseball's more memorable moments.

"How I remember what year I worked there is because we're watching the [1993] World Series with the Phillies and the Blue Jays. We're all watching the screens. There's college football going on. It was a Saturday night if I remember correctly, and so there's a ton of games you've got to keep track of, but now you got this big World Series game," Carrino explained.

"I remember the Joe Carter at-bat against Mitch Williams. I'm waiting and the at-bat's lasting a long time, and I've got to go in and do my recording but I don't want to miss this at-bat. Just as a sports fan, I want to watch it, but it's taking so long and I'm already over the time and I'm like, I gotta go record this."

Williams was trying to protect a 6–5 Philadelphia lead in the bottom of the ninth, hoping to force a Game 7. The SkyDome was rocking as Carter stepped to the plate with two on and one out, packed with rabid Blue Jays fans dreaming of back-to-back championships.

The lefty fireballer quickly fell behind 2-0 but was able to even the count. While Carrino was in the booth announcing the latest rundown for Sports Phone's callers, Carter lined an inside fastball into the left-field seats to seal the deal.

"So I go into the booth, record it really quick in one take so I can get out of there, and I get out and everybody's going crazy. I had missed it. I missed the Carter home run because I had to run in and do this recording, and now I have to go in and update the recording anyway because Joe Carter just won the World Series for the Blue Jays," Carrino recalled.

"So people used to say, 'Oh, that must have been so cool. You had all the games and you could watch all these games on all these TVs,' and I would tell them, 'Yeah, I had to keep leaving the TVs every eight to ten minutes to do recordings, and I missed one of the biggest home runs in baseball history.'"

———

JOHNNY LEE BENCH

John Giannone has won his share of Emmy Awards as part of MSG Networks' Rangers coverage over the past two-plus decades, a career that started at Sports Phone when he was still brand new on campus.

"I had only been at Fordham like three months because I got there September of '81. So by January of '82, I had gotten hired, and I think Michael Kay had put in, or King Wally had reached out to Michael Kay, because Kay was the sports director of FUV at the time, and I had just gotten approved to be on the air. So I was probably only on the air a handful of times," he recalled.

"I would say for the first couple of months that I was at Sports Phone I didn't do much on-air stuff, but I remember the first time going in the booth. I distinctly remember it was a college football Saturday, and I remember having to do like, oh god, it might have been as many as 40 scores in 58 seconds. And I remember screwing up on time and having to hit the reset button and starting all over again."

His blunder didn't go unnoticed.

"A buddy of mine happened to have called at the time when I screwed up," Giannone said. "I remember him calling the office and saying, 'I just heard you totally screw that up,' so that was that was one of my fond early memories."

The longtime hockey voice overcame those early jitters, eventually using Sports Phone's haywire environment to his advantage.

"It honestly was one of the best training grounds you could possibly have. First and foremost, to be able to concentrate enough to get 30 or 40 scores in a 60-second recording. But secondly, just the whole concept of the organized chaos that was at the time pre-computer, trying to gather scores in a 10-minute span," Giannone explained.

"Like every six minutes after the phones would ring and then we'd have to exchange our scores with the other two places, knowing that the score we got from a guy in say, Pittsburgh, was going to be obsolete in two minutes but we were going to report it anyway. It was crazy."

As with many others, Giannone's experiences outside of the office were just as important.

"My most vivid memory of working there actually was when [Sports Phone] would have credentials. The first professional interview I ever did was for Sports Phone and it was with Johnny Bench at Shea Stadium," he said.

"I remember being ridiculously nervous. I was 20 years old and I mean, Johnny Bench for God's sake. So for me, that in itself made working at Sports Phone so satisfying and so cool because at that moment I realized, A: That's what I want to do for a living and B: I actually can get paid for it."

Quickie Quiz

Q: Which Sports Phone announcer once posed as Toys R Us mascot Geoffrey the Giraffe?

A: John Giannone

Giannone: "Andy Roth volunteered me for a Toys R Us promo that we were shooting, because I had easily the highest-pitched voice. I remember going into the booth and just saying, 'Hi, boys and girls. This is Geoffrey the Giraffe from Toys R Us. Visit me at the Willowbrook Mall this coming Saturday.' And I'm like wow, I'm getting paid $7 an hour to be Geoffrey the Giraffe."

Sports Phone Stories

Darryl Defends Dad
(as told by Jim Johnson)

Another WFUV alum who worked in sports media regularly since his time at Sports Phone, Jim Johnson told one of his favorite tales from those early days:

"Sports Phone memories were some of the greatest in my professional life. It was such a fun group of characters working together on busy news nights. The love of sports and the opportunity to work in the profession made those days unforgettable.

"By the time I was in my junior year in 1984, I started to get the opportunity to cover games and I capitalized on every chance I got. I remember covering a Devils game on Friday night, taking the bus back to the city to work my overnight shift, then covering a Nets game on Saturday, and again working the overnight. It definitely was not a party weekend at Fordham!

"Later that spring and summer, I got to cover a fair amount of Mets games. The Mets were coming off several years of sub-.500 play and the veteran guys at Sports Phone weren't too excited about heading to Shea. For me, a 22-year-old lifetime Mets fan, I was living the dream!

"There were two season credentials at Sports Phone. Later that season when the Mets were starting to get good, I ignored media protocol and brought my dad to a game using the other credential. Growing up in upstate Binghamton, we were lucky to get to one Mets game a year, and I knew it would be pretty unique for my dad to be "on the inside" in the locker room.

"My dad was a very unassuming man and was very quiet, just soaking it up. During [manager] Davey Johnson's postgame media scrum, Mets legendary PR director Jay Horwitz saw my dad just standing there and asked who he was and who he worked for. He said he was just with his son, and Jay (luckily) didn't get me in trouble by bringing my dad in. He just politely asked my father to wait outside.

Suddenly, Mets star Darryl Strawberry saw what was happening and he said to my dad, "Don't let him push you around like that." My dad loved that memory and talked about it for many years.

———

CHAPTER 6
THE CALLERS: FANS, FANTASY & FRANCHISE QUARTERBACKS

Even with its talent-laden roster and groundbreaking offerings, Sports Phone would have been nothing without its customer base — the callers. People from all walks of life found themselves dialing those memorable digits regularly, itching to get the latest scores and news.

DID STAN SMYL SCORE?

Kenny Albert may have been known to the Sports Phone announcers as Marv's son and that kid who always won the Quickie Quiz, but the man who once called four sports in four days was also interested in hockey updates on a team across the northern border.

"I was born in '68 so throughout the '70s, without sports radio back then, I was either calling Sports Phone — probably in the mid-to-late, probably '78, '79, '80 is when I started — or listening to 1010 WINS or WCBS every half hour for the scores," Albert recalled.

"I was a Vancouver Canucks fan. I would, late at night, either turn on 1010 WINS, 15 or 45 [after the hour] or call Sports Phone to get the scores. So I was definitely not calling only for the quiz."

Held at the Montreal Forum, the 1983 NHL Entry Draft took place on a Wednesday in June, not ideal timing for Albert.

"I remember calling Sports Phone a couple of times during the day that day just to hear about the NHL Draft because there was no internet, no iPhones. It was Brian Lawton, Sylvain Turgeon, Pat LaFontaine, Steve Yzerman. Those are the first four picks," Albert said. "I can still picture the payphone that I went to … Junior high school, payphone, ninth grade, 1983 NHL Draft."

THE BATPHONE

Like a lot of New York-area kids growing up in the '80s, Rocco Constantino was enamored with the wild group of ballplayers that called Flushing, Queens home.

"I first remember calling Sports Phone the most during the 1985 season, as the Mets were in that great pennant race with the Cardinals. I always knew the Mets' scores and wanted to know if they were gaining or losing ground. I vividly remember huddling on the phone waiting to hear that the Cardinals and Cubs were losing, which they didn't do enough," Constantino recalled.

"The phone we used was right on the wall next to our back door in the kitchen and when I called, I had to be laser-focused on the scores as they were being read. If someone made noise or came in the back door, I could miss a score and the phone call was useless. And of course the phone number … 976-1313. That number remains one of the few numbers from my childhood I won't forget."

Davey Johnson's squad stayed in the hunt until the regular season's final week, failing to reach the playoffs after finishing three games behind first-place St. Louis in the National League East. Constantino and his brothers kept pace the entire way, but it didn't come without a price.

"My brothers and I definitely were reprimanded for calling Sports Phone. Eventually, we had to pay my father the 50 cents if we were going to call. I am sure he just used that as a deterrent because that was fifty cents we weren't going to be able to spend on baseball cards or stickers. I am also sure we snuck in calls without paying," he remembered.

"I am sure that to people who were older than me in the '80s, it was vital for gambling purposes, but to just a kid who loved the Mets and baseball it may as well have been the bat phone to me. The concept of dialing a number and getting the scores you wanted was mind-blowing to an 11-year-old baseball nut."

That young fanatic went on to become a collegiate athletic director and a sportswriter, co-founding the baseball-centric website *BallNine*.

"Sports Phone was part of the experience of growing up loving sports in the 1980s. I couldn't get enough of every aspect of sports, and the ways to find out scores and information were so limited back then," Constantino said. "Just the entire holistic experience of sports in the '80s made me want to get into sports and sportswriting, and Sports Phone was an important fiber in that experience."

THE SHOW MUST GO ON

In 2024, Suzyn Waldman begins her 38th season covering the Yankees in some capacity, her twentieth as a color commentator alongside radio play-by-play man John Sterling. Before embarking on a career in sports, the Massachusetts native graced the world of theater as a gifted singer.

Once appearing opposite the dynamic Richard Kiley in the musical *Man of La Mancha,* Waldman's pre-broadcasting days brought her from

Beantown to Broadway — hundreds of miles removed from her favorite teams.

"I came here from Boston. I was in theater for years, and the only connection I had to [Boston] scores out of town was 976-1313," she recalled. "I can remember in 1985, the Celtics were in the playoffs and I was doing a show called *Nine,* and there was a little boy in the show. I would give him a thing of dimes, and every ten minutes he would call Sports Phone to tell me what the Celtics score was."

These score updates weren't taking place during rehearsals or after the crowd had dispersed, but rather during the actual performances.

"We had a theater in the round, and so it was built up off the stage that we were actually on. He was 10 years old, and he was underneath the stage telling me scores. I was on stage," the Radio Hall of Famer described. "He's now a newscaster in Florida and he's in his forties. I remember handfuls of dimes. There was a payphone in the wall."

Like many transplants, Waldman came to rely on Sports Phone in her new home.

"To those of us who were from someplace else, Sports Phone and King Wally was a lifeline," she explained. "Everybody in theater called Sports Phone. They were tremendous sports fans."

INVISIBLE TOUCH

Sports Phone's aggressive marketing campaigns in and around New York City helped make Pat Leonard a frequent caller early on.

"I started following sports in 1976 and the first time I called Sports Phone was in '78. Howie Rose was the guy who was on. I wanted to find out what it was like because I saw a commercial for it," the former SportsTicker reporter and longtime MLB employee recalled. "The slogan was great, 'If you can't get to the game, get to the phone.'

Lou Piniella and [George] Steinbrenner used to be in the commercials."

On May 31, 1987, Genesis rolled into the Meadowlands for the next show on their worldwide tour. As Phil Collins rocked the New Jersey crowd, nearby Philadelphia's beloved Flyers battled in Edmonton for the NHL's highest honor.

"I went to the Genesis concert in '87 at Giants Stadium and it was the same night as Game 7 of the Stanley Cup Finals. We found a payphone after it was over and we called [Sports Phone] to see who won," Leonard said.

"We could hardly hear the guy on the other end and my friend called back to see if he could hear. It was still hard to hear him, but he was able to hear when he said the Oilers won. One of the guys we were with was a Flyer fan so he wasn't too happy."

THE FOUNDER OF FANTASY

Fantasy sports are as much a part of society as the actual real-life contests themselves, with an estimated 50.4 million Americans assembling at least one virtual team in 2022. That's quite a climb from 1980 when Daniel Okrent and a group of friends gathered in a New York apartment for the first-ever Rotisserie League player auction.

Named after La Rotisserie Française, a now-shuttered East 52nd Street eatery well-liked within the venerated author's circle where Okrent first proposed the idea and ironically located just a short trek from Sports Phone's Third Avenue digs, Rotisserie ("Roto" for short) became the initial and eventually the most widely-used fantasy baseball format. Okrent's invention later earned him recognition as the founding father of fantasy sports.

Long before the fantasy boom, Okrent and his leaguemates often utilized one of Sports Phone's secondary lines to help tally their standings. The burgeoning crew of Rotisserie fiends wasn't interested in the Quickie Quiz or who won that night's tilts on the actual diamond, however.

"It was essential," Okrent recalled. "Just the stats, nothing but the stats."

Moving on from the founder of fantasy to the father of sabermetrics, Bill James's name was once synonymous with his own spin on the popular game. A stat-based concept that pitted teams head-to-head as opposed to Roto's category-based, league-wide ranking system, *Bill James Fantasy Baseball* began as a mail-in service where participants would rely on the post office when it came to submitting lineups or distributing results.

The leagues eventually became phone-driven and finally ended up on the web, moving under the STATS, Inc. umbrella at one point. James was heavily involved, in particular during the product's early years, and was aware of Sports Phone and its offerings.

"I remember hearing about it often as a business entity," James recalled. "The name would come up in meetings."

During those seasons of *Bill James Fantasy Baseball* when stats and results were primarily delivered via snail mail, ideas of a potential dial-in service for league members were often bandied about behind the scenes.

"Oh, [we] constantly [discussed potential ways to deliver stats and results quicker]. We started those games like 10 minutes before the internet was invented," said James, one of the key figures in Michael Lewis's *Moneyball*.

"We did provide a fax service that faxed out information overnight, but the answer we always ran into is that once you head down a certain road, you have to go down that road. I'm not a businessman. I don't understand the ins and outs of it, but there was something always in the way of attempting to [set up a dial-in service]."

Quickie Quiz

Q: What faux fantasy style caused chaos on Sports Phone Live?

A: A league where umpire stats counted.

Gordon Damer: "There was a time where it was a slow day, and me and Jared Max actually called Sports Phone Live just to torment [anchor] Dominic Testani. We asked him different questions to annoy him, just to see how annoyed we could get him. So we asked him 'Who is the umpire in the Yankees-Red Sox game?' and we told him that we had a fantasy league with umpires in it, so that really set him off. Any time I see Jared I always say, 'I have a fantasy league with umpires in it.' It was not just that Dominic got pissed off. The three or four [callers] that were on the line, they got pissed off. 'Who needs a fuckin' umpire? Who cares?!?'"

Scott Engel's love affair with fantasy sports was also sparked pre-internet in 1994, checking individual player progress in the newspaper while the league's commissioner compiled statistics the old-fashioned way. Well before his days as a credentialed media member, Engel even called the public relations departments of certain teams to ask about injuries on occasion.

"There was no live feed back then. My first ever fantasy league that I was in, I was working at Paragon Sporting Goods in Manhattan and we had a fantasy football league," he recounted. "I won the very first year that I ever played. I would be riding in on the subway with *USA Today* looking at the stats, and our commissioner would also have to do it by hand and that was the case with a lot of leagues."

Now a well-known expert in the fantasy sports industry, the writer and radio host was once just another dedicated fan relying on Sports Phone to follow his favorite teams.

"Even though I'm from New York, I've been a longtime fan of the Seattle Seahawks. My only way to find out what was going on in the Seahawks game, because that was before *Sunday Ticket* and satellite and everything, was to call Sports Phone every few minutes," Engel said.

"This was especially important if they were trying to make the playoffs. You'd be forced to watch the Jets and the Giants and hope they would provide an update from your favorite team's game, or that crawl would update, or you'd have to wait for halftime. I just didn't have the patience for it. I leaned on Sports Phone. It was the biggest presence in my life in terms of being a Seahawks fan."

Like many who dialed 976-1313 as a teenager, Engel had to contend with the possibility of a rising phone bill and a pair of unhappy guardians. He quickly devised a strategy to lessen the blow.

"I would call constantly and I would have to sneak calls because my parents would not want the charges to be added to the phone bill," he explained. "I made sure to space them out. My best friend used to call it all the time and his parents got pretty ticked off about it."

Years prior, Engel played board games like *All-Star Baseball* and Strat-O-Matic, which he referred to as the forerunners of fantasy. Sports Phone once hosted a Strat-O-Matic series, one that had a rather high profile.

Sports Phone Stories

Subway Series, Sort Of
(feat. Hal Richman and Mike Weinstein)

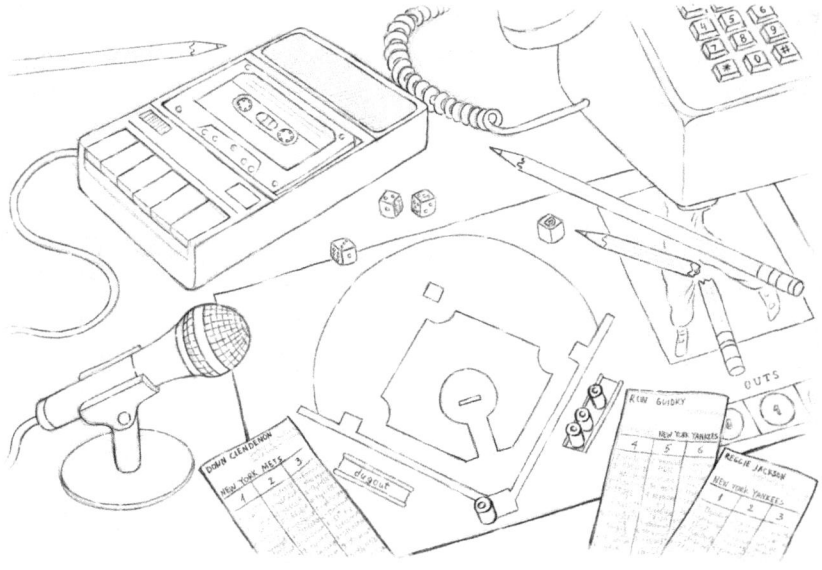

Before warring sides settled on a new collective bargaining agreement in late July and saved at least part of the 1981 MLB season, there was a stretch of almost two months with no action between the lines — not in baseball nor in any of the other major sports, save for the original iteration of the North American Soccer League. To rescue fans from their doldrums and to drum up some interest in Sports Phone at a time when there simply wasn't much to report, Phone Programs teamed up with New York's crosstown rivals to simulate a midseason matchup in late June.

Utilizing the time-honored tabletop game Strat-O-Matic, representatives from the Mets and Yankees were hosted at Sports Phone's offices over the course of several days to play out a best-of-seven New York "Dream Series." On hand for the club from Queens was radio-TV executive Thornton Geary while radio producer Arthur Adler led the Bronx Bombers, overseeing a matchup between two world champion clubs — the 1969 Mets vs. the '78 Yankees.

Beer and hot dogs were served to the media contingent in attendance, the national anthem was played, and the ceremonial "first dice" were tossed.

"I just always remember during the baseball strike when we had the Strat-O-Matic tournament. It was the Mets and the Yankees. I'm a huge Mets fan," Mike Weinstein recalled. "[Sports Phone announcer] Al Abrams and I were the managers. I think it was [Arthur] Adler from the Yankees, but I was really mad at Al because he wouldn't even flip a coin with me on managing the Mets, so I automatically had to have the Yankees."

Mike Walczewski [King Wally] provided play-by-play highlights to Sports Phone callers, filling an early summer void for the baseball-starved Big Apple. Marv Albert even showed up to record a feature for NBC.

"Wally and I would record it, and we kept breaking pencils to recreate the crack of the bat," Weinstein described. "It was just funny for me because I've been playing Strat-O-Matic since like 1967. I don't really play it anymore, although I still have it on the computer. That was well before any of these great video games that are out now. Strat-O-Matic was the word."

The Yankees took the opener 3–2 behind a combined seven-hitter by Ron Guidry and Goose Gossage, with Reggie Jackson plating a pair. They went on to take the next two as well, putting the Amazins in a seemingly impossible hole.

The Miracle Mets climbed off the mat, living up to their moniker in grand fashion by winning three straight elimination games to force a winner-take-all Game 7. Knotted at 2-all in the 11th inning, fan-favorite Art

Shamsky connected for a grand slam and the Mets claimed the title of Dream Series champion. Shamsky and Tom Seaver (0.82 ERA in 22 innings) were chosen as co-MVPs.

"Baseball then was the biggest thing, and so that's why I think this hunger was there, and of course, no other sports were being played at that point," said Hal Richman, the creator of Strat-O-Matic. "It was a time where baseball was the only thing going on normally, and so we did fill that void as best as we could. I mean it wasn't a real thing, but it was as close to the real thing as you could get."

The All-Star Game was originally set to take place weeks later, on July 14 at Cleveland's Municipal Stadium. With the strike still going, a Strat-O-Matic version of the Midsummer Classic was simulated that day on a table situated at home plate within the actual ballpark, complete with an umpire and a smattering of fans in the seats.

"There was one particular situation with the All-Star Game in Cleveland, which was played by an NBC [affiliate WKYC]. They actually created a large Strat-O-Matic board, so it could be played at home plate at Municipal Stadium," Richman recalled. "They invited the man who was to sing the national anthem down there, and they also had [Hall of Famer] Bob Feller come in."

Feller threw out the ceremonial first dice and the game was underway.

The National League trounced the junior circuit 15–2 behind home runs from Dave Parker, Manny Trillo, Gary Carter, and Garry Templeton.

"It was very exciting. I was on television with Bryant Gumbel. The thing about it was, the company itself did not create any of this publicity. It was the game and the customers," Richman reminisced. "After the All-Star Game was over, the fellow from NBC, big Strat-O-Matic player, then drove it to [Cooperstown] to be put in the Hall of Fame and it's still there. Unfortunately, it's in inventory in the stock room, but it was out [on display] for a couple of years."

Richman was busy updating the company's football and basketball games at the time, working close to 70 hours each week. This didn't stop him from reveling in what was taking place from coast to coast.

"We were on television, there was a lot of radio work. There were about 40 different stations in New England, they would play the Strat-O-Matic Red Sox game for that day and then put it on the radio to replace the actual game," Richman added. "And then in California, I think Northern California as I remember, there were Strat-O-Matic people playing the game and then sending the box scores to a newspaper that carried them in lieu of the actual box scores, so it was really something. It was overwhelming to me, but it was certainly an amazing, amazing time for us."

Strat-O-Matic's chairman and founder, Richman is still surrounded by the impact his creation continues to make.

"I was very proud of the contribution that I made, and that the product was so well received," he said. "At this point in my life, I'm 87 years old, I have quite a few doctors, and I would say close to half of them at one point or another played Strat-O-Matic. It's a good feeling."

———

A TIGER TWO-BAGGER

The man behind the wildly popular Super 70s Sports Twitter (or X, as it's now known) account, Ricky Cobb also got into fantasy sports at a young age, hand-writing his weekly lineups and dropping them in the nearest mailbox.

"I was playing fantasy sports with a by-mail service called Simulated Sports Service, SSS. There was an ad in the back of *The Sporting News*. I had read [*Rotisserie League Baseball* by Glen Waggoner and Okrent] around '85 and I thought, 'Oh, my god'. That thing was dog-eared," Cobb recalled.

"I wanted to play but I didn't have enough friends to put together a league where people would really be into it, so I sent off for this thing that I saw in the back of *The Sporting News* and got involved. Nineteen eighty-six was my first year of playing fantasy and I was hooked. I couldn't get enough of it."

It wasn't long before the future sociology professor began hunting the latest information about players on his rotisserie team, getting creative in doing so.

"If you talk to an 18-year-old sports superfan today, they would not be able to relate in the slightest to guys like me craving information and having to scratch and claw to find it. I remember calling the press box," Cobb reminisced.

"I used to get the American League Red Book and the National League Green Book, and I remember calling the press box at Memorial Stadium in Baltimore to find out who the probable pitchers were for the series. I was a teenager, and I got some guy on the line and he found the information and he gave it to me."

Enter Sports Phone...

"For those of us who remember it, that was our internet. I was in the middle of nowhere Kentucky, trying to find out what was going on with my fantasy teams. You know, that was my primary motivation for calling," Cobb explained.

"I started calling in '86 when I was 14 or 15. I wanted to know how my guys were doing. Dude, I was calling on Tuesday night to find out the score of the Tigers-Mariners game. It's not like I was calling to find out how my favorite team was doing, or some particular big game. I was calling multiple times a week and just calling to find out if [Detroit pitcher] Frank Tanana was winning, stuff like that."

An underlying thread for many callers, the cost proved problematic. In Cobb's case, it wasn't only 976-1313 to blame.

"Most of the damage I did were these long-distance phone calls to make trades with guys. I'll never forget, I was 15 or 16 and I remember our phone bill came one month, this would be like '86 or '87. The phone bill came and it was $409," he said.

"Part of that was [Sports Phone] but part of that was these hour-long phone calls with dudes around the country and trying to acquire a second baseman. We were a lower-middle-class family. I don't know how much $400 is in 2023 money, but my poor mother [a single parent] probably almost had a heart attack."

Cobb's mom sometimes tried to get him off the phone, right when he was about to seal the deal.

"If I was on the phone for very long, I can still remember her coming over and trying to signal to me that I'd been on the phone a long time. I'm shooing her away because I'm closing in on a trade for George Bell. I'm lucky she didn't kill me, but I can only imagine that there were a lot of parents back in those days who got some unpleasant surprises when the phone bill came from Sports Phone and the like."

While some former callers remember learning of historical moments via Sports Phone, like the final score of a big game or news of a monumental trade, the call that still resonates with Cobb is a little different.

"Sports Phone was part of the ecosystem for me of being a sports fan in the '80s that kept me connected, and I distinctly remember. It's weird. I have no idea why. But every time I think of Sports Phone I just remember one day calling, and it was just Alan Trammell had hit an RBI double," he said.

"I just remember that was such great news. At that point in my life when I should have been doing homework and whatever, it was just knowing that Alan Trammell had hit an RBI double for me at Tiger Stadium that night. That was all I needed to be happy. It was simpler times, man."

ALL IN THE CARDS

Gloria Rothstein's name was once associated with some of the biggest sports card shows across the tri-state area, a lineup that included the annual East Coast National in White Plains. Known for attracting high-end dealers along with a star-studded cast of guests signing auto-graphs, these events offered collectors in-person access to many of their heroes.

One fan who held a virtual backstage pass was Butch Forte, a diehard who worked for Rothstein from 1986 through 2010 as a concierge of sorts to the memorabilia dealers. Forte and the team he led would assist dealers in setting up their wares, also handling any logistical issues that arose throughout the day.

A Westchester County parks department employee during the week, Forte's side gig meant spending a lot of up-close time with marquee names such as Pete Rose, Mickey Rivers, Willie Randolph, John Starks, and Darryl Strawberry — some leading to lifelong friendships. Well before his days of hobnobbing with the greats, Butch was a high school kid trying to stay on top of what was going on with the Bronx Zoo, and not the one with the lions, tigers, and bears.

"Starting in 1975 or '76, I called Sports Phone to get the West Coast scores. I used to call a lot after 1 a.m., mostly during baseball season," Forte recalled. "I was keeping up with the Yankees when they went out west, especially in '77 when the Yankees-Red Sox [rivalry] got me into it. That team was so crazy in those years, with Thurman [Munson] and Reggie [Jackson] not getting along. There was a whole lot of stuff going on."

Amidst the turmoil in '77 and '78, the Bombers ended up with a pair of World Series titles, with Sports Phone and the *New York Daily News* Forte's two most important companions. He later became a regular listener to Fordham University's late-night programming, where he remembers hearing a pair of Sports Phone alums in their college days.

"Before [WFAN], they had a radio station called WFUV. A show used to come on Sunday nights, from 12-2 or something like that. I remember listening to that in my room with a little portable radio," Forte explained. "I remember Michael Kay from back then, and I remember Bob Papa."

Forte would go on to become one of WFAN's frequent callers, recognizable to its hosts and listeners as Butch from South Yonkers. A regular with the now-retired Steve Somers, Joe Benigno, Evan Roberts, Sal Licata, and others, the growth of his fandom got an early boost by dialing Sports Phone.

EDDIE FROM THE SOUTH SIDE

Eddie Olczyk has seemingly done it all in the world of hockey. The Chicago native played for the 1984 US Men's Olympic Team before a successful 16-year career in the NHL, during which he lit the lamp 342 times. Olczyk spent the first three seasons of that run with his hometown Blackhawks and later won a big Stanley Cup in '94 with the New York Rangers.

Commonly known as "Eddie O" or "Edzo," the once-prolific goal scorer was head coach of the Pittsburgh Penguins from 2003 to 2005 and has served as a color commentator for over two decades for several networks. Olczyk started as a young fan calling Chicago Sports Phone, from which he learned about one of hockey's greatest moments.

Sports Phone Stories

Miracle on Splice
(feat. Eddie Olczyk, David Schuster, and Bob Grochowski)

There are some moments in sport that transcend both time and fandom, leaving their mark on even the most casual observer many decades later. One such occurrence took place in a tiny village in New York's Adirondack Mountains, an upset that rocked the globe during the 1980 Winter Olympics.

Led by coach Herb Brooks, the US squad was comprised mostly of amateur players, an average age of 21 years old making them the youngest team in the entire Olympic tournament. In contrast, the heavily favored Soviet Union featured some of hockey's best and brightest —

including future hall of famer Vladislav Tretiak, recognized by many as the world's best goalie during that era.

As has been widely chronicled since, the upstart Americans downed the Soviets 4–3 and went on to capture the gold medal, defeating Finland 4–2 a couple of days later. The unlikely victory over the USSR was later named the top sports moment of the twentieth century by *Sports Illustrated*, but in a scenario that would seem impossible today, the game was not broadcast live at the time.

With the puck drop set for 5 p.m. ET on February 22, ABC had scheduled the game to be shown three hours later on tape delay. Without the internet, 24/7 sports talk radio, the ESPN BottomLine ticker, or any other readily available methods of instant access, the large majority of those tuning in at 8 p.m. ET had no idea that they were about to witness history.

While most of the nation watched with bated breath as the young Olympians held onto a one-goal lead with 10 minutes remaining, Eddie Olczyk sat satisfied on Chicago's South Side.

"I was not a North Sider at the time, so I was on the South Side. I remember calling and getting updates on the Lake Placid Miracle on Ice in the Olympics. That was '80 and so I was 13 [years old]. It was the first time that I would have called so that's what I remember," Olczyk said. "I was like wow, this [Sports Phone] is the greatest thing. I remember because those games were all on tape delay, and a lot of them would run three, four, five hours later."

The broadcaster delivering the updates to Olczyk was David Schuster, a Chicago Sports Phone veteran who manned the booth there for almost 11 years.

"Eddie Olczyk, who now is obviously a broadcaster, who was a player and a coach. He was just a young kid at that time and he would call Sports Phone for all the scores of the games," Schuster said. "I remember him telling me later on that he found out about that game by calling up Sports Phone. So that was obviously my voice on that."

Not everyone wanted to know the outcome before the broadcast, including future Sports Phone announcer Bob Grochowski.

"I heard Eddie O. give Chicago Sports Phone a call-out during a game one day [in 2022]. You remember the Miracle on Ice game?" he said. "I didn't specifically call Sports Phone that day because I wanted to watch the game that night, and Eddie O. talked about how he didn't want to wait. He called up Sports Phone."

When Al Michaels's iconic "Do you believe in miracles? Yes!" call was finally sent over the television airwaves, Olczyk had already been savoring the win for a few hours, all thanks to Sports Phone.

———

The Miracle on Ice result wasn't the only big news Olczyk heard first on Sports Phone, as the club he'd later kick off his NHL career with unceremoniously axed their head coach during the holiday season in 1976.

"I remember when the Hawks fired Billy Reay. I remember it was right around Christmas," Olczyk recalled.

A two-time Stanley Cup winner as a player, Reay started as the coach of the Toronto Maple Leafs for less than a season and a half before taking over behind the Black Hawks bench for the 1963–64 season. Over the next 13-plus campaigns, the Winnipeg native had a great deal of success that included six first-place finishes, 12 post-season berths, and a trio of Stanley Cup Finals appearances.

"I think there was a story that they put a pink slip under his door, pretty much told him that he was out," Olczyk said. "I remember getting that news over Sports Phone."

The former star center's recollection of the events surrounding Reay's dismissal is spot on. Despite being the frontman for one of the best runs in Chicago hockey history, the Hawks' 10–19–5 record in late '76 caused ownership to opt for a change. The method they chose to inform the 58-year-old head coach of his firing was not exactly the classiest, however, a move that has since become part of Windy City lore.

Having just tied the North Stars in Minnesota, the Blackhawks returned to Chicago in the early morning hours of December 22. When Reay arrived home he found an envelope under his door containing a note from team owner Bill Wirtz, stating that his services were no longer needed. No phone call, no in-person chat, just an old-fashioned pink slip.

Throughout Olczyk's playing, coaching, and broadcasting careers, he's gotten to know most of Chicago's sports media contingent, many of whom he used to hear on the other end of the phone.

"You'd tell some old [Sports Phone] stories like I helped pay the bills for you because I was one of the loyal callers. That was right on the cusp of sports radio," he said. "That was your only way to [get the scores and news]. Either you were listening to the game or watching it, or waiting for the next day's newspaper to get all the scoops."

"It was always good to put a face with a name and hear those voices, all these years after on local radio here in Chicago or even television."

TRAGEDY OVER THE PHONE

Fred Miller was a New York Telephone employee who ironically would call Sports Phone from work, as well as the occasional payphone. He sometimes called two or three times a day starting in the late 1970s, looking for headlines and scores, and to try his hand at the Quickie Quiz.

Miller distinctly recalls a trio of voices on the other end — Howie Rose, Cory Eisner, and Don La Greca — a group of announcers whose tenures spanned decades. Just like Eddie Olzcyk, the Selden resident got the jump on the Miracle on Ice result.

"My most memorable Sports Phone call was getting the final score of the 1980 USA Olympic hockey team's victory over Russia," Miller recalled. "I called my wife after and asked her to tape the delayed ABC broadcast."

Unfortunately, not all news is good news, with Miller also learning of a tragic event upon dialing those seven digits. On August 2, 1979, Thurman Munson was piloting an aircraft, practicing landings at Akron-Canton Airport, when the Yankees captain had an accident.

"On the negative side, [I heard] the announcement of Thurman Munson's death in his plane crash," Miller said.

OH THE PAIN

A name long associated with New York sports radio, Joe Benigno's journey from regular caller to on-air fixture is inspirational in its own right — showcasing that hard work, passion, and just a little luck can make the improbable possible.

"It's hard to believe it all happened. I don't know how else to say it. I got very fortunate, for a guy who was just a caller and basically just went from being a caller to having his own show. Not many guys were able to do that," the New Jersey native said.

"I think what's even more shocking is that it's all behind me now. I [still] do part-time and I'm still very out there but I look back and it's just hard to believe that it ever happened, and it's hard to believe that it's over. It's hard to believe that all those 25 years that I did it full-time are now gone."

Benigno appeared as a guest host on WFAN in 1994 and eventually became a regular on what was launched as the country's first all-sports radio station seven years prior, starting on overnights and later hosting middays from 2004 until his semi-retirement in 2020. His historical knowledge coupled with an everyfan mentality made Benigno favored among the Big Apple faithful, especially those long-suffering supporters of a couple of clubs in particular.

"I'm a hardcore fan of my teams, man. I'm a massive Jet fan, Met fan. The Knicks and the Rangers, I root for them too but maybe not on the level of the football and baseball team, but I am still a massive fan. It's all about that. It's not about me, it's about my teams," Benigno proclaimed.

"I've seen too many people over the years, you're a fan and you get into [sports media] because you're a fan and then once you start working in it, you lose that. That's something I never did and I never will. I live and die with the teams I root for. I've been suffering for 55 years with my football team without winning the Super Bowl or even being in one. [Also] a lot of aggravation with the Mets. I think that's one of the big differences because I've always been a fan. These are my teams, and if you got a problem with that, well that's your problem. You know what I mean?"

Once known to radio hosts as Joe from Saddle River, Benigno didn't have as many options to keep up with his teams before "the FAN" began broadcasting. His go-to during a crucial moment for the Jets franchise was Sports Phone, and what he heard on the other end certainly contributed to the die-hard's trademark phrase "Oh, the pain!", one that would be uttered many times in years to come and eventually become the name of his podcast.

"Nineteen eighty-three, it's the NFL draft, and the NFL draft in 1983 was not the extravaganza it is now, primetime and all of this. They used to do it in the middle of the week during the day. So I think they had it [at] one of those hotels in the city," Benigno recalled.

"So it's the 1983 draft and you know I'm a massive Jets fan. So '83 is the year when all the quarterbacks got drafted, [John] Elway and [Jim] Kelly and [Dan] Marino and all of that. So I'm obviously hoping to get Marino. This is where my mind's set. So I said, I got to call Sports Phone and see what happened and that's where I found out — on Sports Phone — that they drafted Ken O'Brien instead of Marino."

As he talked about the missed opportunity 40 years later, the radio vet's disappointment could still be felt.

"I was working in the city in 1983 and so I was out, and I went to a payphone like the old days when they had freakin' payphones, and called Sports Phone. Let me see, who the hell did we draft? And that's how I found out about O'Brien and I wasn't very happy about it. I didn't even know who he was. I remember going like, 'Who the hell is this guy? Ken O'Brien? [University of] Cal[ifornia] Davis? Who the freak is this guy?'"

While he'd dial those seven digits numerous other times, losing out on a Hall of Fame QB is the one call that will always stick in his craw.

"I called basically for scores, and I remember Howie [Karpin] being on there. I remember at the end he'd always say, 'Stay with us!' They'd always say that at the end," Benigno recalled. "But that's the one time that really sticks out because it was such a big deal for me. That is my number one memory of Sports Phone."

Quickie Quiz

Q: Which announcer accidentally broke the news to a star running back that his coach had resigned?

A: King Wally

Alan Sanders: "I think it was [King] Wally who called Freeman McNeil at home, and McNeil had no idea that Wally was calling to get a comment on [New York Jets head coach] Walt Michaels. I don't think he got fired. I think he retired. I think Wally said to Freeman, 'I'm just calling to see if you have any thoughts about what happened with Walt,' and Freeman goes, 'What do you mean, what happened with Walt?' This is the era where nobody's carrying cell phones with little alerts on them, and Freeman McNeil was blown away that Wally was breaking this news to him. He had no idea."

FRANK THE TANK

Another lifelong Mets fan not shy about sharing his occasional frustrations with the team's play publicly, whether that be online or in the stands at Citi Field, Frank Fleming's NFL allegiances also lie in the AFC East but much farther down the coastline. The Barstool Sports blogger tried not to miss the action back in the day, but when a work shift overlapped a Miami Dolphins game he counted on Sports Phone to keep up.

"I was rarely away from my TV on big game days," he noted.

November 14, 1993, was one of those days, as football history was on the line and it just so happened to involve his favorite team on the road in Philadelphia. Fleming was anxious to stay abreast of what was happening but was stuck at his job in Upper Montclair, New Jersey, less than two hours away from Veterans Stadium by car.

"I worked at an A&P [supermarket] in 1993 and called in every 20 minutes on the day [head coach] Don Shula set the wins record," he recalled.

The Dolphins edged the Eagles 19–14 behind third-string quarterback Doug Pederson, filling in for Scott Mitchell who himself had replaced the injured Marino. It was Shula's 325th win, passing Chicago Bears legend "Papa Bear" George Halas for tops all-time. Fleming may have been busy bagging groceries during the historical contest, but at least Sports Phone kept him connected to the moment as it played out.

The very next weekend Fleming learned of one of college football's more memorable upsets via 976-1313, a phone call that stayed fresh in his memory almost 30 years later. Lou Holtz's undefeated Fighting Irish hosted future New York Giants head coach Tom Coughlin and No. 17 Boston College on November 20 in South Bend. Now ranked No. 1 in the country after toppling Florida State a week earlier in a matchup dubbed the "Game of the Century," Notre Dame was flying high and expected to beat the Eagles to earn a chance at the national title. After all, they had dispatched BC the previous season in a laugher, 54–7.

Things started rough for Holtz's squad, who found themselves down 38–17 with time no longer on their side. Notre Dame rallied for 22 points in the game's final eleven minutes though, taking a one-point lead with just a minute to play. QB Glenn Foley drove the Eagles to the 24-yard line and walk-on kicker David Gordon nailed a 41-yard field goal as time expired — leaving the Irish, their fans, and many Sports Phone callers like Fleming in total shock.

COULD YOU REPEAT THAT?

Living in Maspeth, Queens in the 1970s, the Sherman household kept close watch on the locals including the Mets and St. John's, as well as their national favorites Notre Dame and the Green Bay Packers. As a young boy around 9 or 10 years old, William would often call Sports Phone to check in for both himself and his dad. He also called often from gym payphones during his basketball playing days, from CYO through his senior year in high school.

"My father would frequently ask me to call to find out the score of whatever games we were interested in," he recalled. "I always asked my mother's permission. I was afraid I would call too frequently. My father was the boss but mom paid the bills!"

The increased frequency of those calls was often the result of an overzealous Sherman, or simply the lightning-fast delivery of the Sports Phone announcer at the other end of the phone.

"On a big day, you had to listen carefully. A few times you were so excited that you weren't sure you heard it right. I remember following a Notre Dame-Kentucky basketball game and it was late and close. I couldn't recall if it was ND or Kentucky up with seconds to go or vice versa. Got to call again," he remembered.

"If I had an interest in a particular game and the announcer was going quickly, I did a lot of second-guessing. Maybe I just couldn't believe what I heard."

One thing Sherman was never unsure about was Sports Phone's digits.

"It's kind of like your first home phone number as a kid, locked away in your brain. My mother still has the original home number. I have lived at my home for 30-plus years, same number," he said. "If I have to call home I cycle through my brain and invariably it's always there. Strange, I know, but I singsong, 976-1313. Why? I can't explain it."

BLOCKED

Diane Kraut began calling Sports Phone in the service's infancy, fascinated that she could find out how her favorite club had fared just by spinning the rotary dial.

"I always wondered how many times the tape got updated. Being young, I also wondered if the guy recording the tape did it from home or a studio," she said. "I must have started to call into Sports Phone in the early-to-mid '70s. The main reason was to find out if my beloved Mets had won their ballgame."

The future radio voice of those Mets wore a younger man's clothes back then but left a lasting impression on Kraut nonetheless.

"I remember Howie Rose because he also sounded so upbeat in his recordings," she recalled.

Her clandestine missions to get the scores would eventually backfire.

"I always called from home. I would sneak up to my parents' bedroom and use their phone," Kraut said. "New York Telephone added a charge to your phone bill every time you called Sports Phone. I called it so much that eventually, my dad had the number blocked."

GOOD AFTERNOON, EVERYBODY!

Christopher Russo has been hosting sports talk radio since 1984, smack in the middle of Sports Phone's heyday in many markets. A dyed-in-the-wool San Francisco Giants fan dating back to the '68 season, the man known as Mad Dog dialed 976-1313 often despite the fact he was working for news and sports stations.

"I used to use it all the time to get Giants baseball scores, so I called constantly," Russo recalled. "Andy Roth and Howie Karpin are the two guys that I recall, and those guys did a great job with updates. Phenomenal updates with the scores. You know, bottom of the eighth, 4–1 Giants against the Cubs."

Hosting *Sports Talk with Christopher Russo* in Orlando, Florida at the time, he occasionally had others call for him while on the air.

"Sometimes [we called] on behalf of Chris, other times, because we were on from 6-8 p.m., it was to get a full scoreboard on the early games since Sports Phone was quicker than wire services," producer Jeff Allen explained. "I also liked getting scores of the Braves games [for] myself."

Allen, Russo, and the team called so frequently that management at WKIS was up in arms when the long-distance bill arrived.

"We went from several times a night to maybe once or twice," Allen added. "I also did some damage when I did weekend scoreboard shows and updates during Dolphins games. You had to be quick to get the updates since they were rapid-fire delivery."

Back in New York, Russo continued to call Sports Phone at a regular clip into the early '90s while co-hosting *Mike and the Mad Dog* on WFAN, always keeping tabs on his boys from the bay.

"976-1313. I called it all the time," Russo reminisced. "I can still remember the telephone number. That's all you need to know. That's how important it was to me. I still remember the telephone number 40 years later. How about that?"

Now a television mainstay and member of the Radio Hall of Fame, Mad Dog misses the build-up and intimacy that accompanied the Sports Phone era.

"We lost that connection, calling something like Sports Phone up. It's a little too immediate [now]. You lose a little feeling of anticipation. You got that little feel of the guys who were doing the Sports Phone update, but I do think we've lost something. It's much better hearing a voice give you the scores than looking at it on a computer or your phone.," he acknowledged.

"Now it's almost too available. You take it for granted. There was always a feeling that you wanted to work to get your scores. Okay, let me get a Giants score. It's 5:45, 5:50, or whatever time the update was. I haven't heard it in ten minutes. Let me see if they got out of the bottom of the eighth. There was a good sense, a good feeling in doing that."

LA LENSMAN

Born in Red Bank, New Jersey and raised in Brooklyn, Kevin Reece has been capturing college and professional sports for over 40 years. Now based on the left coast, Reece has snapped his share of iconic moments and big games including ten Super Bowls, nine NBA Finals, and 24 Rose Bowls.

Before his career took shape, the seasoned photographer was a frequent dialer — and Rose was the announcer who stood out to him as well.

"I started calling Sports Phone in my twenties. It was my cousin Robert from Washington, DC, who turned me on to it. He was in the sports business and got me my very first credentials. I always called in for just the scores at night. There was no internet in those days, if you wanted the scores from the West Coast that was the only way to get them," Reece remembered.

"I would call in as many as six times a day. They also gave the college scores. They talked very fast and updated it about every ten minutes. I remember Howie Rose the most. We talked about Sports Phone days in the Dodger Stadium press box on one of his trips out here with the Mets. It was great. I loved it. I always had the number in my wallet, ready to call it."

SHOW ME THE MONEY

Los Angeles native Leigh Steinberg has represented hundreds of athletes over the past four-plus decades. It all started in 1975 with University of California quarterback Steve Bartkowski, his former dormmate and the first of eight No. 1 overall draft picks he'd have as clients.

Prior to earning a law degree in '73, Steinberg was a resident assistant housed with a first-rate group that included a practical joker who would shape the future of technology.

"He would do things like getting all the phones to ring simultaneously in the dorm. He was so far ahead as a prankster in terms of the things he could do with phones and information exchange, and so I often had to talk to him about how do we get these doggone phones to stop ringing," Steinberg recalled, referring to Apple Computer co-founder Steve Wozniak.

"He had wired away a way of torturing somebody on the sixth floor. His brain was so far ahead. That was quite a dorm we had. We had Bartkowski. We had Bob Swenson who played for ten years and was in the Pro Bowl with Denver. We had a guy named Brian Maxwell who was a distance runner, who went out and formed the company PowerBar. Wozniak left Berkeley and went down to Santa Clara and camped out in a garage [with co-founder Steve Jobs]."

As his career took off and the list of clientele grew, Steinberg had to find a way to keep up with each athlete.

"I was a frequent caller to Sports Phone. We're taking people back to a time when the information options in real time were severely limited, and I would guess some of the reasons younger people would not believe that there were no computers, no smartphones, no ESPN, and newspapers had deadlines so they couldn't even get the late games into the next morning's paper," he explained.

"So this would all be inconceivable today. No *NFL Red Zone*, no NFL Network? Not the multiplicity of sports information, television networks, and radio stations, not the ubiquitous nature of the cell phone. There's no breaking news every five seconds on ESPN that this player got cut, waived, traded, or injured. In other words, none of that was possible."

This proved especially tough on NFL Sundays when Steinberg couldn't be in two places at once.

"I'm representing half of the starting quarterbacks in the '80s, so everything is monumental. For example, I had all of these franchise quarterbacks. So San Francisco was always competing with Dallas and I had Steve Young and Troy Aikman, or Pittsburgh on the other side, and I needed to know what was happening so I could put a postgame call into Aikman or [Warren] Moon or Young or Drew Bledsoe or whoever the heck it was. Sports Phone helped me. It enabled me to have a much more intelligent discussion and helpful discussion with players postgame," he said.

"It's hard to remember a time when even if you were at a stadium, you just watched the game on a scoreboard and occasionally got other scores. You didn't have a ticker. You didn't have 15 televisions in a premium zone dedicated to real-time [updates]. Did Steve Young do this or that? Did Bruce Smith sack somebody? Sports Phone was the only alternative to get a larger real-time picture of what was happening on a Sunday or Saturday and get it when I needed it, to be able to know when to call a player.

"Now I might be at one game, but I had no idea what was going on in the rest of the games. I needed to know quicker, and I needed to be in touch with clients, and I needed to understand who got injured, who had a prolific day, who had a miserable day. Your clients expect you to know those things as if you were personally watching every play they made."

That near-immediacy was most important when one of his clients suffered an injury.

"I wanted to be able to monitor if a player got injured and be on the phone with him immediately after they left the stadium so that we could intervene in a medical situation or at least understand what it was," Steinberg explained. "Sports Phone made all of that much more possible."

The superagent didn't only call for business reasons, keeping up on his alma mater, Cal, when he was out and about on Saturday nights.

"The revolutionary nature of Sports Phone was that it realized the massive audience out there of people who followed sports and needed to know results sooner than two days later," Steinberg said. "So for gambling it was massive, but it was also massive for hardcore alums [like me]."

He still represents big-name clients, playing a key role in Chiefs quarterback Patrick Mahomes's 10-year, $450 million contract extension in 2020. With instant access to play-by-play and advanced data, the daily workflow of an agent has changed quite a bit. Without Sports Phone offering what it did back then, however, Steinberg may not have been able to support his clients at the level they grew accustomed to.

"We've lost the sense of how rapidly this whole technological revolution has happened. I'm talking about 20 years ago, you needed America Online to get on to the internet," he reflected. "You have to give Sports Phone some credit for being ahead of its time. It was the great grandfather of what today is the ubiquitous and omnipresent of real-time information."

Quickie Quiz

Q: Which NL West manager was canned early in the 1988 season after a tumultuous year-plus at the helm?

A: Larry Bowa

The scuffling Padres were in town for a three-game set at Shea Stadium in late May when Sports Phone reported on the managerial change, interviewing San Diego's newest skipper from the Grand Hyatt in Midtown Manhattan.

Rich Ackerman: "I remember Larry Bowa getting fired and we we just called the team hotel and [replacement manager] Jack McKeon was certainly happy to talk to us. There were a couple of occasions such as that, but that one really stands out... I thought that gave us a lot of validity, that we were able to break stories and also back it up with that type of stuff. I thought that was really important... I remember it was at an off time. I want to say it was a Saturday morning that he got fired. Back in the day we had the hotel numbers and you just called. Sure enough, boom, there it was. There he was. He was too happy to come on, so I was kind of surprised and I remember being happy that he did it."

 Sports Phone Stories

Man or Mouse
(feat. Charlie DeNatale and Mike Weinstein)

Raised in Brooklyn and educated at NYU, Howard Cosell was one of the most recognized and celebrated sports journalists in American history. Armed with a distinctive voice, a vast vocabulary, and an often controversial candor not found in many sportscasters of his era, Cosell never shied from sharing an opinion or inserting humor into a situation.

Two of the country's biggest leagues dealt with labor strife at the outset of the 1980s, leading to a pair of memorable moments involving the brash broadcaster and Sports Phone reporters.

Charlie DeNatale: "I was in a hotel in New York City covering either the

1981 baseball strike or the 1982 football strike. Anyway, a bunch of reporters are there, and lo and behold there is Howard Cosell about ten feet away from me. So the negotiations are going on behind closed doors, and I wander over and put my ear up to the door to try and listen in. Cosell yells out in front of everyone, 'Don't put your ear to the door. Go in! Are you a man or a mouse?'"

Mike Weinstein: "The funny thing I remember about the baseball strike is at one point Reggie Jackson comes out of the meeting room and he's going into the bathroom. Howard Cosell looks at everybody and kind of winks, and he follows him into the bathroom. And they're in there, you know, whatever. Nobody else followed them in, then they came out, and Cosell comes back. So all the reporters were waiting, and Cosell had that way of talking slowly and making sure everybody was listening to him. He goes something along the lines of, 'I was in the stall to the left. Reggie was to my right. I washed my hands. Reggie did not.'"

———

CHAPTER 7
THE CALLERS: BOOKIES, BETTORS, AND TOUTS

No group of callers dialed Sports Phone more often than those with gambling interests. When money was on the line, it was a favorite for both bookmakers and those wagering on sporting events.

"976–1313 was ingrained in every sports bettor's mind in the local markets," recalled Jim Feist, one of the nation's most well-known handicappers during the Sports Phone era. "It was a fabulous service."

Not everyone at Sports Phone realized that betting was so influential in their call volumes, at least not initially.

"I didn't know the betting world, and of course back then it didn't even come close to what it is today. It's crazy. But let's face it, that was used as a tool for people who bet on games," Linda Cohn said.

"I was almost out of college and I thought it was like, let's keep people up to date with the scores of their favorite teams. I'm a fan first and everything. That was just another aspect that I learned later that people used Sports Phone because they bet on games."

Sports betting was almost exclusively an underground thing back then, not like the legalized versions we see today.

"The evolution of this industry has been remarkable. I started betting on certain sports when I was a kid in a little town in Pennsylvania, and of course, throughout the land, it was illegal to make bets or take bets ... It was always on the outside of the law and it stayed that way until the offshores came into the picture in the '80s. That didn't make it any less illegal, but they were out of reach for the most part," Feist added.

"The bookmakers in the United States moved several of their operations to offshore countries so that they were outside the scope of law enforcement. Fast-forward to today where sports betting is legal in many states. DraftKings, FanDuel, [Bet] MGM, and of course in Nevada everything is different."

Superstition and gambling have always gone hand in hand, and Sports Phone's callers were no exception.

"We did see the [call volume] numbers from time to time if I recall correctly, but the reason I knew the reach was because I heard from friends, especially friends who were gamblers, and the volume of calls that came from people who had action," Gary Cohen said.

"They would call every ten minutes and sometimes more often than that. I also know that some of them had favored voices where if they heard a particular voice they knew it was unlucky for them, and so they would call back hoping to hear a different voice. So it was something that I was very aware of."

Black cats and broken mirrors aside, Sports Phone's horse bettors expected accuracy above all else, something the announcers were keenly aware of.

"What I remember about the horse racing was people telling me, probably someone like [Jim] Memolo, yanking my chain. He goes, 'You don't want to make a mistake on this, Berman, because if you do you're probably going to wind up in the East River.' Because all the gamblers were calling in and it's like you don't want to get the who in the trifecta, that you read the wrong number or say the wrong horse, because they're gonna hunt you down and you're going to be finished," Jim Berman said, recounting his early days at Sports Phone.

"I was like, Okay, I need to make sure I get this right. I took everything [literally], because [the Sports Phone announcers] were my idols. I took everything that was being said 100 percent literally. If they told me this, I assume that that was probably true, that if I got it wrong when I walked out at night of 919 Third Avenue a couple of good old boys were gonna find me and that would be the end of it. But the point was you've got to be accurate, and I learned this discipline and that was important."

The Sports Phone staff had to serve as customer service agents from time to time, with irate gamblers tracking down their direct office numbers and dialing them often.

"You would have people betting on North Dakota Central versus New Mexico Agriculture and no one wanted the score except the people that had bet on it, but if you didn't have it then you'd hear from them. There was a way the fans were able to call the office easily. I don't think we were listed in the phone book," Peter Newman explained.

"People would call me and correct something that I had said that was inaccurate or tilted one way. Not only were we doing three people handling thousands of Quickie Quiz calls, but we were also the compliance and complaint department. Thank God we were 21 [years old] is all I've got to say."

QUICKIE QUIZ

While it might be a stretch to call the Quickie Quiz a form of gambling, participants did fork over the cost of a call to win on-air recognition along with the occasional prize.

"I did get called in for a couple of chats about the phone bill...I think it was 10 cents a phone call, right, so it added up," Kenny Albert remembered. "I was calling the quiz four or five times a day to try to be the first one on there. You know, when [my parents] went through the phone bill it was definitely noticed."

Initially created to keep calls coming in during a lull in the action, the quiz segment quickly became a hit.

"The Quickie Quiz was something we developed to fill in the afternoons. If we were doing a Sports Phone in the 1950s, we would have had baseball scores that [were] in the afternoon," Mike Farrell said. "There weren't that many scores in the afternoon. It was something to fill in that day part and keep people actively involved, and part of the challenge was then to keep ratcheting up the degree of difficulty of the question."

Interest may have grown a little too rapidly for the technology in place, causing the staff to be overwhelmed with calls initially.

"[One] thing that was a great idea but poorly thought out was the Quickie Quiz, because if you had that many people listening and you put out a question, and then you had three people answering the phone and you had hundreds, if not thousands, of calls coming in at the same moment," Newman recalled, describing the workflow in the mid-1970s.

"It was insanity. It was like people running around and then taping a reaction from the winner of the Quickie Quiz, 'How'd you get [the answer]? How do you remember that stuff?' The Quickie Quiz, in its own way, was a bizarre thing. We were making it up as we were going along."

Over time the logistics were improved upon, with the quiz serving as an everyday ritual for many callers. Even those focused on actual gambling occasionally took aim at the quiz.

"I'm sure that I dabbled a few times," Eddie Olczyk admitted.

Long before scoring a job at Sports Phone, Tony Matteo was hooked.

"I was kind of naive about the gambler aspect of it. The gamblers would rely on it because they wanted up-to-the-minute information. For me, it had something every three o'clock called the Quickie Quiz, and if you got it correct they would mention your name," Matteo acknowledged.

"The same guys used to win all the time, but a couple of times I was honorable mention and I got my name mentioned on Sports Phone. To me, it was a huge deal. I used to call multiple times daily. My father used to get mad because back then the calls are itemized and I believe it was 25 cents a call instead of a dime, but I was a sports information junkie and they were true pioneers."

There was a particular group of quiz players whose interests expanded beyond bulls and bears.

"Peter [Newman] was the first self-made star of Sports Phone because he was on most of the time. He had a good personality for it. He'd make friends with the callers and there were a couple of regulars. You know, it was like WFAN if you're listening to it. They have regulars all the time. We had our regulars," Denis McNamara reminisced.

"The guys from Wall Street, they were wild. They were calling the Quickie Quiz. They won a couple of times. Peter and I once went down and had lunch with them. Wall Street's a pretty crazy place, but they were nice people. They were so excited to meet us. So we were thinking, we're just talking on the telephone doing these announcements. Meeting us didn't seem like such a big deal, but they loved it."

Detroit Sports Phone saw a sustained spike in call volume throughout the 1984 baseball season, as Sparky Anderson's Tigers made a mockery of the American League en route to their first World Series championship since '68. Led by sluggers Lance Parrish and Kirk Gibson, the up-the-middle combo of Alan Trammell and Lou Whitaker, 19-game winner Jack Morris, and closer Willie Hernandez who won the Cy Young Award as well as AL MVP, fans in Motown couldn't get enough of their hometown club.

This fever pitch carried over to their Quickie Quiz, which often focused on Tiger baseball in both guesswork and giveaways.

"I think the best year we had when I was there was '84 when the Tigers were on their roll. Everybody was fascinated with them because that was an unbelievable season," explained John Cwikla, who left Sports Phone a year later for an executive producer position at ABC affiliate WXYZ Channel 7. "The trivia was a big draw in '84. We gave away a lot of Tiger memorabilia and stuff like that."

The Quickie Quiz wasn't only reserved for the daytime either, with another version broadcast for insomniacs and those working the graveyard shift during Sports Phone's early years. The questions posed were a lot less difficult during the wee hours, and the competition was not nearly as fierce.

"[It was] 3:30 in the morning and it was funny as hell. You had eight or nine regular callers that were calling in on those phones around the corner, between New York and Jersey [Sports Phone], so I'd have to sit there the whole time," Tommy Tighe recalled, describing the phone bank featuring multiple lines that would all ring at once.

"You'd wait for some idiot to come on and say, 'So who wore number seven on the Yankees? A: Roger Maris, B: Clete Boyer, or C: Mickey Mantle.' Stupid things like that. It's 3:30 in the morning. You weren't gonna put somebody on that had thought [like that]. Then I'd have to put the thing [the new recording with the answer] back on."

EDDIE C

Massachusetts native Ed Coleman read his share of score updates over WFAN's airwaves in the 1980s, but when a wager was in play Sports Phone was sometimes the best option.

"When I first came to New York I can remember there were times I'd be out, it might be a Friday night or a Saturday night, and I'd bet a game or whatever and I'm looking for a phone. I'm checking Sports Phone. I think everybody did and it definitely served its purpose because there was no other place to get information," Coleman recalled.

"You couldn't just pick up your phone. You couldn't flip open a laptop. I guess you could run to your car and get an update from FAN but you're not doing that on a regular basis. [Now] I always do a double take when I see a payphone like, 'What the hell is that?'"

LIKE FATHER, LIKE SON

Steve Finamore started calling Sports Phone in 1976, driven by his love for the Kansas City Royals and their perennial All-Star George Brett.

"All my friends were Yankees and Mets fans. I didn't care for either," he recalled. "Towards the end of the regular season I wanted to see how KC was doing in their games, so one day I called from my phone at home to get their score."

He learned about Sports Phone not from an ad on the subway or a commercial on radio, but from his old man.

"My father was a bookie. I had seen and heard him using Sports Phone," Finamore explained. "He hung out in Timboo's Bar on 5th Avenue and 11th Street in Brooklyn. On Saturdays, he took me to the bar and I hung out all day long, watching whatever game was on TV, playing pinball, pool, and shuffleboard. It was great. I was the only kid in there but I didn't care. My bar visits started when I was 10."

Soon he was calling daily, on weekends multiple times per day, eventually leading to some static about the bill — which meant taking it to the street.

"My mother was pissed. The phone bill was always super high. I called from home in the beginning," Finamore said. "But then when I started gambling at 16, I would call from the payphones on any street corner. If I was out in Manhattan I'd look for the nearest payphone, especially if I had action on a game. If I was at my girlfriend's house I would use her phone to check on a game."

Betting became a year-round thing, as did calling Sports Phone.

"Summer I bet on baseball, fall it was football, and still baseball. Winter it was basketball, and college too, hoops and football," Finamore explained. "The bets weren't placed with my father though. There was another bookie in the same bar named Lefty. I made my bets with him."

This included those little yellow betting slips so prevalent around New York City in the pre-internet days.

"Pro and college on one sheet. All the games and the point spreads were on it. You would get one, pick the games, circle the number on a stub at the bottom, and put your name and a dollar amount you wanted to wager. You could bet anywhere from four games to twelve," Finamore described.

"You had to get them all right to win. Your wager had to start at two dollars. Say for instance you picked four games, and you would multiply four by the dollar amount you bet. You never put your real name, because if the betting parlor was raided and the cops looked at the stubs you didn't want them to track you down. I went by Red, because of my red hair."

After a lifetime of coaching hoops, Finamore looks back on those experiences as influential in his lasting love for the game.

"It did increase my love for sports," he said. "It was all part of it."

NOSTRADAMUS OF THE NINTH RACE

Jeff Melnik had sports in his blood from the very beginning, but the game changed when he learned about the wagering side of things.

"Since we grew up on the ballfield playing football and baseball, the basketball court, the tennis court [to play hockey] and the race-track, sports — and eventually gambling — was our life," he recalled. "One day someone said to me, 'You know, you can bet on the games.' I was hooked."

He started calling Sports Phone in the mid-1970s, first for horse results but eventually to check on other outcomes as well.

"It was better than waiting for the *Daily News* the next day. I remember calling in for a horse that I bet on at Saratoga," Melnik said. "Race results weren't always immediately available, so I called back over and over again, especially when you paid twenty-five dollars for a [handicapper's] tip."

He was sometimes a little too eager, eventually forcing the need for a new plan.

"I remember getting pissed when I would get the same recording, and I remember re-calling over and over thinking that the new results would be in," Melnik explained. "[I called] mostly from home until mom busted me, then found payphones or called from work until the boss looked at the bills one day."

Calls to Sports Phone became part of a regular routine, like eating or sleeping.

"So, I'm pretty active with horse racing [at the time]. The access to results allowed me to grow my gambling addiction," Melnik acknowledged. "I would always remember going to OTB on a Saturday morning to get all my bets in, then call on the phone to get the results during the day."

One Saturday in particular he decided to have a little fun at a neighbor's expense, using Sports Phone to predict the future.

"On Saturdays OTB would show replays on Channel 9 at 6 p.m. of the eighth and ninth [races] at Aqueduct, Belmont, or Saratoga. The ninth race was usually a maiden race and it was an open field," Melnik said.

"Having dinner at my parents' [home] one Saturday evening and my parents' neighbor was over with his wife, and this guy was a tool, kept talking about how well he did at the track. Well, being the ball-buster I am, we're sitting there and the ninth race is on TV. This guy starts with how he likes this horse and that horse. Me being me, I go upstairs and call for the results of the ninth."

What happened next would make Melnik look like the second coming of Andy Beyer.

"I go back downstairs and say something like, 'I like the 5-7-12 triple.' This guy is like, 'No way.' Well, of course, 5-7-12 hit because I called [Sports Phone] and knew. The guy freaked out because the triple paid like $15,000. He couldn't stop saying how amazed he was. I kept that secret for a while, but my parents laughed their asses off when I told them a few weeks later that I called."

EVERYONE HATED THAT GUY

Bismark Pierre learned about Sports Phone from Yonkers rapper Jadakiss, who called the service to check on the latest NBA scores. Soon after that introduction, he was bombarded with ads for 976-1313 in the newspaper, on TV, and elsewhere, part of the company's New York City–area marketing push.

Pierre began to call daily, mostly from payphones. That frequency skyrocketed to several times per hour when an illicit calling scam spread quickly around town.

"I checked [Sports Phone] a lot when we had the illegal cell phone era, when people in the hood got corporate cell phone numbers from big companies' accounts," he explained. "Those big companies never noticed if you had a big company number. They just paid the bill, so I was checking every five to ten minutes."

One memorable night that Pierre called Sports Phone was through the traditional method, dropping dimes into a payphone.

"I remember betting on the UNLV games all year the year they went undefeated, when they had Stacey Augmon, Larry Johnson, Anderson Hunt, and them boys. I thought they would win it all, Pierre said. "I was loving that squad, arguably one of the best college squads ever. They ran through the competition that year like water till they came into the tournament."

Hall of Famer Jerry Tarkanian was in his 18th season coaching UNLV when the Runnin' Rebels entered the 1991 NCAA tournament with an unblemished record. Defending national champions backed by soon-to-be NBA first-round picks Johnson (1st overall), Augmon, and

Greg Anthony, Tark the Shark's squad were favorites to take the crown yet again.

On March 30, UNLV met Duke at the Hoosier Dome in Indianapolis in the national semifinals. The Rebels had embarrassed the Blue Devils in the previous year's championship game, winning by a 30-point margin.

"I hated Duke. I was watching the game. Everyone thought it was an easy win, but it wasn't going to happen versus Christian Laettner, Bob Hurley, and Grant Hill as a freshman," Pierre recalled.

"Duke came to play. They were up from the beginning to the first commercial break, but UNLV went on a spectacular run to take the lead. It stayed close the whole game. I was at my friend's house watching, and when I left UNLV was up 76–74 in the fourth quarter."

As Pierre hopped in a cab, Brian Davis converted a three-point play to put Duke up by one with just 1:02 on the clock. A Johnson free throw would tie the score at 77-all, but UNLV fouled Laettner with 12.7 seconds left. Now the stuff of NCAA legend, during a timeout Duke coach Mike Krzyzewski asked Laettner if he had it, to which the 6-foot-11 center reportedly responded, "I got 'em."

Had 'em he did, nailing both free throws to give Duke a 79–77 advantage. On the final possession, Johnson passed to Anderson Hunt, who missed a 3-pointer to end the contest and break a 45-game winning streak by the Runnin' Rebels. Many to this day, Johnson included, wish that he had opted to take the shot himself.

"I stepped out of the cab and called Sports Phone from a payphone, got the score 79–77 Duke. I damn near broke the payphone receiver. I was so pissed off," Pierre said.

"As we all well know, Duke went on to win the whole tournament after those free throws. I always hated Laettner, but everyone hated that guy. Crazy to say I met him once [later], coolest dude ever except for on the court."

SIMULCASTING AND SKATING

The third overall pick in the 1984 NHL Entry Draft and a member of the United States Hockey Hall of Fame, Eddie Olczyk's passions expand beyond the ice from the barns to the backstretch. His foray into thoroughbred racing began at a young age, back when TV simulcasting was not available to the masses. Olczyk would call Sports Phone as well as some of the other hotlines that advertised on the back of the *Daily Racing Form*, many which offered the full race calls for 99 cents or just the stretch call for about half a buck.

Now a horse racing analyst and handicapper for NBC Sports in addition to his hockey broadcasting duties with the Seattle Kraken, Olczyk has covered big events including the Kentucky Derby, Preakness Stakes, and the Belmont Stakes. Back in his playing days, he'd utilize the dial-up services to keep track of ongoing races, especially those that featured a horse he owned.

"I never did that from the clubhouse. I always did it either probably from home or a hotel. Was there a time or two that I was in desperation mode and had to figure something [else] out? Yeah. But I think the majority of it is because Woodbine runs pretty much when hockey is ending and hockey is beginning. When I was either at home or if I was in Toronto I'd be there, but if I was at home in the summer in Chicago or whatever that's when I would call," Olczyk explained.

"Obviously, trainers and coaches had phones in their offices, but nothing that exciting where it was in between periods and I got on the phone and tried to listen to a race call ... But I would call, for sure, because there was no simulcasting. It was a personal thing because my horse was running up there and I wanted to listen to it. But then if I was in Chicago you could go and bet Hawthorne and I'd bet Arlington. If you didn't want to wait until the 5:30 race recap show then you'd call the number."

Olczyk would also get creative with some help from a pal in the press box, then a sports reporter with the *Toronto Sun*.

"If I was getting my feet wet or whatever and I couldn't have a direct line to the press box, a guy by the name of Perry Lefko — a journalist with the *Toronto Sun* — he was on the beat for horse racing and CFL for a long time. I had a couple of horses that were running up in Toronto at Woodbine," Olczyk recalled.

"There was no simulcasting. You couldn't go to Arlington or Hawthorne and watch the races from Woodbine. I'm going back to the late '80s, and what Perry would do is, I'd call the press box. Perry would answer the phone. He'd drop the phone, and on the TV that was up in the press box he'd put the volume up really high so I could listen to the race and listen to my horse run."

Sports Phone Stories

Arrested At Arlington
(feat. Fred Huebner)

Purchased by the Chicago Bears in February 2023 and reportedly slated as a site for their new stadium, the Arlington Park track (once known as Arlington International) hosted horse racing from 1927 until its closure in 2021. During the days when Chicago Sports Phone had its own office, stringers were dispatched to the suburban racetrack so that updated results could be relayed to callers.

"Many tracks were agreeable in having one of us in their press box to gather the info and often broadcast the updates from the track," Fred Huebner explained. "Arlington Park was not one of those."

Because Sports Phone wasn't credentialed, the stringers had to get creative.

"We, myself included many times, stood outside the track watching what we could of the race, gathering the payouts from the tote board," Huebner recalled. "And then walking to the payphone near the train station across the parking lot from the track [to call in the results]."

This back-and-forth routine became a regular thing on race days, eventually garnering some unwanted attention from the local police. After observing a stringer's actions for a spell, the authorities were convinced that he was, in fact, an illegal bookmaker.

They moved in and arrested the unlucky reporter, who was eventually set free after a call to the Sports Phone office cleared things up.

———

SORRY, DAD

Kevin Egan's short-lived Sports Phone patronage began somewhere around 1990, always calling on account of neighborhood pick-'em pools, football betting slips, or wagers with a local bookie.

"Saturdays and Sundays during college and pro football season, my brother Jamie and I called Sports Phone often and it wasn't just for the final score. I remember always calling with a pen in the other hand," Egan recalled. "They rattled the scores off quickly. I would try to avoid it, but if I missed the score of a particular game it usually meant a redial."

Those frequent calls became costly, leading to some Oscar-level acting by the Yonkers brothers.

"We would call from home, and at the time the only phone was in the kitchen — right next to the living room. We had to make these calls quietly and quickly. I vividly remember us, on numerous occasions, sneaking downstairs to find out the late night, early morning scores for the last college football games of the evening, which usually involved Hawaii," Egan said.

"I recall my father asking us about the charges a few times. He was not happy, but we usually played dumb and denied any involvement with the calls. This eventually came to a screeching halt after a long run of Sports Phone calls and so-called erroneous phone call charges."

After a year-plus, the calls to 976-1313 ceased for good.

"We used Sports Phone for over a year, off and on, but no more than two. It was around the time we could tune in to WFAN on the 20s, but I think we stopped shortly before," Egan explained. "We finally realized that our parents would really lose it on us if the Sports Phone madness continued. Good times."

CHARLIE HUSTLE

Prepared by special counsel John M. Dowd at the behest of Commissioner Bart Giamatti in May 1989, the Dowd Report detailed Pete Rose's alleged history of betting on baseball which eventually led to a lifetime ban for MLB's all-time hits leader. Included in the report were multiple exhibits, one being a forensic analysis that noted Rose called both New York Sports Phone (718-976-1313) and Chicago Sports Phone (312-976-1313) frequently, sometimes several times per day.

An early section in the exhibit even called out a specific day when wagers were supposedly placed, during which Charlie Hustle rang 976-1313: *"[On April 8, 1987] It is indicated that a call was placed from the home of Pete Rose to (718) 976-1313 (Sports Phone) at 8:15 pm. It is to be noted that the Cincinnati Reds were at home on this date."*

Considering his widely reported gambling, it should be no surprise that Rose was a repeat caller.

"There was always Pete Rose, who used to always call us… Of all the Sports Phones supposedly he liked the Chicago one the best and he called all the time," David Schuster said. "Actually, I loved Pete Rose, both as a player and as a guy who was sort of fun to be around."

Rose's love for Sports Phone helped with interviews on occasion.

"Pete did know me from Sports Phone," Steve Cangialosi said. "It was a pretty intimidating thing for us to walk into a manager's office at Shea Stadium after a loss. I was probably 20 years old and I looked like I was 14. There I am, with my little tape recorder and microphone and he might've said, 'Who the heck are you?' I said, 'I'm Steve Cangialosi.' He goes, 'Oh, I know you, Sports Phone.' This was when he was still managing the Reds and John Franco was still pitching."

The Sports Phone affiliation came in especially handy whenever Rose was in a bad mood.

"I walked in with my mic with a Sports Phone flag on it. I think it was a doubleheader at Shea Stadium, Cincinnati Reds in town. Pete Rose was the manager," Jerry O'Neil recalled. "I walked in and I started to ask a question, and he kind of cut me off and he was real grumpy, but then he looked and he saw it was from Sports Phone. He said, 'All right, I'll answer your fucking question,' or something like that."

MOB NIGHT

Chris Erwin first began calling Sports Phone in 1979 when the New York Giants drafted quarterback Phil Simms seventh overall out of Morehead State.

"Depending on the day and what was going on would determine how often I called. I do remember they were good with updating the info every 10 to 15 minutes during games or things like the draft," Erwin recalled. "It wasn't uncommon to call right back to get the latest up-to-date scores."

He'd call from home and at school, remembering the announcers' delivery and those seven famous digits.

"I would call from payphones at school and from home. Had to limit the calls from home to not get in trouble, like some 10-cent call was going to break them," Erwin said.

"The cadence of the guys talking is what I remember the most. It seemed choppy like you would hear in a 1940 baseball game. No one stood out, but that number 976-1313 is one of maybe four phone numbers I remember from my youth. It was easy and engraved in my head."

There was a gap in calling as Erwin took more than one shot at college, an undertaking that didn't exactly work out.

"I went to college in 1982 and had ESPN and MTV so I didn't need Sports Phone. I would watch music videos and ESPN day and night, making my stay in that college a short one," he explained. "I flunked out after one semester and went on to flunk out of three more in one semester. I collected more sweatshirts and assault charges than credits."

He became a repeat customer once again a few years later, working at one of the hottest clubs of the '80s.

"The next time I remember using Sports Phone was the summer of 1986. I was an assistant manager of a popular shore bar The Pier Pub in Long Branch [New Jersey]. We claimed to be the first video dance club in the area. They had a bunch of TVs and most nights showed dance videos or videos of people on the beach," Erwin said.

"Not Monday night though, I called that mob night. It was rumored the owner was half a gangster. I got the job through a high-level Genovese guy I knew from his children, so I would have to suspect the rumors were true. Anyway, on Monday night instead of closing we would have fight night. The owner and his friends, who all seemed like connected guys, would come in and watch old fights like [Jack] Dempsey, [Rocky] Marciano, etcetera. It would be me and a hot bartender, and these guys were all degenerate gamblers."

Connected or not, the Monday night crowd wanted their MLB scores.

"They would bet on what time it would stop raining. They would give me $100 to call Sports Phone and get the scores of the baseball games. They tend to be very competitive and showy so once one did it the next one would," Erwin explained. "It was the Monday routine and I would decline the money, but they would insist and say I was insulting them. It was very *A Bronx Tale* in retrospect."

Sports Phone Stories

Killer on the Court
(feat. David Schuster)

When betting was involved, not all of Sports Phone's callers were happy-go-lucky. David Schuster found that out when he was threatened on a Chicago basketball court.

"I had a Sports Phone T-shirt on and I'm playing hoops and some giant of a guy comes up to me and he goes..."

"Do you work at Sports Phone?"

Schuster: "Yeah."

"What's your name?"

Schuster: "David Schuster."

"I ought to kill you here right now"

Schuster: "What the blank? Why?"

"You gave me a score the other night that I didn't like."

Schuster: "Was it the right score?"

"Yeah, but I didn't like it."

The disgruntled caller didn't take things any further, but incidents like that opened Schuster's eyes to who actually comprised a large chunk of Sports Phone's caller base.

"You found out very quickly who your clientele was," he said. "Not that I was naive to it. We were the gambling outlet, obviously. There was no pager. There were no 10-minute scrolls. There was nothing."

———

Quickie Quiz

Q: Which Chicago broadcasting vet had a lucky night thanks to Sports Phone?

A: David Schuster

Sports Phone was wildly popular, especially among gamblers, which led to some announcers being treated like celebrities on occasion.

Schuster: "Back in those days anybody who wanted to know the score of any game, they called Sports Phone. We were big in the gambling community, obviously. And so one night I think I took a girl out to some restaurant … and the maître d' had one of those phones at his station. He found out who I was, and he goes, 'Oh my God, we call you all the time. We've got you on speed dial.' Yadda, yadda, yadda. So he sat us down, sent a bottle of wine over to the table, compliments on the house. Well, the girl was obviously impressed because I think I got laid that night, if I remember correctly."

CHAPTER 8
THE CALLERS: GOODFELLAS

The point-shaving scandal involving the 1978–79 Boston College men's basketball team has been widely documented, covered ad nauseum in print and on film. One aspect of the case put forth against infamous Lucchese crime family associate Jimmy Burke and his co-defendants not necessarily discussed in-depth happens to apply to our tome of tales, a web of interconnected phone records that included a cluster of calls to Sports Phone.

Burke masterminded the biggest cash robbery in America at the time when a crew nabbed $5 million, along with close to another million in jewelry, from the Lufthansa cargo terminal at John F. Kennedy International Airport. The heist was later immortalized in Martin Scorsese's blockbuster *Goodfellas*, with Robert De Niro portraying a character based on the mobster known as "Jimmy the Gent."

As the movie depicts, many of those involved began turning up dead, a result of Burke cutting any ties between him and the caper in fear of the feds closing in.

"I was working on the Lufthansa investigation and we were out talking to a lot of people all along, in the months after the robbery," recalled former FBI Special Agent Ed Guevara. "A lot of people were getting killed. We would leave our cards to talk to someone, that person would be killed within a week."

MAURY'S WIGS

One collaborator who met an early demise was bookmaker Martin Krugman, who got the ball rolling in the first place by letting Burke's associate and pal Henry Hill know that the German airline frequently stored large amounts of untraceable cash at JFK. His reward for tipping off Hill was a gruesome one, as Burke and Angelo Sepe dispatched and dismembered the Queens wig shop owner, whose body was never located.

"[Henry Hill] was kind of that middle guy for the Lufthansa robbery, but Jimmy did not want Hill to go on the robbery himself as he was still on probation. So Henry wasn't really part of the scheming for the robbery," Guevara explained. "But he did know a guy by the name of [Marty] Krugman, who had a men's hairdressing shop next to Hill's restaurant. Krugman had a contact within Lufthansa and that's how the connection started."

Featured as the main character in *Goodfellas* and portrayed by Ray Liotta, Hill would famously become a government witness, cooperating with Guevara and the team to avoid being killed. It was during one of these debriefing sessions that another serious crime would be uncovered, almost by accident.

"I arrested Henry. At one point my supervisor said, 'Ed. Do you mind picking up this guy Henry Hill on your way home tonight? We have a material witness warrant, and afterwards put him in the lockup overnight.' I lived in the Oceanside area in Long Island and Henry was in Rockville Centre, which is a town adjacent to where I lived. [My supervisor] gave me the warrant, and said pick him up on this material witness warrant. We think he has information on the Lufthansa robbery," Guevara added.

"So the next day my partner John [Kapp], who also lived out in the Baldwin area, and I waited near Hill's home for him to arrive. Sure enough, he rolls up and we arrest him right outside his house. If you've never met Henry, he can kinda talk a mile a minute and can be a very persuasive guy at times. Very charismatic to an extent. We cuffed him, but he convinced me to remove the cuffs and let him into his house, which is the wrong thing to do.

"But there was something about him and I said okay. It was a material witness warrant, but still, knowing what I know now I screwed up, but nothing happened. He was excited and kind of crazy inside the house. I grabbed him, threw him back down on the chair, and said 'Hey, you're not moving. Stay here.' And he gave Karen, his wife, some instructions, kissed her and we took off after that. A day or two after that is when he started his cooperation with Eddie [McDonald]."

IF HE'S LEGITIMATELY BRONCHIAL

The former US Attorney overseeing the Lufthansa case, Ed McDonald also appeared in the Scorsese film, portraying himself in a memorable scene where he tries to persuade Hill and his wife Karen (played by Lorraine Bracco) to enter the witness protection program — during which the Hills ask that they be placed somewhere warm, on account of Henry's supposed bronchial condition.

"Henry wanted to put two of his girlfriends in the program, along with his wife and his two children, his mother-in-law, his father-in-law, and his two sisters-in-law. The in-laws were all omitted immediately. They decided they didn't want to go, but the two girlfriends were junkies and drug dealers," McDonald recounted.

"They worked for his drug business and to placate him we interviewed the girls too, just to go through the motions, even though they weren't going to go into the witness protection program. They weren't going to qualify. They didn't have enough information. It was only on drugs. We didn't give a shit about some half-ass drug business that Henry had."

It was in McDonald's office where the Boston College scandal first came to light.

"[Henry] worked out a deal to get immunity and so I was going through the motions one day of questioning one of the girls, Judy Wicks. Henry had gone out to Pittsburgh as part of his drug business with [Paul] Mazzei. He met Mazzei in prison," the former prosecutor elaborated.

"While he was there, Mazzei fixed Henry up with Wicks, who was a prostitute and was also involved in the drug trade in Pittsburgh. And so she said, 'Henry came out to meet with Paulie. I'm not sure why he was there, and Paulie fixed me up for the night. We were high all the time.' I said, 'Well, what did you do after that?' She says, 'We went up to Boston.' I said, 'What were you doing up in Boston?'"

WAS THAT WRONG?

McDonald's interests were piqued. As a Boston College alum with a wife who hailed from the city, the mere mention of Hill possibly doing business there raised his antenna.

"I could see she didn't want to give up Henry and I'm trying to explain to her that he already has immunity, and whatever she says is not going be harmful to him. So I said to the agent, 'Go and get Henry, bring him in here and he'll explain to her that he can't be harmed by what she says,'" McDonald shared.

"'Henry, what the hell are you doing in up in Boston?' He looks at me and he goes, "Oh, in them days we was fixing basketball games at

Boston College, uhh, Boston University.' I said, 'What school?' and he says 'BU, BU.'"

Hill went on to describe an All-American player on the club, which led McDonald to realize that he had to be talking about BC, not Boston University.

"I looked at the agents and Henry and said, 'Cut the bullshit, will you please?' They all knew I was a big BC fan and I thought that they were just breaking my chops," McDonald said. "Then as I was saying it I realized, wait a minute, this is too convoluted. There was no way that they're going to set me up with this scenario, with me talking to Judy Wicks and Henry coming in."

It wasn't beyond Hill to misrepresent past events, even if it wasn't intentional, so maybe he had the wrong school in mind.

"Henry was not quite there," Guevara mentioned. "He was still dealing with the effects of drugs, and so he would only give us bits of information and we'd try to corroborate the information in other ways."

Not quite there may been an understatement, as Hill did not think twice about point shaving being something the prosecution would care about.

"'What were you doing in Boston?' the agent says to him. Henry said, 'We were fixing games,' and I'm like, holy shit, and he goes, 'What are you getting so excited for? There's nothing wrong with that," McDonald revealed, laughing at Hill's absurdity. "He didn't know it was a crime. He said, 'Burke's killing people all over the place and selling drugs, we're doing the Lufthansa robbery, and you're talking about college basketball games? Who gives a shit?'"

Hill did have a point, albeit a twisted one, considering the violent acts his cohorts committed regularly.

"They were using a guy by the name of Rich Perry, who was called 'The Fixer' in New York. He kinda gave the final okay after Henry had gotten the okay from Jimmy and from Paul Vario, who was the capo of his faction of the Lucchese family," Guevara added. "In any event, The Fixer knew it was against the law. I can guarantee you that most of these guys did to some extent, but they didn't view it as a heinous crime. It wasn't shooting someone or stealing a truck. Who gets hurt from sports bribery, right? But Henry didn't think it was illegal."

NOTHING PERSONAL

A former basketball player at Boston College himself, the possibility of fixed games hit home.

"Yeah, it did [feel personal in a way]. I didn't have any more incentive to go try to prosecute Jimmy Burke because he was our main target in the Lufthansa robbery case. It wasn't like I was on a crusade or anything like that. It was an opportunity that they had," McDonald noted. "If anyone, I was disgusted with [BC forward Rick] Kuhn, who of course later cooperated and I got to know him very well. Actually, as a cooperator, he was in my office all the time and I became friendly with him. I really came to like him."

From the mobsters' perspective, any school would have been fine had the chance presented itself.

"It was my school. Let's put it this way. They weren't fixing games at Boston College or shaving points because they had some animosity towards Boston College," McDonald opined. "Henry thought it was BU when he first told us about it. He didn't know one school from the other."

The quirk of fate was palpable, as there's a decent chance that this entire scheme would have never been revealed had a hooker from Pittsburgh not made an off-hand remark about a trip to Beantown.

With the cat now fully out of the bag, the government launched a full-scale investigation into happenings at BC, eventually charging Burke, Kuhn, Mazzei, and brothers Anthony and Rocco Perla with conspiracy to commit sports bribery, among other offenses. The Perla brothers hatched the initial plan, leaning on the fact that Rocco and Rick were high school buddies.

SCARFACE

Reminiscent of ruthless crime boss Al Capone receiving an 11-year federal prison sentence after being convicted on five counts of income tax evasion, the prosecution now had another path to potentially taking the murderous Burke off the streets for an extended period. If they couldn't cage Jimmy for the countless felonies he'd been linked to previously, they just might be able to lock him away for something as relatively innocuous as fixing some games.

"This went to trial in 1981, it was the very first federal case of sports bribery in the history of US college basketball," Guevara explained. "The others were state prosecutions, like New York for the CCNY one [in 1951]. Eddie was fairly confident in the prosecution, except for Jimmy, but in the end, we were able to get him. If anybody needed to be prosecuted it was him, of all the homicides connected to the Lufthansa robbery he was prosecuted for sports bribery."

While the case was strong against Kuhn, Mazzei, and the Perlas, the evidence on Burke did not elicit feelings of a slam-dunk conviction among the feds. What they did have on their side was a plethora of phone records, which collectively helped paint a picture of guilt.

"We had a lot of telephone records of the people we were looking at because they were involved in the Lufthansa robbery. The same people who executed the Lufthansa robbery were involved in the point-shaving case, and Jimmy Burke was the main guy," McDonald acknowledged. "We had all his phone records along with a bunch of other people, and then we got some more phone records. At trial, we put together a charge of relevant phone calls among the parties.

"Henry Hill identified who all the bookmakers were, where to lay off bets, and all this other stuff, so we put together a chart. There were no records for them calling each other on Monday and Tuesday, but on Wednesday when Boston College was playing Connecticut, from like five o'clock on, there was a whole flurry of phone calls between Pittsburgh, New York, and Boston, and so we felt that that was proof of what they were doing."

CONNECT THE DOTS

This wasn't the typical phone-based evidence that you hear of so often today, with wiretaps and other surveillance methods sealing a defendant's fate in court. McDonald and squad may have had records of calls being placed, but they had no idea what was being said by either party.

"The phone records were essential to the prosecution of Jimmy Burke. We had very little on Jimmy, but the phone records that we got during the Lufthansa robbery case, in those days we called them MUDs and LUDs — multiple unit dialing and long distance unit dialing, and all of it paper. We had to send them to headquarters, because there were just massive amounts of records, that they organized for us by phone number, by date, by subscriber information, that sort of thing," Guevara described.

"What I did is I put Jimmy Burke in the center of a chart. It was like the spoke of a wheel and then the numbers, they were either going to Jimmy Burke or leaving Jimmy Burke — going from Jimmy Burke to someone else, different numbers he's used. We placed him in the middle of all these numbers that were called during either the games or before or after placing some bets. The chart was challenged in the courtroom by Burke's attorney, a guy by the name of Michael Coiro who was later arrested [on RICO charges] in a different case. So all we were able to prove was that there were phone calls made to and from numbers associated to Jimmy Burke.

"I couldn't testify that Jimmy Burke was on the phone. I couldn't testify to what was said. All it was is a chart showing calls going out from a Jimmy Burke number, or to a Jimmy Burke number. In fact, when I testified, Mike Coiro asked me, 'Do you know if Jimmy Burke answered the phone, or was it his wife or his kids?' I said, 'Yeah, I don't know.'"

Reprinted on the following pages (with permission from the National Archives at Kansas City and cited in this book's bibliography) are these phone records, pulled from the United States Court of Appeals. This key piece of evidence included phone calls from a Rockville Centre Holiday Inn where the prosecution contended Paul Mazzei was staying, calls from a Logan Airport Holiday Inn in Boston made by Anthony Perla and Henry Hill, calls from a pair of different Boston hotels made by the Perla brothers, and calls placed from the Burke and Krugman households.

"It would be a flurry of phone calls before every game so it's like, this is unbelievable," McDonald reminisced. "Somebody said to me, 'You didn't have wiretaps,' but I said, 'You know something? If you don't have the words with this, just the fact that there were phone calls, it's almost proof positive. You can tell, you can speculate and argue it to the jury.'"

STAY WITH US!

Scattered among these calls were well over a dozen made to Sports Phone, meaning those involved in the conspiracy at one point heard the likes of King Wally, Gary Cohen, Chief Martin, Charlie DeNatale, or one of the other voices manning the booth in late '78, likely including what in this context would be the announcer's paradoxical 'Stay With Us!' sign-off.

"I vaguely remember Henry would talk, 'We're on Sports Phone all the time, getting the scores, getting the scores,'" McDonald said.

Because of the timing of these calls to Sports Phone, some of which took place during the preseason, along with several of the defendants being known as degenerate gamblers, the fact that they were checking on scores was not singled out to the jury. They were included in the prosecution's evidence, however, mainly for completeness.

"In a way, it would be counter to what we wanted, because [the defense] could show that there were Sports Phone calls constantly just because they had bet on a bunch of games," McDonald asserted. "It showed interest in the games that day, not compelling proof of a fix."

GUILTY

In the end, what they had wasn't perfect, but the connections were compelling enough to convict Burke and his co-defendants.

"Sports bribery cases, normally, I knew would attract attention, and the fact that we had Jimmy Burke as a defendant was big," Guevara summarized. "This was on the back page of every newspaper in the United States for a while, so it was a big case, and it kind of defined my career."

Burke — who by then was locked up for a separate parole violation — was sentenced to twenty years, the heaviest penalty of the group by far. He'd later be convicted of murdering a drug dealer in '79, tacking on an additional 20. Jimmy the Gent was still serving time when he died of cancer in April 1996, at the age of 64.

82-1028

IN THE

United States Court of Appeals

For The Second Circuit

Docket No.: 82-1028

UNITED STATES OF AMERICA,
Plaintiff-Appellee,

-against-

JAMES BURKE, ANTHONY PERLA, ROCCO PERLA,
PAUL MAZZEI AND RICHARD KUHN,
Defendants-Appellants.

ON APPEAL FROM THE UNITED STATES DISTRICT COURT
FOR THE EASTERN DISTRICT OF NEW YORK

APPENDIX FOR DEFENDANT-APPELLANT
JAMES BURKE

GERALD L. SHARGEL
Attorney for Defendant-Appellant
James Burke
150 East 58th Street
New York, New York 10155
(212) 486-1717

HON. EDWARD KORMAN
United States Attorney for the
Eastern District of New York
Attorney for Plaintiff-Appellee
225 Cadman Plaza East
Brooklyn, New York 11201
(212) 330-7060

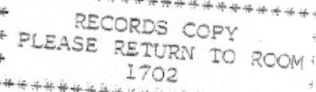
RECORDS COPY
PLEASE RETURN TO ROOM
1702

List of Telephone Calls
Placed From Hotels

Red-Calls to telephone numbers subscribed to or used by defendants.

LIST OF TELEPHONE CALLS FROM THE HOLIDAY INN,
OCKVILLE CENTRE, NEW YORK, ROOM 226, REGISTERED UNDER THE NAME "MUSCA", FOR THE PERIOD NOVEMBER 4 THROUGH NOVEMBER 6, 11|78.

NUMBER CALLED	PERSON SUBSCRIBING TO OR HAVING ACCESS TO PHONE	DATE	TIME	DURATION
(412) 782-0585	HAROLD MAZZEI (MAZZEI'S FATHER) 12 Third St. Sharpsborough, Pa.	11/4	4:19P	11
(412) 243-8862	ANTHONY R. PERLA 1202 Circle Drive Pittsburgh, Pa.	11/4	4:32P	5
(212) 999-1313	SPORTS PHONE	11/4	4:47P	3
(212) 999-1313	SPORTS PHONE	11/4	5:29P	2
(212) 999-1313	SPORTS PHONE	11/4	5:32P	1
(212) 999-1313	SPORTS PHONE	11/4	5:34P	2
(212) 999-1313	SPORTS PHONE	11/4	6:02P	1
(212) 999-1313	SPORTS PHONE	11/4	8:11P	2
(212) 999-1313	SPORTS PHONE	11/4	8:14P	1
(212) 999-1313	SPORTS PHONE	11/4	9:57P	2
(212) 999-1313	SPORTS PHONE	11/4	10:38P	1
(212) 738-3353	BURKE HOME 78-02 160th Ave. Howard Beach, NY	11/5	3:22A	1
(212) 999-1313	SPORTS PHONE	11/5	8:16A	2
(412) 243-8862	ANTHONY PERLA	11/5	11:43A	2
(212) 738-3353	BURKE	11/5	11:45A	3
(212) 738-3353	BURKE	11/5	12:05P	2
(412) 782-0585	HAROLD MAZZEI	11/5	12:45P	5
(412) 243-8862	ANTHONY PERLA	11/5	12:53P	11
(212) 738-3353	BURKE	11/5	1:04P	3
(212) 738-3353	BURKE	11/5	2:17P	2
(212) 738-3353	BURKE	11/5	2:28P	1
(212) 520-8121	F. GENOVA (HILL'S FRIEND) 70-25 Yellowstone Blvd. Forest Hills, NY	11/5	2:31P	3
(212) 592-9075	ELSA MARTINEZ (Employee of MARTIN KRUGMAN) 61-20 Grand Central Parkway Queens, New York	11/5	3:43P	7

(212) 738-3353	BURKE	11/5	3:53P	4
(212) 592-9075	ELSA MARTINEZ	11/5	4:03P	3
(212) 592-9075	ELSA MARTINEZ	11/5	4:12P	2
(212) 520-8121	F. GENOVA	11/5	4:18P	2
(212) 520-8121	F. GENOVA	11/5	4:29P	1
(212) 738-3353	BURKE	11/5	5:14P	2
(212) 738-3353	BURKE	11/5	5:44P	2
(212) 738-3353	BURKE	11/6	7:56P	4
(212) 738-3353	BURKE	11/6	8:20P	2

LIST OF TELEPHONE CALLS FROM THE HILTON INN, LOGAN AIRPORT, EAST BOSTON, MASSACHUSETTS, ROOMS 1408 AND 1410, REGISTERED FOR BY ANTHONY PERLA AND HENRY HILL, ON NOVEMBER 16 AND 17, 1978.

NUMBER CALLED	PERSON SUBSCRIBING TO OR HAVING ACCESS TO PHONE	DATE	TIME	DURATION
(516) 766-7637	HILL'S HOME 19 St. Mark's Place Rockville Centre, New York	11/16	8:05P	2
(412) 371-1003	ROCCO PERLA	11/16	8:05P	5
(603) 893-0368	JAY LEAVETT 21 Bailey Road Salem, New Hampshire	11/16	8:29P	2
(603) 893-0368	JAY LEAVETT	11/16	11:51P	7
(412) 372-1193	ERNIE'S BUSTER BROWN SHOES Monroeville Miracle Mile Shopping Center, Monroeville, Pa.	11/17	12:21A	3
(212) 738-3353	BURKE HOME 78-02 160th Ave. Howard Beach, NY	11/17	12:25A	3
(617) 685-8035	BROADWAY ELECTRICAL SUPPLY CO. 33 Springfield St. Lawrence, Mass.	11/17	2:14A	4

LIST OF TELEPHONE CALLS FROM THE SHERATON BOSTON HOTEL, BOSTON, MASSACHUSETTS, ROOMS 1840 AND 1841, REGISTERED FOR BY ROCCO PERLA AND ANTHONY PERLA, ON DECEMBER 16 AND 17, 1978.

NUMBER CALLED	PERSON SUBSCRIBING TO OR HAVING ACCESS TO PHONE	DATE	TIME	DURATION
(412) 243-8862	ANTHONY PERLA 1202 Circle Drive Pittsburgh, Pa.	12/16	3:51P	1
(412) 782-0595	HAROLD MAZZEI (MAZZEI'S FATHER) 12 Third Street Sharpsborough, Pa.	12/16	3:51P	3
(914) 793-3776	C.B. GOLDBERG (JOE RAZZANO - KRUGMAN'S PARTNER) 322 Reed Ave. Tuckahoe, New York	12/16	5:35P	1
(516) 666-4214	FREDERICK ROTUNDOORS (HILL'S FRIEND) 613 Askewoken Blvd. Bayshore, New York	12/16	5:36P	1
(516) 766-7637	HILL'S HOME 19 St. Mark's Place Rockville Centre, New York	12/16	5:37P	1
(212) 520-3121	F. GENOVA (HILL'S FRIEND) 70-25 Yellowstone Blvd. Forest Hills, New York	12/16	5:39P	2
(212) 999-1313	SPORTS PHONE	12/16	10:50P	2
(212) 936-2525	FOOTBALL PHONE	12/16	10:50P	1
(412) 243-8862	ANTHONY PERLA	12/16	11:26P	10
(412) 243-8862	ANTHONY PERLA	12/16	11:58P	5
(412) 243-7032	JOAN THOMPSON (MAZZEI'S GIRLFRIEND) 1804 Clark Street Pittsburgh, Pa.	12/17	12:01A	1
(412) 271-6611	LINCOLN CIVIC CLUB 2031 Mononghela Ave. Pittsburgh, Pa.	12/17	12:10A	5
(516) 766-7637	HILL'S HOME	12/17	2:09A	9
(212) 520-8121	F. GENOVA	12/17	8:37A	7

LIST OF TELEPHONE CALLS FROM THE COLONNADE HOTEL, BOSTON, MASSACHUSETTS, ROOM 831, REGISTERED FOR BY ROCCO PERLA ON FEBRUARY 3 AND 4, 1970.

NUMBER CALLED	PERSON SUBSCRIBING TO OR HAVING ACCESS TO PHONE	DATE	TIME	DURATION
(412) 241-8990	ANTHONY PERLA 1202 Circle Drive Pittsburgh, Pa.	2/3	11:47A	2
(305) 946-9381	NICK LAMBERTI 2640 NW 20th Street Pompano Beach, Fla.	2/3	1:06P	1
(412) 271-9511	LINCOLN CIVIC CLUB 2051 Mononghela Ave. Pittsburgh, Pa.	2/3	1:0??	3
(412) 371-2202	ROCCO PERLA 7306 Schoyer Ave. Pittsburgh, Pa.	2/3	1:??	2
(305) 946-9381	NICK LAMBERTI	2/3	5:16P	1
(412) 243-8002	ANTHONY PERLA	2/3	5:29P	5
(412) 271-9511	LINCOLN CIVIC CLUB	2/3	6:16P	2
(412) 731-8924	MARK A. BERENATO 1635 Ardmore Blvd. Pittsburgh, Pa.	2/3	6:16P	1
(412) 731-8924	MARK A. BERENATO	2/3	6:24P	1
(412) 243-8002	ANTHONY PERLA	2/3	6:3?P	1
(412) 734-3591	H. CAMPBELL 1001 New Brighton Rd. Avalon, Pa.	2/3	6:41P	6
(412) 243-8002	ANTHONY PERLA	2/3	6:5?P	1
(412) 731-8924	MARK A. BERENATO	2/3	6:5?P	3
(212) 999-1313	SPORTS PHONE	2/3	10:39P	2
(212) 999-1313	SPORTS PHONE	2/3	10:41P	1
(212) 999-2525	FOOTBALL PHONE	2/3	10:41P	1
(212) 999-2525	FOOTBALL PHONE	2/4	1:50A	1
(212) 999-1313	SPORTS PHONE	2/4	1:52A	2

List of Selected Calls Placed From Burke and Krugman Homes

Red-Calls to telephone numbers subscribed to or used by defendants.

SELECTED TELEPHONE CALLS FROM 212-738-3353 SUBSCRIBED TO AT THE HOME OF JAMES BURKE, 78-02 160TH AVENUE, HOWARD BEACH, QUEENS, NEW YORK.

DATE	NUMBER CALLED	PERSON SUBSCRIBING TO OR HAVING ACCESS TO PHONE	TIME	DURATION
1970				
11-2	516-766-7637	HENRY HILL	9:21P	:53
11-3	516-766-7637	HENRY HILL	7:40P	:55
11-3	516-766-7637	HENRY HILL	7:46P	1:17
11-4	212-447-4570	ROBERT SMITH (RICHARD PERRY)	2:02P	1:22
11-4	516-766-7637	HENRY HILL	8:58P	3:03
11-4	516-791-7382	MARTIN KRUGMAN	10:50P	1:38
11-4	516-678-1300	ROCKVILLE CENTER HOLIDAY INN (PAUL MAZZEI)	10:55P	7:12
11-5	516-766-7637	HENRY HILL	10:51A	:29
11-5	212-447-4570	ROBERT SMITH (RICHARD PERRY)	12:33P	:45
11-5	212-447-4570	ROBERT SMITH (RICHARD PERRY)	12:43P	1:40
11-5	516-678-1300	ROCKVILLE CENTER HOLIDAY INN (PAUL MAZZEI)	12:46P	:07
11-5	516-678-1300	ROCKVILLE CENTER HOLIDAY INN (PAUL MAZZEI)	12:47P	5:10
11-5	516-678-1300	ROCKVILLE CENTER HOLIDAY INN (PAUL MAZZEI)	12:57P	:12
11-5	516-593-1314	JOHN SAVINO	2:53P	1:04
11-5	212-447-4570	ROBERT SMITH (RICHARD PERRY)	3:57P	2:14
11-5	516-678-1300	ROCKVILLE CENTER HOLIDAY INN (PAUL MAZZEI)	4:00P	:47
11-5	516-678-1300	ROCKVILLE CENTER HOLIDAY INN (PAUL MAZZEI)	4:03P	2:40
11-5	212-447-4570	ROBERT SMITH (RICHARD PERRY)	4:06P	:05
11-5	212-447-4570	ROBERT SMITH (RICHARD PERRY)	7:26P	:33
11-6	516-766-7637	HENRY HILL	7:09P	2:25
11-6	516-791-7382	MARTIN KRUGMAN	7:27P	:20
11-6	212-447-4570	ROBERT SMITH (RICHARD PERRY)	8:06P	:45
11-9	516-766-7637	HENRY HILL	9:31A	:56
11-9	516-766-7637	HENRY HILL	4:10P	:99
11-9	212-447-4570	ROBERT SMITH (RICHARD PERRY)	6:54P	2:28
11-10	516-766-7637	HENRY HILL	7:37P	1:34
11-12	212-447-4570	ROBERT SMITH (RICHARD PERRY)	12:21P	:29
11-12	212-447-4570	ROBERT SMITH (RICHARD PERRY)	12:25P	:34
11-12	516-766-7637	HENRY HILL	2:01P	2:32
11-12	212-447-4570	ROBERT SMITH (RICHARD PERRY)	8:29P	:31
11-13	516-766-7637	HENRY HILL	3:50P	1:55
11-13	516-791-7382	MARTIN KRUGMAN	6:34P	:33
11-13	516-791-7382	MARTIN KRUGMAN	7:44P	:14
11-14	201-886-0564	MILTON WEKAR	8:47P	1:00
11-14	201-886-0564	MILTON WEKAR	9:17P	1:00
11-17	617-569-9300	LOGAN HILTON INN, BOSTON (MAZZEI, A. PERLA, HILL)	8:14A	2:00
11-18	516-766-7637	HENRY HILL	9:50A	:29
11-18	516-791-7382	MARTIN KRUGMAN	11:14A	:09

11-19	516-766-7637	HENRY HILL	12:25A	:03
11-19	516-766-7637	HENRY HILL	2:32A	1:20
11-19	516-766-7637	HENRY HILL	12:25P	:17
11-19	516-791-7382	MARTIN KRUGMAN	12:32P	:15
11-19	516-766-7637	HENRY HILL	1:43P	:27
12-14	516-593-1314	JOHN SAVINO	6:38P	2:32
12-19	212-447-4570	ROBERT SMITH (RICHARD PERRY)	7:25P	:11
12-21	412-243-7032	JOAN THOMPSON (MAZZEI'S GIRLFRIEND), PITTSBURGH	8:03P	1:00
12-22	516-825-7897	MURRY FRIEDMAN (HILL'S FATHER-IN-LAW)	9:35A	:07
12-22	516-766-7637	HENRY HILL	9:36A	:31
12-23	516-766-7637	HENRY HILL	8:30P	:59
12-23	516-766-7637	HENRY HILL	10:59P	2:37
12-24	516-791-7382	MARTIN KRUGMAN	4:01P	1:06
12-24	516-626-0144	JOHN YARMOSH	4:10P	1:19
12-25	516-791-7382	MARTIN KRUGMAN	11:52A	:37
12-25	516-593-1314	JOHN SAVINO	6:45P	:42
12-26	212-447-4570	ROBERT SMITH (RICHARD PERRY)	6:37P	1:24

SELECTED TELEPHONE CALLS FROM 212-738-3353 SUBSCRIBED TO AT THE HOME OF JAMES BURKE, 78-02 160TH AVENUE, HOWARD BEACH, QUEENS, NEW YORK.

PAGE 2 OF 2

DATE	NUMBER CALLED	PERSON SUBSCRIBING TO OR HAVING ACCESS TO PHONE	TIME	DURATION
12-26	212-447-4570	ROBERT SMITH (RICHARD PERRY)	7:03P	:51
12-26	212-447-4570	ROBERT SMITH (RICHARD PERRY)	7:44P	:57
12-26	516-791-7382	MARTIN KRUGMAN	8:30P	1:53
12-27	516-766-7637	HENRY HILL	6:01P	:30
12-27	516-766-7637	HENRY HILL	6:52P	
12-27	516-766-7637	HENRY HILL	7:10P	
12-29	516-766-7637	HENRY HILL	P	:12
12-31	516-593-1314	JOHN SAVINO	7:10P	:50
12-31	516-766-7637	HENRY HILL	8:02P	2:02

1979

1-2	516-766-7637	HENRY HILL	7:10P	:12
1-5	516-681-5860	MARIE SARACINO (HILL'S SISTER)	1:02P	5:03
1-7	516-791-7382	MARTIN KRUGMAN	5:12P	:49
1-7	516-766-7637	HENRY HILL	P	:20
1-9	516-766-7637	HENRY HILL	P	1:07
1-10	412-243-8758	JOAN THOMPSON (PAUL MAZZEI'S GIRLFRIEND), PITTSBURGH	3:44P	2
1-19	412-243-8758	JOAN THOMPSON (PAUL MAZZEI'S GIRLFRIEND), PITTSBURGH	6:10P	1
1-20	412-781-0925	ALFRED VITARO (MAZZEI'S FRIEND), PITTSBURGH	11:24P	1
1-22	412-243-8758	JOAN THOMPSON (PAUL MAZZEI'S GIRLFRIEND), PITTSBURGH	6:06P	1
1-23	412-243-8758	JOAN THOMPSON (PAUL MAZZEI'S GIRLFRIEND), PITTSBURGH	10:26P	1
1-31	412-243-8758	JOAN THOMPSON (PAUL MAZZEI'S GIRLFRIEND), PITTSBURGH	7:55P	1
2-8	412-243-8862	ANTHONY PERLA, PITTSBURGH	5:41P	1
2-8	412-782-0585	HAROLD MAZZEI, SR. (MAZZEI'S FATHER), PITTSBURGH	5:45P	2
2-9	702-739-4111	MGM GRAND HOTEL, LAS VEGAS, NEVADA	11:38A	2

ADDITIONAL CALLS

1978

12-4	516-593-1314	JOHN SAVINO	6:56P	:07
12-5	516-791-7382	MARTIN KRUGMAN	7:22P	:11
12-5	516-766-7637	HENRY HILL	10:11P	1:06
12-7	516-791-7382	MARTIN KRUGMAN	9:49P	:08
12-8	516-791-7382	MARTIN KRUGMAN	2:00A	:02

SELECTED TELEPHONE CALLS FROM 212-835-6081 SUBSCRIBED TO BY
CATHERINE BURKE, 78-02 160TH AVENUE, HOWARD BEACH, QUEENS, NEW YORK.

DATE	NUMBER CALLED	PERSON SUBSCRIBING TO OR HAVING ACCESS TO PHONE	TIME	DURATION
1972				
10-19	516-825-6220	MURRAY FRIEDMAN (HILL'S FATHER-IN-LAW)	9:09A	2:14
10-19	516-593-1314	JOHN SAVINO	9:12A	2:10
10-19	212-447-4570	ROBERT SMITH (RICHARD PERRY)	10:39A	1:18
10-19	516-766-7637	HENRY HILL	6:30P	:39
10-19	516-593-1314	JOHN SAVINO	8:40P	1:18
10-19	516-437-8110	NICHOLAS BOTTA	8:52P	:37
10-19	516-766-7637	HENRY HILL	10.04P	:51
11-4	516-766-7637	HENRY HILL	1:22P	5:45
11-8	516-791-7382	MARTIN KRUGMAN	6:12P	:16
12-4	516-437-9478	ANGELINA BOTTA (N. BOTTA'S WIFE)	7:03P	:44
12-4	516-437-9437	ANGELINA BOTTA (N. BOTTA'S WIFE)	7:14P	:59
12-11	516-593-1314	JOHN SAVINO	9:23P	:43
12-14	412-243-7032	JOAN THOMPSON (MAZZEI'S GIRLFRIEND), PITTSBURGH	8:49P	9:03
12-30	412-243-8852	ANTHONY R. PERLA, PITTSBURGH	6:39P	3:00
1973				
1-10	412-243-7045	JOAN THOMPSON (MAZZEI'S GIRLFRIEND), PITTSBURGH	6:50P	1:00
1-10	412-732-0585	HAROLD MAZZEI SR. (MAZZEI'S FATHER), PITTSBURGH	6:56P	2:00
1-10	412-781-0825	ALFRED VITARO (MAZZEI'S FRIEND), PITTSBURGH	6:52P	3:00

SELECTED TELEPHONE CALLS FROM 516-791-7382 SUBSCRIBED TO AT THE HOME OF MARTIN KRUGMAN, 948 WHITEHALL DRIVE, NORTH WOODMERE, LONG ISLAND.

DATE	NUMBER CALLED	PERSON SUBSCRIBING TO OR HAVING ACCESS TO PHONE	TIME	DURATION
10-30	212-738-3353	BURKE	5:34P	2:40
11-2	412-243-7032	JOAN THOMPSON (MAZZEI'S GIRLFRIEND) PITTSBURGH	7:23P	3:00
11-5	212-738-3353	BURKE	2:31P	:15
11-5	212-738-3353	BURKE	2:32P	1:21
11-6	212-738-3353	BURKE	10:17A	:02
11-6	212-738-3353	BURKE	6:03P	:02
11-6	212-738-3353	BURKE	6:04P	1:45
11-6	212-738-3353	BURKE	7:29P	:13
11-7	212-738-3353	BURKE	6:12P	:50
11-8	212-738-3353	BURKE	6:07P	:10
11-8	212-738-3353	BURKE	6:20P	:44
11-10	412-243-7032	JOAN THOMPSON (MAZZEI'S GIRLFRIEND) PITTSBURGH	6:52P	1:00
11-12	212-738-3353	BURKE	12:26P	1:21
11-14	212-738-3353	BURKE	9:47A	:23
11-14	412-782-0585	HAROLD MAZZEI, SR. (MAZZEI'S FATHER) PITTSBURGH	2:42P	2:00
11-19	212-738-3353	BURKE	6:55P	1:04
11-21	212-738-3353	BURKE	7:51P	1:37
11-22	212-738-3353	BURKE	7:08P	:30
11-27	212-738-3353	BURKE	8:11P	:12
11-27	212-738-3353	BURKE	9:18P	:03
11-29	212-738-3353	BURKE	6:41P	:13
12-6	212-738-3353	BURKE	7:42P	:14
12-8	212-738-3353	BURKE	9:05A	:17
12-12	212-738-3353	BURKE	6:07P	:07
12-16	212-738-3353	BURKE	5:49P	:15
12-17	212-738-3353	BURKE	11:49A	:26
12-17	212-738-3353	BURKE	7:56P	:11
12-18	212-738-3353	BURKE	9:23A	:04

1979

1-5	212-738-3353	BURKE	5:21P	:09
1-7	212-738-3353	BURKE	7:23P	:02
1-7	212-738-3353	BURKE	8:24P	:02
1-7	212-738-3353	BURKE	8:57P	:05
1-9	212-843-9248	ROBERTS LOUNGE	9:59A	:39
1-14	212-738-3353	BURKE	11:48A	:06
1-16	212-843-9248	ROBERTS LOUNGE	10:12A	:27
1-17	212-843-9248	ROBERTS LOUNGE	10:21A	:15
1-17	212-843-9248	ROBERTS LOUNGE	11:11A	1:30
1-18	212-843-9248	ROBERTS LOUNGE	10:01A	:24
1-20	212-738-3353	BURKE	10:20A	:12
1-20	212-738-3353	BURKE	12:17P	:14
1-21	212-738-3353	BURKE	10:41A	:07
1-21	212-738-3353	BURKE	11:35A	:04
1-21	212-738-3353	BURKE	12:49P	:20
1-21	212-738-3353	BURKE	1:57P	:18
1-22	412-243-8759	JOAN THOMPSON (MAZZEI'S GIRLFRIEND) PITTSBURGH	9:53P	1:00
1-23	412-243-8759	JOAN THOMPSON (MAZZEI'S GIRLFRIEND) PITTSBURGH	11:03A	1:00
1-24	212-843-9248	ROBERTS LOUNGE	11:54A	:02
1-26	212-738-3353	BURKE	11:03A	1:37

CHAPTER 9
HOLLYWOOD CONNECTIONS

Maybe it was the on-air aspects of Sports Phone. Maybe it was the bright lights of Manhattan and Chicago. Maybe it was the collective ambition of being on the big stage, whether it be in sports or elsewhere.

"When it comes to the performing arts, [Phone Programs] was a job. Actors, creative people always need work," Mike Farrell said. "Parts and roles aren't always available. Projects aren't always out there, and this was a way to pay your rent."

Whatever the reasons, several who called Phone Programs home would end up with ties to Tinseltown in later years, some citing their time at the company as influential in future roles.

HOWIE AND ROSE

For 1980s sitcom buffs, Nat Mauldin's writing credits should elicit fond memories. Whether it was classic shows like *Barney Miller*, *Night Court*, and *Newhart*, or the lesser-known *It Takes Two* (starring Helen Hunt and Patty Duke, among others) and *Have Faith*, the former Sports

Phone announcer made a lasting mark on the genre throughout the decade.

Before penning tales for television, Mauldin found work as a copy-writer for the ad agency N. W. Ayer.

"There was a terrific guy I worked with [at Ayer] named Paul Gourvitz. One of Paul's side gigs was doing PA for the Islanders at Nassau Coliseum, and another was announcing at Sports Phone. I'm sure he had others. Paul was one of those energetic, dialed-in types who knew everybody, including 'Bullet' Bob Meyer, who was in charge of Sports Phone at the time. Bob was also the track announcer at Yonkers Raceway and had a great voice," Mauldin recalled.

"At some point, he mentioned to Paul that they were short-staffed and Paul thought of me. I believe this was because I used to do a few barely passable impressions of Warner Brothers cartoon characters around the office and made him laugh. Anyway, Paul sent me over one evening and I auditioned for Bob. I'm pretty sure I was terrible but Bob, either because he felt sorry for me or because there was absolutely no one else around, gave me a chance."

While Mauldin had some prior experience deejaying for a college radio station, his sports chops were virtually non-existent.

"I had never called in and had no idea what Sports Phone was. I honestly didn't even know that much about sports...I liked baseball and possessed just enough basic knowledge about the Yankees to engage in superficial conversation with my new Sports Phone colleagues, all of whom knew everything about every player on every MLB, NFL, NHL, and NBA team that ever existed," he explained.

"Sweet Jesus, was I out of my league. I was initially quite pleased with myself for managing to hang in with these guys, and only later realized that they knew I was a fraud from day one and didn't care."

This being Sports Phone, speed always played a factor.

"What saved me, I believe, is that I was pretty fast. My radio station played Top 40 music, which meant that you usually had a few seconds over the intro of a song to squeeze in dedications, a tidbit about the group, a weather report, etcetera. before the singing started. If it did and you were still jabbering away then you were a dead man, never to be allowed near a mic again," Mauldin said.

"So I and my fellow collegiate broadcasters learned to speak at lightning speed with both clarity and coke-binge enthusiasm, an otherwise useless skill until I arrived at Sports Phone when on-air guys had to go into the booth, wait for the beep and rattle off an absolute shit-ton of scores in 58 seconds."

The son of two-time Pulitzer Prize-winning editorial cartoonist Bill Mauldin, Nat occasionally made his way uptown under the Sports Phone flag.

"I never covered any games per se, but was the proud owner of a 1977 Yankees media pass and attended quite a few games, sitting in the press box and eavesdropping on all the writers who actually knew what the hell they were doing. I learned so much about the game," he said.

"The complexities of signals to players, all the subtle shifts in the infield and outfield, etc. A lot of these guys were friendly and happy to explain the nuances to a hopeless but enthusiastic neophyte like me, and it was incredibly appreciated."

The apple didn't fall far from the tree.

"Dad was even less knowledgeable about sports than I was, but on top of being a great cartoonist, he was also a damned good writer," Mauldin explained. "How many little kids want to be just like their dads? Since I never had much talent at drawing, I was left with one last option."

The younger Mauldin's writing wasn't limited to TV, boasting screenplay credits on box office notables including Eddie Murphy's *Doctor Dolittle*, as well as *The Preacher's Wife*, which starred Denzel Washington and Whitney Houston. He first got involved in screenwriting thanks to another Ayer colleague.

"Another friend at Ayer had moved over to the publicity department at CBS and was working on a new sitcom called *WKRP in Cincinnati*. He knew I had a little experience at a radio station and suggested I think of something funny that happened to me there and try writing a spec script. He snuck me a couple of shooting drafts from the show and I slavishly copied the format to make it look like I knew what I was doing, and I wrote about something I thought was funny," Mauldin recalled.

"It wasn't, but an amazing fellow named Bill Dial, one of their supervising producers, called and offered me a pitch meeting. I immediately accepted, flew to California, and reeled out a dozen more story ideas and none of those were funny, either. But Bill, bless his soul, worked with me to put something together. It was my first sale, and I didn't make another one for a year and a half. But I did stay in LA, wrote about five hundred more spec scripts, and finally ended up joining the staff at *Barney Miller*. You are one lucky writer if your first staff job is on a show like that."

Also a producer on several projects including 22 episodes of *Night Court*, and a TV adaptation of Kevin Smith's *Clerks* that featured a young Keri Russell and Jim Breuer, Mauldin's time at Sports Phone helped prepare him for these roles.

"Working on television shows means facing myriad deadlines, and those nights at Sports Phone definitely helped to thicken my skin. There are few deadlines quite as immediate as hearing that beep when you're in the booth and knowing you have exactly 58 seconds to make it all happen," he explained.

"Looking back on it, I just smile and shake my head. It's not like we were curing cancer in there. But in that moment, hearing that beep and pulling it off, I felt like a god."

Mauldin also saw action on some of the other hotlines before jetting out to Hollywood in 1978.

"Eventually the parent company of Sports Phone felt emboldened enough by its success to try launching a few other dial-in services, including Music Line and New York Report, neither of which ended up doing particularly well," he noted. "I switched over to Music Line when it started, then left the company in '78 and moved to Los Angeles."

Forty-plus years removed from the booth on Third Avenue, Mauldin still remembers his colleagues well.

"They were all memorable. Seriously, every one. The guy I worked with on my first night, John Bothe, was even younger than me but knew he wanted to be a track announcer when he was, like, eleven. While other sixth graders were at home watching *Happy Days*, John would be sitting in the nosebleed section of Roosevelt Raceway with a pair of binoculars, calling the trotters to himself," he explained.

"The Meadowlands had either just started or was about to start nightly harness racing. 'Someday I'm gonna call races there,' John announced within two minutes of shaking my hand. And he did, for years, there and elsewhere. 'Precision' Peter Newman also took me under his wing in the beginning and helped me along, an incredibly affable, generous guy."

He also remembers those late nights in the office, along with some key historical events that happened while there.

"It's funny, so many important events occurred when I was in that building on Third Avenue. I was there the night Elvis Presley died and when the power went out all over New York City for a day and a half, but none of them happened when I was at Sports Phone, by this time I was already working on the other soon-to-disappear [Phone Programs] services," Mauldin said.

"Mostly, I still wonder how I was able to pull it off. Sports Phone was actually my second job when I started out. I finished at Ayer around six, jogged across town to Air Time [Phone Programs], and hit the ground running. If I was the only one there late, which happened often, I would have to wait until all the West Coast games wrapped up before recording the final update of the night. There were more than a few nights when I wouldn't make it home until 2:00 or 3:00 a.m., which meant barely four hours of sleep. It's the kind of shit you can only get away with when you're in your twenties."

Speaking of Sports Phone colleagues, Mauldin was a writer and executive producer on a 1991 film titled *Howie and Rose*. Coincidence or not?

"Howie Rose! [Sarcastically] Boy, his career kind of went nowhere, huh? Howie was another terrific dude. That place was crawling with them," he said. "The title was just a coincidence, though. I did another pilot in the early '90s with Howie Mandel. He played a radio host who inherited his miscreant 12-year-old niece after his sister was sent to prison for mail fraud."

SPORTS PHONE TO SUNDANCE

The Mets broadcaster would make it to the big screen in a pair of Newman's movies, however.

"Peter had aspirations to become either an actor or a producer, and how he got the sportscasting job I don't know. But many years later,

Peter used me to voice a couple of roles in movies. I wasn't on screen, but my voice was heard," Rose said.

"One was called *Smoke* with Harvey Keitel, and there was I think kind of a sister film to that which would come out a year or two later called *Blue in the Face*. I still get residual checks for that and believe it or not, some of the checks I get are for less money than it costs for postage to mail me the check. I get checks for 37 cents."

In addition to the laundry list of heralded actors found in titles produced by Newman, he's worked with a slew of filmmakers such as Wes Anderson and Jonathan Demme.

"This is one of one of several reasons I didn't become a sportscaster as a career. It was so clear to me that there were some people at Sports Phone who were both so talented and so focused on a career in sports-casting that I saw for myself what the real deal was, and Howie Rose, during my time there, how he was clearly number one," Newman recalled.

"I met him 20 or 30 years later, he did some voiceover for a movie I did. He was always an incredibly nice guy, so easygoing, just what you see on television or what you hear on the radio. That's what he is. I thought you could tell which people were headed for big things. Howie was the one who stood out the most."

In these pursuits, Newman even co-executive produced a film with the preeminent Oliver Stone.

"Personally, it's just a maturation process, and any of these enter-tainment industries rely on collaboration. As it turns out, [Sports Phone] was a wonderful opportunity," he said.

"If you do a good job as a producer of something, you put the nine best people on the field or the five best people on the court and you let them play. The owner or the general manager doesn't run out on the court. Your decisions have been made, and I found that much more just akin to what I was about. The interesting thing is when I talk to people in the film business, I've made 40 films. They say, 'Oh, you must have grown up loving film,' and I say no. Actually, it was always number three on my list."

"One was sports, two was politics, and three were films. It's my belief that it's not true, that working at something you love is necessarily the best thing to do because sometimes you fall out of love with it. The work becomes more complex than what it is you love about it. You're detached from the enjoyable part."

Quickie Quiz

Q: What unlikely ally helped guide Peter Newman on the path to Hollywood success?

A: Muhammad Ali's personal magician

Newman: "I was sort of struggling around [after Sports Phone]. I was doing some public access TV shows. I would do interviews, but not necessarily sports. Through an odd set of circumstances, I was introduced to Muhammad Ali's personal magician, whose name was Theo, who brought me down to Pennsylvania to Ali's camp when he was training for [Larry] Holmes. [There was] an NYU student who wasn't a Sports Phone guy but had a broadcast-quality camera. He shot for the Spanish Broadcasting Network. He gently removed it for a day, and we went down and I did half an hour with Ali and he cut it into a show that PBS ran nationwide. The thing I realized about it was that I much preferred putting things together, and I didn't like being in front of the camera. I had an element of stage fright."

 # Sports Phone Stories

Holy Rejection, Batman!
(feat. Charlie DeNatale)

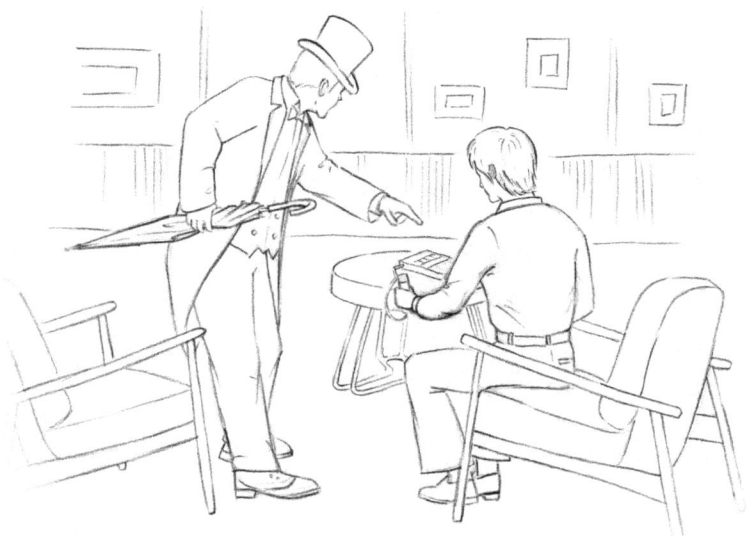

By the time the movie *Rocky* was released in 1976, actor Burgess Meredith had almost a half-century's worth of theatre and film credits to his name, several gaining critical acclaim. A particular role the former Air Force captain was well known for was that of the Penguin in the 1960s television series and movie *Batman*, one he apparently didn't rank very high on his personal list — as some genuine praise led to one of the shortest interviews in Sports Phone history.

"I was asked to interview the great actor, Burgess Meredith, about the time *Rocky* was released in theaters," Charlie DeNatale said. "We were going to use sound bites on Sports Phone and also New York Report [a news-centric hotline]."

"So I meet him at the hotel in New York and turn on my tape recorder. Obviously, I'm in awe meeting this guy and I say, 'You know Mr. Meredith, I think your best acting performance ever was as the Penguin in the *Batman* TV show.'"

"Well, I guess that was not a flattering comment so he got up off his chair and in that rough voice says, 'Shut that tape recorder off and get the fuck out of here.'"

––––––

CARE BEARS

Mike Weinstein's career in television has spanned more than three decades, a journey that started with Phone Programs and Sports Phone.

"I did a lot of announcing with instant football updates and 8,000 basketball games on Wednesdays and Saturdays, but I got to be involved in a whole other part of our business, where I was the guy going on the road with a lot of our really big hotlines," he recalled.

"I worked with Will Smith on the Jazzy Jeff and the Fresh Prince hotline. I worked on our Kiss hotline, Robert Englund [the actor who played Freddie Krueger] on the *A Nightmare on Elm Street* series, and all of these different things. They all helped me get started in my TV career."

Now an executive VP at Lionsgate, Weinstein was exposed to a variety of entertainment categories through these hotlines.

"I did a commercial with Henny Youngman for Dial-A-Joke," he said. "I remember I sat on Henny Youngman's knee and my line is, 'They're ready for you, Mr. Youngman.'"

Those experiences played a critical role later on, eventually leading Weinstein to swap coasts.

"One of the shows that we worked on, there was a company called LBS Television and they were doing a live special on UFOs, and at the time the technology was pretty simple. You either dialed one phone number if you believed in UFOs or you dialed another number if you didn't believe in UFOs. At the time I met a guy who ran ad sales for this company," he recalled.

"Maybe six months later, because I had now been at Phone Programs for about nine years and I think we all realized while we loved being there it was not a lucrative place. So I remember calling this guy and saying, 'Hey, would you ever be interested in teaching me the TV business?' And it's really funny because I picked a good week to call. They were owed about a million dollars and the guy [who owed] had no assets, except he owned the equipment for a 900 tele-phone number. They basically said to me, 'If you come in and help us monetize this phone line, we'll teach you the TV business.'"

What they were asking was second nature for Weinstein at that point.

"I looked at the different properties that they represented and they happen to have *Care Bears*. I had created all kinds of things like the Easter Bunny hotline and other kids programs for Phone Programs, so I went in and I programmed the Care Bears Christmas hotline," he conveyed.

"It was like 25 cents a call. It was inexpensive. They made a ton of money. They taught me the TV business. A year later, I moved to Cali-fornia and I started working on *Baywatch* and *Family Feud* with their parent company and I remain in the TV business to this day."

Before making a name for himself in LA, Weinstein was a bright-eyed New Yorker in the presence of some childhood heroes.

"I remember my first game [for Sports Phone], could have been my second, going for the free meals [at Shea Stadium] and I saw [broad-casters] Lindsey Nelson and Bob Murphy eating in there and it was just the coolest thing," he said. "Because you have this dream when you're a kid, to go to Opening Day every year and try to watch the Mets, and so these were thrills that just live on with us."

 # Sports Phone Stories

Tire Trouble for The Fresh Prince
(feat. Mike Weinstein)

In addition to working on Sports Phone, Mike Weinstein was also involved with some of the other lines owned by parent company Phone Programs. One of its most dialed was 1-900-909-JEFF, the DJ Jazzy Jeff and the Fresh Prince hotline.

Before going on to mega-stardom as an actor and movie producer, West Philadelphia native Will Smith was part of a successful hip-hop duo that sold over five million albums in the US and won a couple of Grammy Awards. To capitalize on the pair's popularity, the paid line (which cost callers two dollars for the first minute and .45 cents each additional) featured everything from insider news from the rap world to relationship advice courtesy of Smith and his deejay.

Weinstein worked directly with the up-and-coming rapper on the hotline, which reportedly grossed $10 million in just a two-year span, and the two became friendly.

Prior to striking it rich in feature films, Smith's big break came in 1990 when NBC greenlit a sitcom where he played a fictionalized version of himself. *The Fresh Prince of Bel-Air* was a hit, totaling 148 episodes across six seasons.

Prior to the show becoming a primetime smash, however, some car trouble almost stopped Smith dead in his tracks.

"A few years after I had worked with him [Will Smith] on the Fresh Prince hotline, I was moving out to LA and I was actually on a field trip to decide if I wanted to move. So I was at the Mondrian Hotel and I was just walking in, and all of a sudden somebody runs up and grabs me in a bear hug and lifts me up. I turned around and it was Will Smith. We talked for a few minutes," Weinstein recalled.

"As I was leaving, I could see that they were hanging out because they had a flat tire and Will was supposed to go. I can't remember if it was a pilot or a regular episode. I think it might have been the pilot. He was going in the studio to tape *Fresh Prince of Bel-Air* and I drove him [to the studio]. Stupidity on my part, I didn't get his phone number. Literally, the last time I saw him, I dropped him off for one of the early episodes or the pilot of Fresh Prince."

Despite the tale told in the show's well-known theme song, the Lionsgate exec's car didn't have a license plate that said "FRESH" nor any dice in the mirror. Even so, Weinstein still managed to transport Smith just in time to sit on his throne as the prince of Bel-Air.

———

ROAD WARRIORS

Weinstein and others traveled long and far to get content for the Phone Programs hotlines, an effort that wasn't lost on the talent.

"I remember when the idea for [1-900-909-JEFF] popped up, it was one of those things that we really did not take seriously. Because when you think back, this is pre–social media, this is pre-internet, so you're just trying to figure out who cares enough about you to pick up the phone and call to listen to a message that you recorded," explained Jeffrey Townes, better known as DJ Jazzy Jeff.

"I think one of the things that made me understand that this is bigger than I know is Mike met us wherever he could. When we were on the Run's House tour [with EPMD, Run DMC, and Public Enemy], Mike would show up in Albuquerque, New Mexico, and stay with us for three to four days until we recorded enough. People don't realize that talking for a minute and a half thirty times is a lot because you start running out of stuff to say."

Townes and his partner Will Smith caught on quickly, as the call volumes spiked to surreal levels.

"That was the internet before the internet. That was social media when social media was picking up the phone and calling somebody, so it wasn't the easiest thing for us to understand," Townes added. "We just realized, when someone says you guys are getting millions of calls, you're like, 'Oh, my gosh.' It was a great time."

The Grammy Award–winning DJ and producer never stopped making music and has traditionally been at the forefront of the newest delivery vehicles for his content, not afraid to take a shot at the unknown. As technology advances, so does Townes, a trait reminiscent of those road gigs with Smith and Weinstein.

"I appreciate knowing that I was a part of something on the cutting edge, cause so much of this is faith. So much of this is jumping out on a limb, doing something that no one has ever done or no one believes in, and making it work," Townes said.

"I have been a part of so many things like that. Why not try this method? So many people are very quick to say no before they even make an attempt, so I think to be a part of [Phone Programs], that was another feather in the cap to make you believe that you're doing something cutting edge and it can work."

In early 2020 when much of the country was quarantining, Townes applied that attitude to a new medium, launching the Magnificent House Party livestreams — producing well over a hundred sets and featuring big-name guest DJs.

"About a week after Will and I got together officially, we sat on a stoop about 2 o'clock in the morning and he said, 'You know what, I want to be the biggest movie star in the world,' and I said, 'I want to do music for the movies.' No one believed that," Townes recalled.

"He bought a camcorder and would film commercials and figure out ways to edit them, just to make an attempt at doing something like that. You look at it now, and everybody's capturing and recording their own content. I was not interested at all in the video world until we started streaming during the pandemic, and then you start realizing about lighting and cameras and frame rates and the rest of that, and you're kind of like, wow, you know what, I've got a TV station now."

NICKELODEON

As a recording engineer, Joe Gauci worked with many of the voiceover artists that stepped into the midtown booth, a group that included several with SAG cards like New York natives George Gerdes and Jan Leighton.

"We did so many hotlines. We did the Santa Claus line. We did the

Easter Bunny hotline, Story Phone. The actors, the professional people from the Screen Actors Guild. These were real actors who you don't see on the big screen [much] but their voices have been in commercials thousands of times and they maybe have had a cameo in a couple of TV commercials," he explained. "They came through the studios. They were professionals and we had a wonderful time."

Gauci himself went on to be part of a well-received kids cartoon that had an impressive run.

"I worked on every episode of the *Doug* cartoon till it ended. It went from Nickelodeon to Disney. Disney owns it now but Nickelodeon started it first and I was on every episode as a sound effects editor," Gauci said. "Four seasons till I left the company, so the last two seasons I had nothing to do with but all my sound designs were already on there and they just reused them."

ONE LIFE TO LIVE

Jerry O'Neil did a bit of everything for Phone Programs, from serving in virtually every capacity at Sports Phone to working on the business side of things for Floyd O'Neil. Despite having success on both sides of the ball, the SUNY Purchase alum's dreams lay elsewhere.

"I really had my heart set on going out and trying to become an actor, a performer, a voiceover artist. So that's what I [eventually] did and it lasted 12 good years," O'Neil explained.

He got involved in some of the soap opera world's biggest titles as both a writer and an actor, focusing on the NYC-based shows.

"Robbie [Caploe] and I lived together from '85 because we met at Phone Programs. We started living together in upper Manhattan, and then she moved to LA. By that time I had left and I was a freelance writer, and I had a seven-year career writing profile pieces for *Soap*

Opera Weekly. Robbie was a *Soap Opera Digest* editor. She went to LA and then I met the editors of this weekly magazine," he recalled.

"I would take actors and directors out to lunch. I was also working the soaps at that time as an extra and a day player, so I always parlaying those relationships. I did all the New Yorks. *All My Children, One Life to Live, As the World Turns*."

O'Neil even became friendly with Emmy Award–winning actor Robert Woods, best known as Bo Buchanan on *One Life to Live*.

"He was a great guy. Essentially, the waiting areas and makeup and everything else were down a level in the studios on West 66th Street. The extras, day players, etcetera would just sit around. We'd read or whatever we did," O'Neil said.

"Bobby would come out and sit with us. Very, very down-to-earth guy. He just would talk to us like, 'Hey, I don't care if you're extras or day players. Let's have a chat.'"

ACTING THERAPY

Like O'Neil, Charlie DeNatale played a multitude of positions during a decade-long run at Phone Programs.

"I was working in radio in a small town in Bristol, Tennessee, and I responded to an ad that I saw which was for a Sports Phone announcer. I started at Sports Phone in 1978, and I kind of had two careers there," he explained.

"The first half was totally 100 percent Sports Phone, where I was a reporter and announcer. Then the second half, they switched me over to the management side where I started to get involved in the 900 business overall."

DeNatale later moved to San Diego and became a part-time actor.

"I do it as a hobby. I do get paid for it and stuff, and I have some credits. I try to do some theater and some film whenever I can. It's good therapy for me," he said. "It takes me away from the bullshit every day. You get to play somebody else, and it's fun. My real job is I'm still a media buyer. I still do a lot of television and radio advertising for clients and stuff."

ALADDIN AND ANASTASIA

Sports Phone employees weren't the only ones with connections to stage and film, as many of the service's callers also made their mark.

Meg Ryan may have voiced the lead character in the hit movie *Anastasia*, but each time Anya/Anastasia sings a song it's actress and recording artist Liz Callaway you're hearing. The Chicago native also belted out tunes as Odette in *The Swan Princess*, Jasmine in a pair of *Aladdin* sequels, as well as some other animated characters.

Callaway also has a mix of TV and stage credits to her name, debuting on Broadway in Stephen Sondheim's *Merrily We Roll Along* in 1981. She was later nominated for a 2024 Grammy Award in the Best Traditional Pop Vocal Album category, a group that included Bruce Springsteen, for *To Steve With Love: Liz Callaway Celebrates Sondheim*.

During those early years in theater, the Emmy Award winner often found it hard to keep up with her favorite sports team.

"I was and am a die-hard Mets fan. I think I used Sports Phone for maybe a three-year period, approximately 1982 to '84. As an actress, I was often doing shows at night, on and off Broadway, so I wasn't able to listen, watch, or go to as many games as I would have liked," she explained.

"So Sports Phone was a lifeline for this die-hard fan who couldn't wait to find out the score in the newspaper the next day. I stopped using Sports Phone when I got my first VCR around 1984 or '85. Then I taped every game and watched when I got home."

Callaway called 976-1313 at least a few times a week, sometimes multiple times in one night if the Mets were playing an important game.

"The idea that I might have heard Howie Rose [on Sports Phone] is wild. When Howie talked about Sports Phone on the air a few months back, I loved hearing how he and so many other sportscasters got their start working on that," she said. "As much as I love my MLB app, in hindsight, there was something special about the anticipation of waiting until they got to your team's score."

AN ELDERLY LADY FROM SWEDEN

Comedian Jeff Garlin is a bona fide Chicago sports fan, dating back to his childhood days in Morton Grove and truly blossoming when he returned to the Windy City in the 1980s to pursue a career in stand-up — a period during which he lived in Wrigleyville, roomed with Conan O'Brien, and performed with legendary comedy troupe The Second City.

The boisterous baritone spent a great deal of time working, both at home and on the road, which meant catching an afternoon game at The Friendly Confines or keeping up with his beloved Cubs on WGN wasn't always an option.

"The joy it brought me on a daily basis was ridiculous. It kept you up to date the way the internet does. This was a version of the internet for people who love sports. Yes, I read the sports pages in the newspaper, but it was not as fast as my friend, the Sports Phone," Garlin recalled.

"At the forefront for me were the Cubs. The Bears, when it's a once-a-week thing, especially on a Sunday, you know what happens with your team. But the Cubs, they're on the road and I wanted to know The Cubs' scores as soon as possible. Sports Phone was the only way to get it unless you listened to the game."

As his professional life started taking him all over, Garlin had alternatives when it came to staying up to date, but none rivaled dialing Illinois Bell's trusty hotline.

"I would say Sports Phone was my number one, [followed by] CNN with Nick Charles and Fred Hickman, local sports TV, and the next day's newspaper," he explained. "I began using the newspaper — which I still do to this day, I read *The Athletic* — for perspective on what the game meant."

An actor with some serious credits to his name, Garlin often stole the show as Larry David's agent Jeff Greene on HBO's *Curb Your Enthusiasm*. When it comes to those behind the mic on his hometown sports scene, he's got a list of preferences.

"In terms of favorite broadcasters it goes back to Jack Brickhouse, Harry Caray, Steve Stone, and up to now with Boog Sciambi, Jim Deshaies, Ron Coomer, and my all-time favorite broadcaster, Pat Hughes," Garlin said. "If I had to pick a voice to tell me any sports news, I'd want it to be Pat Hughes."

Also a director and producer, including an executive producer role on *Curb,* Garlin paid little attention to who was announcing Sports Phone's updates on any given day.

"With Sports Phone, I only gave a crap about finding out the score. I didn't care who told me," he acknowledged. "It could have been an elderly lady from Sweden giving me the scores."

MYRON BOLITAR

Famed author Harlan Coben has had multiple books adapted for the screen, also creating a pair of TV crime dramas. Some of his best-known work involves a series of thrillers whose main character is a basketball player turned sports agent named Myron Bolitar. Sports Phone is referenced more than once throughout these novels, including the following dialog between Bolitar and his mother.

"It's not what you think," Myron said.

"What's not what I think?" she countered. "You shoot around in the driveway a little. Okay, no big deal. But I don't understand. You never even mentioned you were playing again."

"I'm not."

"Don't lie to me. You scored two points last night. Your father called Sports Phone. You know what it cost to call Sports Phone from here?"

"Mom, it's no big deal."

JIMMY V AND A BAG OF WEED

Comedian Joey Diaz once told a story to fellow actor Michael Rapaport on *The Church of What's Happening Now* podcast that involved a weed run to Washington Heights, a cop dressed like a mailman, and a call to Sports Phone from Manhattan night court.

Diaz: "So I was telling somebody, they were like, 'When was the last time you bet on college basketball?' I'm like, 'Don't fuckin' remind me.' The last time I bet college basketball, I had just cleaned up on the Super Bowl. It was the Killer Bees, Miami vs. the Redskins [Super Bowl XVII], and I took the Redskins. The Redskins covered and the guy paid me that Monday. And I take the bus to Port Authority. I take the A train down, and I go to like 150-something Street and I'm walking around. It's January. It's fucking freezing.

"I'm walking around and I see this store that sells Chocolate Thai weed. I knew they sold it. It's 164th and Amsterdam. I walk in there. I take a soda, I take a *Daily News*. They only had three sodas in there. They used to be health food stores. In the '80s, they were called health food stores and they sold weed. They had one thing of protein powder, one of those protein bars, the peanut butter ones, Tiger Milk with the protein, and there was bulletproof glass and the little skinny Black guy, I used to call him Mister Wendell. On this particular January, the day after the Super Bowl, it was freezing in New York. It's one of those days, the fuckin' wind is coming off the East River. It's just cold."

"So I go in there, I buy the fuckin' twenty-dollar sack. I buy sixty dollars worth of weed. I had eight hundred dollars from the Super Bowl. I'm living like a doctor. I go in there, 'Give me a quarter.' I take it outside. Now I can't roll in there, so I take it outside. I go in the building on the steps and I roll a joint, and then I do what every other New Yorker does in 19-fuckin-83. I go for a fuckin' walk, and I'm walking, smokin' this fuckin' joint and the wind blew it out, so now I go into a building corner where the wind can't get me and I go to light the joint, and as I light the joint I hear, 'Get on the floor. Put your hands behind your head.'"

At this point, Diaz went on to explain that he was handcuffed by an undercover officer dressed as a postal worker as part of a neighborhood sting, and eventually let go with just a ticket after a brief discussion cleared things up.

Diaz: "'Now we're just gonna write you a ticket. Take the ticket.' But I've got to go to court. Guess what night I got to go to court? NCAA Finals. It's Houston against fuckin' North Carolina [State]. Houston's giving nine in the paper, but the line goes up to nine and a half. So I love Houston, and that December I went to buy Pat Benatar tickets at the fuckin' Giants Stadium and I heard a commotion. I turned around and it was North Carolina State with Jim Valvano. They were walking through there and I go, 'What the fuck?' and that wasn't a sign. That should have been my sign, but I didn't let it."

"I went with the national public and I go, 'Houston is going to slaughter them.' So I take like three hundred dollars, I call the book-maker. Now, I gotta go to court that night. New York had six o'clock court the night of the NCAA Finals. I got the letter in the mail. You gotta go to court at six o'clock. You get there at six and there's 80 people on the fuckin' docket."

Rapaport: "And you're not watching the game…"

Diaz: "No, [I called] Sports Phone! And they always gave you your score last. They give you the Islanders and the Penguins and hockey and basketball, and then they give you college basketball. When they said North Carolina [State] was up by one I just hung up the phone. I'm like, 'Oh, did I get fuckin' taken.' They weren't beating the spread, and I remember getting out of there for the second half with like eight minutes left, and just running to a bar down by the court. I caught a fuckin' beating. I'll never forget that. I owed the bookie so much fuckin' money."

RAPPIN' MAE

Fran Capo's career has taken her all over the map, starting with a comedy gig at WBLS-FM. Her June East character (actress Mae West's long lost sister) led to some early notoriety and the chance to tour with hip-hop pioneers LL Cool J and The Fat Boys, where she performed her record "Rappin' Mae" — a rebuttal to Shawn Brown's popular "Rap-pin' Duke," a parody in which Western movie icon John Wayne is supposed to be rapping.

Going on-air in the guise of June East garnered the attention of a *New York Daily News* reporter, who would eventually publish multiple features on Capo. Before those were written, however, stretching the truth in a phone conversation forced the future voice of Phone Programs' Candy Claus into successfully breaking a world record.

"Dinah Prince called me up and said, 'Oh, I'm doing a story on weather and traffic people. How long have you been doing it?' Well, I didn't want to tell her 30 seconds so said I've been doing it a while," Capo recalled.

"She said, 'Oh, really? Well, what are you planning on doing next?' Now I didn't have a next, but I had a lady from the *Daily News* so I said I'm thinking of breaking a world record. She said, 'Really, for what?' But I didn't have a for what, so I said I can't tell you because it'll jinx it."

Prince had a 6 p.m. deadline that evening and gave Capo the option of spilling the beans by that time if she wanted to.

"I run out, go buy a Guinness book, start looking through the records, see fast talking. I knew that people my entire life have told me I talked fast. I called up Guinness. I said what do you have to do," Capo recalled.

"At five or six, I had a [stand-up comedy] gig that night. I remember thinking, what the hell, I'll call her. So I said 'All right, I'll tell you. I'm thinking of breaking the fast-talking [female] record.' She said, 'What's the record at?' I'm looking at the book. 'Oh, the record's 552 words a minute,' and she goes, 'What are you at?' So I go, '550. Those last two words are a killer.'"

Things spiraled quickly after that.

"So she prints it in the paper and the very next day the *Larry King Live* people call me up and ask me to go on the show and break the record. And to be honest with you at that time, I didn't even know who Larry King was," Capo recounted.

"All I heard was cable, and I'm like, 'Hey, is this some kind of porn?' And they're like, 'Oh, no, honey, it's a national show.' And I said, 'Well, what if I don't break it?' Larry doesn't care if you break it or not. He just cares if you try it on his show first."

Capo was now on the hook and would have to try speed talking in front of a large TV audience.

"So I called up Guinness and said, 'Well, what do you have to do exactly?' They said Shakespeare or *The Bible*, so I agreed to it. They had a limo pick me up at my house. I had three hours," she said.

"I'm over there rehearsing the 91st Psalm, a prayer that my mother had taught me over and over and over again. I go on the show and I broke the record doing 585 words a minute, and then I re-broke it at the Guinness Museum in Vegas doing 603.32 words a minute, which is 11 words a second."

She went on to break another nine records, publish over 20 books, and land a wide variety of on-air and voiceover spots. Still going strong, Capo holds a special place in her heart for the time spent at 919 Third Avenue, and the lifelong friends she made there.

"I appreciated that my first wasn't a one-shot gig. It wasn't like I got hired for a commercial and then that's it. It airs and I'm done. I was going there every week reading because it was five days a week that these kids could call in, and that was all the way from Thanksgiving to Christmas Day," Capo said.

"One of my dreams was to do voiceovers for a cartoon, so here I am getting my first on-air voiceover and it's me playing a character, me doing a cartoon. Granted, I didn't get to see kids' reactions, but when I saw the little cartoon commercial that aired on TV I was like, 'That's the little girl I do the voice for! That's Candy Claus!'"

TINSELTOWN TIDBITS

There were plenty of other links between Phone Programs and those on screen.

- A frequent Sports Phone caller, Leigh Steinberg served as a technical consultant on several celebrated films and television series in addition to *Jerry Maguire,* for which he was the inspiration for the film's lead character portrayed by Tom Cruise. These include *Any Given Sunday, Arli$$,* and *For Love of the Game.* Steinberg himself also made a cameo appearance in *Jerry Maguire.*

- John Gordon appeared as a fictional broadcaster in the movie *Little Big League.*

- Along with others from the golden age of broadcasting such as future *Saturday Night Live* announcer Don Pardo and singer Kitty Carlisle Hart, Guy LeBow made a cameo in Woody Allen's *Radio Days.*

- Allen could be found playing clarinet almost every Monday night at Michael's Pub, which happened to be downstairs from Sports Phone's Midtown office. "I went to Michael's all the time," Joe Gauci recalled. "Oh, he's five feet away from me playing the clarinet and somebody told me the next day, "Oh, did you see Woody Allen last night?' I'm like, 'Yeah, he was there last night!' I'm a kid. I'm like 21 or 22 in Michael's drinking a martini in a suit that probably didn't fit me."

- Former Sports Phoner Lou Davidson was in one of Al Pacino's earliest films, *The Panic in Needle Park.*

- King Wally's voice is heard in the Billy Crystal film *Forget Paris* as well as an episode of *Sex and the City.*

- Keshia Knight Pulliam, who played Rudy Huxtable on *The Cosby Show*, spent time in the Phone Programs booth recording content for the sitcom's hotline.

- Lisa Wernick worked directly with New Line Cinema on content revolving around the *A Nightmare on Elm Street* movie series, including a collaboration with mask maker David Miller, who did the makeup for Wes Craven's nightmarish Freddy Krueger character. Wernick also traveled to California to work on *The Terminator* hotline.

- While in high school, Fran Capo appeared in the music video for David Bowie's song *Fashion*.

- A Phone Programs employee, Karen Sorensen, brought her actor and comedian husband to the office one evening. Henry Morgan, who played the lead in Stanley Kramer's *So This Is New York* and appeared as a Brooklyn assistant district attorney in the 1960 gangster classic *Murder, Inc.*, wasn't so friendly to a Sports Phone staffer. "Karen Sorensen introduced me to him one time. I was walking out to go home. I did the day shift. She goes, 'Pat, I'd like you to meet my husband, Henry Morgan,'" Pat Harris described. "So I walked up to him and I said, 'Nice to meet you, sir.' I put my hand out. and he just looked at me up and down, like he was checking me out, and shook his head and didn't say anything to me. So I just said, 'All right, whatever you want to do.' I walked out. The next day I came in. She said, 'I apologize so much for my husband. He does that sometimes. I always tell him not to treat people like that.'"

- Many other recognizable names spent time in the booth on Third Avenue, including Jackie Mason and Rod McKuen.

 # Quickie Quiz

Q: Which Sports Phone announcer had his recording ruined by The King?

A: Bob Grochowski

Grochowski: "I was going on through the night and Charlie [DeNatale] had a supervisory fit because he figured he'd better check my tapes once in a while and make sure I'm not fucking up anything. So I didn't shut the booth door all the way. I didn't realize I hadn't shut it all the way, and Charlie started blasting Elvis on that transistor radio he had in the background. And so he checks the tape and instead of hearing the scores all you hear is 'Jailhouse Rock,' so he's like, 'Grouchy, you fuckin' idiot, go back in there and redo the tape... fuckin' music.'"

Sports Phone Stories

Good Luck, Champ!
(feat. Pat Harris, Howie Karpin, and Mike Weinstein)

December 11, 1981, would go down in boxing history as the date Muhammad Ali laced up the gloves for the final time in a professional fight, with the 39-year-old legend pitted against a heavyweight more than twelve years his junior in Trevor Berbick. The match was held in the Bahamas, as Ali was unable to secure a boxing license in the States following a lopsided defeat to Larry Holmes the year prior.

A few days before what was dubbed "Drama in Bahama," both Pat Harris and Howie Karpin were working a shift at Sports Phone when they thought about trying to reach Berbick at his Nassau hotel. Harris knew a lot about boxing, so they figured he'd be the perfect staffer to conduct an interview.

There was only one main hotel in the island country's capital so it wasn't hard to track Berbick down, but he wasn't in his room and was unavailable to take their call. Karpin then urged Pat to take a shot at Ali instead.

"Why don't you try the champ? Hey, try the champ and see what you can do," Karpin said. Why not, right?

"I'll try. I got nothing to lose," replied Harris, as he called the same hotel with a new plan in mind.

"Can I have Muhammad Ali's room, please?" "I'll connect you, sir."

After a few beats, Ali picked up the phone. Harris whispered to Karpin: "That sounded like the champ, but that can't be him."

"Yeah, I'm looking for Muhammad Ali." "Yeah, what do you want?"

Harris staggered and started hemming and hawing as he was just a little nervous, but regained his footing and conducted the interview. In the end, a gracious Ali said, "Thanks for interviewing me. Thanks for talking to me."

Harris closed the call by saying, "Good luck, champ," with both he and Karpin stunned that the plan had worked.

A shell of his former self by then, the man known as "The Greatest" went the distance in the ten-round match but was bested by the Jamaican native in a unanimous decision.

Harris's chat with the prolific pugilist born Cassius Clay Jr. wasn't the only time Sports Phone snagged an exclusive with Ali, as Mike Weinstein would take a similar leap a few years later — one that paid off handsomely.

In September of 1984, Ali checked into New York City's Columbia Presbyterian Hospital's Neurological Institute to undergo a battery of tests to determine what medicine to use to treat his recently diagnosed Parkinson's Disease. Doctors also wanted to check for signs that Ali may have been dealing with low blood sugar at the time.

"I remember Ali was coming back from Germany," Weinstein said. "I don't know if he was already starting to experience some of the problems that he had later in life, but I remember that he was saying he had hypoglycemia."

"One thing I loved at Sports Phone and [Howie Karpin] had it, I had it, [Jim] Memolo had it. We all basically didn't care. There were no obstacles that we wouldn't try to overcome. No question, no interview was out of line, we would do it all. I discovered what hospital Ali was in, in New York. I remember calling him up from that tiny little room where we used to erase all the little carts and stuff. I got on with his security people and I don't even know how I did it. Somehow I convinced the security people that Ali was expecting my call, and somehow they actually put me on with him."

"I remember we spoke, this was like a big moment for me. I sold this to WINS radio and I sold it to Canadian radio, but obviously Sports Phone had it immediately and we had the exclusive. Ali was talking to me about his career, but what made it even more unique and so memorable in my life was [what happened] the very next day. I can't remember if I was supervising that day or if I was on air. Fred Weiner, one of the owners of the company, comes over to me and he's got a big smile on his face. He goes, 'I got Muhammad Ali on the phone for you.' I looked at him and I was sure he was busting my chops, and so I started laughing. He goes, 'No, I'm not kidding. I have Muhammad Ali on the phone for you.'

Ali had actually called back and so we had a second conversation. It was so amazing to me. At one point, Ali's a little mumbling because he's still not feeling well and he goes, 'I got a scoop for 'ya. I got an exclusive,' and I go, 'What's up, champ?' He goes, 'I'm making a comeback.' I go, 'Who are you fighting? Frazier? Foreman?' He goes, 'You,' and then he did a poem for me. Ali's poems were so epic, but I can't remember [word for word] because it's so many years ago. He literally challenges me to fight in a poem and we put it on air."

Quickie Quiz

Q: Which Hall of Fame manager zinged Charlie DeNatale in 2019?

A: Tommy Lasorda

DeNatale: "I'm at Petco Park in San Diego, watching a Dodgers-Padres game behind the Padres dugout. Tommy Lasorda was sitting about two rows in front of me. I am wearing a Padres hat. So Tommy gets up to leave towards the end of the game. Keep in mind, Lasorda is in his eighties at this point in time. So back in the 1980s, I traveled the spring training circuit for Sports Phone down in Florida and chatted with Lasorda in Vero Beach. We talked Sinatra, and spaghetti and meatballs. So that night in Petco I thought it would be a kick if I walked up to him to see if he remembered that. When I stopped him and he saw the Padre hat he said, 'I only talk to Dodger fans,' but I persisted and said, 'No, Tommy, back in the '80s when I was with Sports Phone we chatted in Vero Beach." He stops in his tracks and says, 'Sports Phone? Oh, yeah. 976-1313. I remember that but I don't remember you.'"

CHAPTER 10
MORE SPORTS PHONE STORIES

This chapter contains a collection of stories ranging from the adorable to the absurd, complete with stuffed animals and surly sluggers.

We hope you enjoy them…

Sports Phone Stories

It Pays to Drink
(feat. Jim Memolo)

Tracking interview subjects down by whatever means possible became a badge of honor for the folks at Sports Phone. Of course, it was a lot easier when they were listed in the White Pages.

"It comes down to this. We would track down people at hotels. I remember I found Bo Jackson. Bo Jackson was in the phonebook in his hometown in Alabama," recalled Jim Memolo.

"You looked him up and his name was there, and you're like, well, that can't be Bo Jackson. He wouldn't put his name in the phone book. So I called him up and it's Bo Jackson. That's just an example of how transparent athletes were for the longest time, I can't believe, even in the '90s."

Some athletes that weren't listed still gave out their home numbers, even a name as notable as Smokin' Joe.

"Joe Frazier, I remember I covered a press conference when his son was fighting and it was this big party at this bar in SoHo or whatever. I go there and they're wining and dining the media, which they used to do all the time. There was plenty of alcohol to be had in the press box, in the media room at Madison Square Garden, and at every other venue. It was a given," Memolo explained.

"I met Joe Frazier covering this thing. I did it on a whim. I struck up a conversation, and I stick around and have a couple of drinks with him. He gives me his home phone number."

Memolo called on that connection often in later years.

"When I worked at WFAN, as a producer and doing updates and hosting occasionally, I remember calling him a couple of times. I called Joe at home and asked him if he would come on," he noted. "He was a good guy. He was a friendly guy."

After these experiences, what advice does Memolo have for aspiring media members?

"When younger people in the business ask me about the key, how I bounced around, how I wound up at FAN, how I wound up in Chicago, worked at The Score here, and then I was at WGN for 13, 14 years," he said. "I've been at SiriusXM now for 15 years. I say to them, half-jokingly, it pays to drink."

———

Sports Phone Stories

Lasorda, Lawrence, and a Lopsided Win
(as told by Howie Karpin)

During the 1980s I covered the New York Giants for Sports Phone. Working the games was a great experience, but I also covered media day, which was usually every Wednesday leading up to that week's matchup, along with their training camp. At that time, the Giants' training facility was at Pace University in Pleasantville, New York. Luckily, that was only a 35-minute drive from my house in the Bronx.

In the '86 championship season, I worked all of the home games, one road game in Philadelphia, and of course, Super Bowl XXI in Pasadena. Sports Phone sent me to California for the week leading up to the game. I was required to cover the press conferences each day for both the Denver Broncos and New York, with a little more emphasis on the Giants.

Phone Programs paid the freight for the flight, a rental car, and a room at the hotel. The Anaheim Marriott served as the NFL's headquarters that week, so all the league activities were based there. There was one problem with my lodging.

Sports Phone would send someone to the Super Bowl every year, but I wasn't the original choice, and it was kinda late when they made the decision to send me instead of someone else. Luckily, Dan Kensil was working for us at that time. He was the son of New York Jets President Jim Kensil, so he had NFL connections and was nice enough to set me up in the Anaheim Marriott.

So here I was in California, covering the Super Bowl.

Media day was Tuesday of that week and it was held at a local high school athletic field. This was where I had my first taste of notoriety. Giants all-time great Lawrence Taylor was boycotting the media that season but the NFL threatened to fine him if he didn't fulfill his obligations.

Sitting on the media bus that was taking us to the field, I was thinking that I was going to have to get Taylor and that would mean getting in position, close enough to make a valid recording of the sound. When I got to the field, we had an idea about what time he was going to speak, so I staked out where Taylor was going to be and positioned myself accordingly.

It worked out well as I was in a perfect position right next to the chair when Taylor arrived, and was able to get some great soundbites to feed back to New York. The next day, every newspaper that was sold at the hotel (in those days, there were many newspapers) featured a picture on the front page of Taylor sitting and talking to the media. Lo and behold, I am smack dab in the middle of that picture holding my Sports Phone microphone and speaking with the future Hall of Famer.

I was told that the moment was featured in almost every newspaper across the entire country. A number of years later, that exact photo showed up in a book that profiled the Giants' first 75 years in the NFL.

There was an incident during the week where I nearly saw an iconic baseball manager get hit by a car.

The Marriott featured a circular driveway, and one night I was standing and talking with Dave Sims, who, at the time, was working for WNBC Radio in New York. Sims has since gone on to do NFL football for Westwood One and he has become the TV play-by-play voice of the Seattle Mariners. We were off to the side, away from the revolving entrance door when Los Angeles Dodgers manager Tom Lasorda came out with a lady friend to hail a taxi cab.

A few moments later, an out-of-control car came careening into the circular driveway and nearly went up on the sidewalk where Lasorda was standing. Maybe the driver did not want to hit the couple, so he turned the speeding car to where it came to a stop, but the front was up in the air leaning against a water fountain that adorned the driveway.

The driver was eventually freed from the car and was arrested. Lasorda's companion was a bit distraught, but thankfully, neither was hurt.

Sunday was game day and it was an absolutely picture-perfect one in Pasadena. The media bus drove us to the Rose Bowl and I was in awe of a place that I had only seen on TV.

My credential did not allow me to be on the field or in the press box, but I managed to find a place to watch the game live, witnessing New York defeat the John Elway-led Broncos 39–20. When it was over, I snuck onto the field to not only get sound if possible but to experience the significance of this win for the Giants, my hometown and favorite team.

The locker rooms at the Rose Bowl were incredibly small for an event of this magnitude, so some players and coaches were brought to a podium. Today that is standard procedure, but it wasn't in January 1987.

When my work was done, I was able to relax a little. I also had to stay over another day because I couldn't get a flight out of Anaheim until the red eye left Monday evening, so I spent the day at Knott's Berry Farm, a theme park within walking distance of the Marriott.

———

Sports Phone Stories

A Reel Frankenstein
(feat. Don La Greca)

Editing audio in the Sports Phone days was not as simple as queueing up a file on your laptop and cutting until a clip was ready for airplay. Reels had to be physically spliced, and in some instances that meant a lot of extra manipulation by hand before the recording could be used.

Don La Greca was manning the NBA Hotline one night when some sound arrived from Denver that required a great deal of work.

"There was a time where if you said the city, I could tell you the stringer that was in the city. I started to lose it over the years, but if you saw Denver, [it was] Lee Frank. I became friendly with these people, so one night Mahmoud Abdul-Rauf had this amazing game for Denver. Lee Frank calls up. It's mandatory if you get a triple-double, you've got to be on there. I think he had a triple-double. I gotta have him," La Greca recalled.

"He's like, 'I have the sound but I don't know if I should send it to you.' I was like, 'Dude, I got nothing. There weren't a lot of games tonight. You gotta give it to me.'"

The Denver stringer explained his hesitation.

"He's like, 'Well, Mahmoud Abdul-Rauf has Tourette's. It's really kind of a mess.' So I'm like, 'Listen, just send it to me I'll try to work with it,'" La Greca explained. "So he sends Mahmoud Abdul-Rauf's audio and he's doing this Tourette's thing so I had to edit."

La Greca got to work on the not-so-easy task of cleaning up Abdul-Rauf's postgame reaction.

"This was back when you're splicing the reel with a razor blade, so by the end of it it looked like Frankenstein. I was finally able to cut out all his little hiccups and stuff and put it down a line," he described.

"It was hilarious. The poor guy was trying to talk and Lee Frank's back there like, 'I can't send this to you.' I needed it! The pressure we'd be under to try and get that stuff out there, radio stations were counting on it."

———

 Sports Phone Stories

"Boo" Ackerman
(feat. Rich Ackerman, Kenny Albert, Jim Cerny, and Andy Roth)

A fast-paced environment that involved close quarters and high pressure resulted in practical jokes becoming a way of life in the Sports Phone offices. Rich Ackerman was on the receiving end of a few, the most memorable preserved on tape.

"The time when we started Boston Sports Phone it was a really late night. Andy Roth was doing New York," Ackerman recalled. "I think I was training for Boston. We had the tape and you get the cart and everything, you hit record and boom, you hit play."

Roth was supposed to be in the New York booth. He wasn't.

"I was training with Ack to be an announcer. I went into the booth before him. He didn't know it," Roth explained. "I was under the table, and while he was doing his report, I yelled out, 'Boo!' and he just screamed and jumped out of the chair. Since that day my nickname for him was Boo."

An unsuspecting Ackerman was recording his rundown when it happened, storing the frightful memory.

"What I didn't realize was Andy was hiding underneath the table waiting to scare the bejesus out of me, and he succeeded pretty well," he remembered.

"Luckily for him, I hit the record button and the play, and so that whole thing was recorded. You hear me on tape introduce myself, and then you hear, 'Whoa!' I turned around and there was Tom McQuade in the window behind the booth, just laughing hysterically."

Details of the incident made their way around the Sports Phone staff, even those who weren't on duty that night.

"Rich Ackerman, awesome guy, but he was a little bit younger than everybody. He was Kenny Albert's roommate in college. Great voice and everything but he was kind of a younger, shy guy, and he went into the booth to do an update, and didn't know that one of the other guys was hiding underneath the booth," Jim Cerny recounted.

"So he starts off the recording with that great voice of his, 'Rich Ackerman for Sports Phone', and then all of a sudden you hear on the recording, 'Ahh!' because somebody grabs his ankles as he's doing this."

The recording eventually made its way to NYU.

"I roomed in college with Ack for four years... I hear a lot of stories from him about when Andy Roth hid under the desk, when Ack went in to do one of his updates, and scared him," Kenny Albert noted. "We had that cassette tape for a while. We used to play it all the time."

———

 Sports Phone Stories

Bunny Business
(feat. Tony Matteo)

An FDNY veteran who's answered countless calls, Sports Phone alum Tony Matteo became the subject of a children's book after a minor blaze turned him into a little girl's hero.

"I was working that day as a captain in the city, and there was a fire in a restaurant in SoHo. It was not much of a fire. It was a kitchen fire, but they had to evacuate the restaurant. It was lunchtime," Matteo recalled.

"[Author Jeanne LaSala Taylor] was in earshot of me and she was talking to one of the chiefs saying, 'Can I go back inside because my daughter's bunny is in there, her stuffed animal.' I had a young daughter also who had a bunny fascination and I knew she had the same thing, she had a stuffed animal that she couldn't go anywhere without. She couldn't go to sleep without her."

Matteo was sympathetic and told the Chief he'd go in and search for the stuffed bunny.

"There was no danger involved. I casually walked in there after the fact, and I found the bunny and I handed it to her," he explained. "She was very appreciative and I said, 'Hey, it's no big deal. I have a daughter with a bunny fascination, and I know what it would be like to try and get her to go to sleep without it.' That was it."

End of story, or not...

"A couple of years later I had transferred back to Brooklyn, and I got a call from my old firehouse in Manhattan saying there's a woman here to see you. She wants to talk to you," Matteo shared. "So she said, 'Hey, listen, I remember what happened that day and I appreciate it. I would like to write a children's book about it.'"

Matteo permitted Taylor to use his name, noting that he didn't want any royalties in return. *Just Bunny and the Great Fire Rescue* was later published, at which point the author invited the fire captain to several release events. While Matteo was flattered, he also didn't want to make too much of the situation.

"So then she was publishing the book and she calls me and says, 'Would you like to do a book signing?' Would you like to do this? Would you like to do that? And I kept rebuffing her because I guess she doesn't understand that there are guys every day in my job that put their lives on the line in obscurity," Matteo said.

"And to have a book written where I'm included, where I basically saved the stuffed animal. I know how my fireman buddies would perceive it, and I know it would just be a little bit embarrassing."

When Taylor scheduled a book signing near Matteo's home in Staten Island, however, he was on board — thanks to a little encouragement from his daughter.

"Jeanne is always very nice. I'm always very cordial with her and I always correspond with her, but I think she was always kind of confused as to why I never wanted to be bothered," he reflected.

"I found it a little funny that basically in the book I'm like a hero, and when in reality it was just a very benign gesture. I have two daughters and a son, and they did get a kick out of it, and then even my girlfriend came to the book signing that day. The fact that I have the book and that I was in the book, it's still kind of funny to me. I'm glad it happened. I'm not embarrassed by it."

Sports Phone Stories

Mournful Meadowlands
(feat. Bob Grochowski)

November 29, 1992, goes down as arguably the worst date in the history of Giants Stadium, when Jets defensive linemen Dennis Byrd and Scott Mersereau violently collided while charging Kansas City quarterback Dave Krieg. Byrd went head-down into his teammate's chest, causing a broken neck and leaving him paralyzed.

Initially drafted as the hopeful heir apparent to three-time All-Pro Mark Gastineau, Byrd would eventually walk again but never play another down. He was tragically killed in an auto accident in October 2016 at the age of 50.

Bob Grochowski covered that game against the Chiefs for Sports Phone, snagging a solemn postgame interview with a shook-up defensive end.

"I liked going to the games in those days. Unfortunately, for better or worse, I was at the Dennis Byrd game, which was just heartbreaking to me. Everything about that was heartbreaking. And the way he died, the poor guy. He was just the best," Grochowski recalled. "Marvin Washington, he and Dennis Byrd were like blood brothers. They were inseparable. They were best friends."

Washington was one of the first people Grochowski saw upon entering the locker room.

"The Jets were kind of wedged into another locker room, shared it with the Giants. The defensive ends, a couple of them were right there.

You take two steps into the locker room and there would be the defensive ends. I was there with [*New York Daily News* beat writer] Paul Needell, and so Marvin Washington is in there and his eyes are red. I got there first, and I looked at Paul and I said I can't do this. I'm not going to do this," Grochowski explained.

"There's a mob of people behind me, so then I went to Mersereau because Mersereau was the guy that collided [with Byrd] ... Mersereau was a scab, crossed the picket line, but by then nobody gave a shit. And Mersereau was like, 'Not me.' He couldn't speak. So we went to a couple of players, but Mersereau and these guys are numb."

Ready to give up on an interview, Grochowski was approached by a surprisingly willing player.

"I start to go to that far elevator where the team buses would leave, and this guy taps me on the shoulder and it was Marvin Washington, and he said that Paul Needell [asked him] if you still want to talk," he recounted. "I said to him, 'Do you still want to do it? I don't care. It's up to you.' So he was nice enough to talk for about five minutes."

———

Sports Phone Stories

Big D and The Juice
(feat. Don La Greca)

If there was a story involving a notable player, Sports Phone was typically on top of it. When the most infamous running back in NFL history was accused of murder, a separate number was dedicated to related details.

"We had an O. J. Simpson line when O. J. was going through his stuff," Don La Greca recalled. "So we wanted to be on top of that."

When Hall of Fame hurler Don Drysdale passed away at the age of 56 in 1993, La Greca delivered the sad news to callers.

"I remember having the break on Sports Phone when Don Drysdale died. It's one of my first updates, and the crazy thing was he died in his hotel room in Montreal. We had all the satellite dishes, so they were feeding down the line. I guess he had gone to the stadium earlier to do some sort of a preview and they were feeding it down the line," La Greca described.

"So when they called me to say that he was dead I'm like, 'No, he's not. I'm looking at him right now on television. He's doing a stand-up in Montreal at Olympic Stadium.'"

"[The stringer] is like, 'I'm telling you, he was found in his hotel room,' So it turned out that that was just raw feed that they were sending down from earlier, that I guess he went back to his hotel and he died. I still have the cassette of it, because it was the first time I ever on Sports Phone broadcasted hard news like that. And then getting sound from [Mets

manager] Dallas Green later that night, because he had played with Drysdale, so that was a big deal."

———

Sports Phone Stories

Tough Pill
(as told by Howie Karpin)

The Giants were favored by a field goal heading into a divisional-round showdown with the Los Angeles Rams on January 7, 1990. Following their Super Bowl win in '86, New York had failed to make the playoffs two years in a row but Bill Parcells's squad seemed well equipped to make it back to the big game.

A first-round exit was the last thing Big Blue's elite coaching staff, which included Bill Belichick and Tom Coughlin, were expecting. The low-scoring affair ended up in overtime, which was when Rams quarterback Jim Everett connected with wide receiver Flipper Anderson for a 30-yard touchdown pass, crushing many of the 76,000-plus in attendance.

Howie Karpin was in the building that day, a rough one from start to finish for the Sports Phone reporter. Here is his story:

In January 1990 I was covering the NFC Divisional Playoff game between the Giants and Los Angeles Rams. That was a strange day that began with me attending my aunt's funeral in the morning and then going to cover the game.

Once Flipper Anderson scored the winning touchdown in overtime, it was my responsibility to get downstairs to get postgame reaction. The protocol for Giants postgame coverage in those days was to first speak with Head Coach Bill Parcells in a separate press conference room before going into the actual locker room to talk with the players.

I was waiting on the media line and when we started to walk in, for some ungodly reason, I did not go into the press conference room. I was not redirected into the press conference room and as I entered the locker room, a distraught Phil Simms was getting dressed in a hurry.

I quickly realized that he did not want to speak with the media after the way the game and the season had abruptly come to an end. The Giants won the NFC East with a 12–4 mark and had a bye into the divisional round at home, so this was a bitter defeat for Simms and company. I had been covering the team on a steady basis for a number of years, and although I did not have a close relationship with the Giants quarterback he knew who I was, so I took a chance and approached him.

There was one other media member with me and I remember asking Phil if this loss was tough to swallow. He answered in a strict tone, "Yeah, it's fuckin' tough to swallow," and he then looked at me as his tone mellowed. "Yeah, it's tough," Simms reiterated and bolted out of the locker room.

———

Sports Phone Stories

What's the Fuckin' Score?
(feat. Tommy Tighe)

Tommy Tighe's tenure at Sports Phone ended rather abruptly. He recalled the incident that led to his unfortunate dismissal.

"[An unnamed announcer] was on his first shift by himself. He had trained for a couple, so they put him on New York Sports Phone. He goes on, and he had the Phillies beating the Pirates 5–4 in the third inning. Next time he went on in 15 minutes [recordings were made on 15-minute intervals and later reduced to 10], he had the opposite way, 5–4 in the fourth inning, so he had the Pirates beating the Phillies after he had the Phillies beating the Pirates. The next time he comes on, he's got the game tied. Some guy calls up on the main line," Tighe recalled.

The conversation went something like this:

Tighe: "Hello, Sports Phone."

Caller: "Who is this?" The caller doesn't tell Tighe who he is at this point. "What the fuck is wrong with you people?"

Tighe: "Excuse me?"

Caller: "You got a guy in there who's just given the Phillie-Pirate score as 5–4 with each team winning, and now it's 5–5."

Tighe: "Well, maybe they tied it up now, I don't really know. I'm not monitoring anybody else's system. I'm not the boss, I'm sorry. If that happened, I'll apologize. I'll speak with him."

"He hangs up. [The announcer] makes another mistake, maybe not the same game but a different game. The guy calls back again and I said, 'Look, chief, I'm awfully sorry. What do you want me to do? What do you think our job is, to dupe you guys to keep calling us? Is that what it is?'"

"So I was sarcastic with the guy after like five phone calls to me," explained Tighe. "You weren't allowed to give results out on the phone to these guys, so I couldn't give it to him."

Caller: "What the fuck? What's the score? What's the fuckin' score?"

Tighe: "I can't give it to you."

Caller: "What the fuck is wrong with you people?"

Tighe: "Well, that's what we do here. We try to get you to keep calling."

"So he called the phone company and complained. I didn't think anything of it. It was a Friday night. Pat [Harris] was the supervisor. I told him about it," Tighe said. "I said, 'This fuckin' idiot calling all these times.' 'I'll take him next time,' [Pat] says. The guy never called back after that. He calls the phone company, and gets me screwed."

"Saturday goes by, Sunday goes by, Monday goes by. I did a Monday night shift. Nothing, nobody said anything all day Monday. Tuesday morning, [Mike] Farrell calls me and tells me what happened. 'We're gonna have to let you go, Double-T.' For what? What the hell did I do? They demoted Pat from supervisor and put him on Cleveland. He'd do Cleveland Sports Phone."

The Cleveland line was known as the "Siberia of Sports Phone," adding insult to injury in what was already a hapless tale.

———

Sports Phone Stories

Green Acres Wasn't the Place to Be
(feat. Joe Bomrad)

One of the staples of Sports Phone's New Orleans line was thoroughbred results from Fair Grounds Race Course. Well known around the track as one of its more colorful characters, Alan "Black Cat" Lacombe worked as a stringer for Sports Phone and his unique voice led to a television comparison.

"He would always call. [In a gravelly, high-pitched voice] 'All right champ, the eighth race.' He had that voice. I know that voice. I know where it's from, I just can't place it. Then finally, I got it," recalled Joe Bomrad. "'Doesn't he sound like Mr. Haney of *Green Acres*?' We started calling him Haney Downs."

Lacombe was on a cold streak when he looked to Bomrad for some advice.

Bomrad: "Hey, Haney, how you hittin' 'em?"

Lacombe: "Cousin, I haven't had a fuckin' winner in three weeks ... I got another problem. I haven't got paid from Sports Phone in a month. What should I do?"

Bomrad, holding back laughter: "It's the weekend but here's what you do. On Monday at nine o'clock, call this number and ask for Mr. Douglas in accounting. He'll work on that and you'll get paid."

For those of you not familiar with 1960s sitcoms, Oliver Wendell Douglas was the main character in *Green Acres*. Played by Eddie Albert,

Douglas scrapped his big-city attorney lifestyle to run a farm in the Midwest.

"Can you imagine him calling at nine in the morning [in the gravelly, high-pitched voice], 'Mr. Douglas,'" Bomrad cracked.

———

Sports Phone Stories

Mookie and Micheal Ray
(feat. Cedric Dew)

Cedric Dew was in audio production at Phone Programs, editing and inputting sound for many of the company's hotlines including Sports Phone. Like most involved with 976-1313, opportunities to chip in elsewhere would pop up on occasion.

"One of my most memorable moments was when [Sports Phone] gave me the opportunity to interview [Mets centerfielder] Mookie Wilson. That was a highlight of my career. Somebody who was supposed to do it couldn't get it done. I got to get on the phone with Mookie Wilson, and I had about three or four questions about the game. I remember him being such a gentleman about it. He could sense my nervousness and he calmed me down just so easily," Dew recalled.

"It was such an amazing moment because there I was, this kid who got a chance to interview a major league baseball player, and was just taken aback by it. I remember just getting off of that call and feeling like I had arrived in this industry."

Sports Phone gave Dew another chance to interact with a pro athlete, one who suited up for both the Knicks and Nets.

"I remember getting in a 25-second cut of Micheal Ray Richardson, and he probably had 12 'you knows' in a 25-second piece. There were a couple of guys in [the office], I won't say the names, but there were a couple of guys in there sort of giggling at how inarticulate he was, and I took it personally," he explained.

"So what I did was I took the audio and I went in the other room and I chopped out at least nine of those 'you knows.' When I gave it back it was probably like a 17-second piece but the audio was flawless, and it made Micheal Ray Richardson sound the way I wanted him to sound."

Dew met the four-time All-Star years later, telling him about the amended audio.

"I met him in Philadelphia at NBA All-Star Weekend and we were talking about it, and he was so grateful that he gave me tickets to every event and NBA All-Star Weekend. I got to spend that weekend with him, Darryl Dawkins, and Micheal Ray Richardson's family," Dew added.

"He was over in France or somewhere at that time. He was a player-coach, and he said that people didn't know he had a speech impediment. People just thought he was illiterate, and so those are the moments that really helped me realize the importance. My partner-in-crime was Ken Samelson. We were Starsky and Hutch, and we took pride in what we did in that back [editing] room."

———

 Sports Phone Stories

Proved You Wrong
(feat. Peter Schwartz)

In most situations, the hope is that a teacher offers encouragement whenever a student is passionate about a seemingly viable career path. Peter Schwartz experienced the opposite at East Meadow High School, something he still calls on for added motivation to this day.

"I had a social studies teacher in high school that I was very friendly with, and we used to talk about sports every single day. I was starting to tell people in my senior year, 'I'm gonna go to Buffalo State and major in broadcasting and be a sports reporter someday.' With a couple of weeks to go in the school year, I remember him telling me. 'You're wasting your time,'" Schwartz recalled. "He says my daughter tried to do it and she failed at it, so it's a waste of time. And I said to him, 'Just because your daughter failed, that doesn't mean I'm gonna fail at it.'"

Undeterred, the Long Island native stayed on track in Buffalo, returning to East Meadow during a break.

"I went to go visit my high school. I went to go see some of the teachers and I saw him in the hallway," Schwartz said. "He goes, 'How's the broadcasting thing going?' I'm like, 'Oh, it's great. I'm on the college radio station. I'm calling play-by-play at my school's games. I'm doing this and that.' He just had this empty stare."

While the teacher's intentions may not have been driven by any ill will, Schwartz was understandably disappointed by the lack of encouragement.

"I just didn't think it was right that a teacher, especially one that I was close with and always enjoyed conversations with, is telling me I'm wasting my time. You don't tell a student you're wasting your time," he explained.

Despite dealing with detractors and not having any built-in connections, Schwartz persisted.

"I didn't know anybody in the business. My father wanted me to be in sales. When I was in college he was like, 'When you graduate you'll go into the liquor business with me and Uncle Stevie.' I'm like, 'No, I want to be a sportscaster. I don't want to do that,'" he said.

"This is what I wanted to do since I was sitting on his lap as a kid, watching a baseball game with my dad, saying I want to do this when I get older. I didn't want to go to work with my father. I didn't want to go to a mall and sell shoes like my mother had suggested. I wanted to be on the radio. I wanted to talk about sports."

It's apparent he chose the right calling.

"I always use what that teacher told me as motivation, so every time I get another job, whether it's a play-by-play job, or I finally start hosting at WFAN, and when I've gotten some other things, I always think about the teacher telling me that I was wasting my time doing this."

———

 Sports Phone Stories

Sound From Shea
(feat. Jerry O'Neil and Mike Weinstein)

Shea Stadium was the place to be in the mid-1980s, with the infamous bad boys of baseball running roughshod over the rest of the National League and causing plenty of controversy along the way. Sports Phone was in the building those eventful summers, encountering the occasional hiccup while trying to capture audio.

"I remember sitting next to a certain reporter at many a Shea Stadium game, and he would have his binoculars up and just checking the stands for the most gorgeous woman he could find," recalled Jerry O'Neil. "We all did that shit."

When they weren't glued to the action between the lines or scanning the loge level for ladies, Sports Phone's reporters and stringers could be found in the home clubhouse seeking a sound bite.

"It was just before the All-Star break. It was '85 and Lenny [Dykstra], I think was going to be joining the All-Star team. I was assigned to go out and get some actualities because there's going to be the All-Star Game break. I went around to the usual suspects, [Gary] Carter and others that were always talkative," O'Neil said.

"I go over to Lenny. He had a far-off locker corner and he's sitting there, shirt off, scratching his balls, right? Just hanging out in his locker spitting. He had a spittoon and he's spitting tobacco. So I go over to him, introduce myself, and he kind of shrugs. He says, 'Yeah, I'll talk to you but first I gotta take a dump.' So he goes off and then comes back. So to this day, if you ask [Phone Programs producer and O'Neil's ex-girlfriend]

Robbie Caploe what Lenny Dykstra's name is, she will tell you it's 'Lenny I gotta take a dump first' Dykstra."

New York's first baseman also wasn't the easiest interview subject.

"The other guy who used to constantly ruin our actualities, Keith Hernandez," O'Neil explained. "You'd go into the fucking locker room and within six, or seven, eight seconds, he'd drop an 'f-bomb,' because he knew he'd ruined it."

Mike Weinstein learned a trick when it came to working with the former MVP, one that served him well during the club's championship season.

"I also remember what a thrill it was for me to cover the '86 Mets," he said. "Keith Hernandez was there smoking a cigarette, and I don't remember which one of our reporters had given us the hint, but if you talked about the Civil War you could always get Hernandez engaged."

———

Sports Phone Stories

Nearly Cold-Cocked in Cockeysville
(as told by Charlie DeNatale)

The 1982 NFL season was already underway when a 57-day strike began on September 21, cutting into a good chunk of the schedule and leading to some tense negotiations that took place in Cockeysville, Maryland. Charlie DeNatale was on site for Sports Phone and had a very interesting off-hours experience in the aptly-named Baltimore suburb.

"I'm at Cockeysville at the hotel, and we're all getting exhausted by being at this hotel and not doing anything," DeNatale recalled. "So I'm sitting in the lobby and [another reporter] comes up to me and sits next to me. He goes, 'Charlie, isn't this a drag? We're here for 12 days and we got nothing to do and shit.'"

"He says, 'By the way, did you catch the band in the lounge?'"

"No, why?"

"I want you to do something tonight, get you away from all this shit that's going on with the strike."

"Okay, what is it?"

"I want you to go into the room, listen to the band, and sit at the front table with a drink in your hand. Make eye contact with the female singer in the band."

"Okay."

"I felt, I'll give it a shot. I didn't even know what the female singer looked like or anything like that. So I go into the room, I sit in the front seat with the drink in my hand, and sure as shit I make eye contact with the female singer," DeNatale described.

"When they take their first break, the next thing I know, she's coming up to my table and she's sitting down with me making social chat. So that went on after each break. She comes to my table at the end of the night and she says, 'Why don't you and I get together?' She says, 'My hotel's down the street here. I'm not staying here.'"

"We go to her hotel and we start getting a little bit intimate. So she starts slapping me, punching me, throwing my head up against the wall. Like, this was her fun idea of sex. I managed to get myself out of there without getting in any trouble."

"The next day, [the reporter] is in the lobby. So I go over and I sit next to him and he says, 'Did you make contact with the singer?' I said, 'Yeah.' So he said, 'Did she take you back to the room?' I said, 'Yeah, she did.'"

"Then he said to me, 'Did she pull your hair and smack you around?' I said, 'You motherfucker!' I asked, 'You went with her the night before?,' and he said, 'Yeah, wasn't that a trip?'"

———

 Sports Phone Stories

Rat Shot
(feat. Don La Greca, Tony Matteo, and Jim Memolo)

Sports Phone's second home in New York, located out near Belmont Park racetrack in Elmont, Long Island, wasn't as sanitary as their original Midtown digs. Unwanted creatures were so prevalent, in fact, that one night around 3 a.m. a napping staffer awoke from a sound sleep exclaiming, "There's a bear! There's a bear!" — likely shaken from seeing a large rat running across the floor.

You wouldn't think a rodent infestation could have any positives associated with it, but it just may have saved one supervisor's job during the epic 1994 Stanley Cup Finals showdown between the hometown Rangers and the Vancouver Canucks.

"Game one of the [1994] Stanley Cup Final against the Rangers. The Canucks win Game 1. There was a guy that worked there, he had just started working there. So when Vancouver scores, he throws the chair at the wall and puts a hole in the drywall and everybody's freaking out," recalled Don La Greca.

"I'm the supervisor. At this point, I had just been made supervisor just a couple of months ago. Tony [Matteo] had just come in, he's doing all this night stuff and everything and I'm freaking out. I just became a supervisor. How am I gonna explain there's a hole in the drywall?"

"So Matteo comes in and he's like, 'Don't worry. I got it covered.' He writes a note to the boss saying that we were in the newsroom and a big rat came out from behind the television. I took my hockey stick and I took a slap shot with the rat and it put a hole in the drywall. He goes on, I don't appreciate working in an environment where we have rodents. He ended up turning it around, where the boss called me and apologized to me that I had to work under those conditions. So I went from worried I was gonna lose my job, because one of my subordinates puts a hole in the drywall, to where the boss ended up calling and apologizing to me that I had to work under those conditions."

The series eventually went the distance, with New York ending a 54-year championship drought by securing a tight Game 7 victory at nearby Madison Square Garden. The city celebrated en masse, and La Greca kept his job through the end of the decade.

Sports Phone's original location in Manhattan may have been a little tidier than the Elmont office, relatively speaking, but the crew at 919 Third Avenue wasn't immune to rat problems themselves — something Jim Memolo found out at the start of what was to be a very busy and unorthodox day.

"There was one shift where I was the first one at work that morning. Thankfully, I hadn't slept over, because when I got to the office I walked in and the lights were all off. I turned on the lights and there was a rat as big as Secretariat outside the New York booth," Memolo recalled. "Apparently what had happened is they'd opened up the wall to do some internal construction, and it opened up the wall for rats to come in."

College football Saturdays were often Sports Phone's most hectic days, with a packed slate of games and the expected spike in call volumes to go along with it. Memolo and crew had to figure something out fast, as kickoff was fast approaching and the callers would soon be frantically dialing.

"So I remember I went outside to a payphone and called the boss. I'm like, we've got rats in the office. This is a Saturday. So what are we going to do?" he said. "So we delayed for a while, and then eventually what had happened [is] we all went down to P. J. Clarke's. We used the payphone at P. J. Clarke's to call into the system and we did our updates."

The popular saloon had always offered Sports Phone employees a respite after a long shift in the booth, but it wasn't exactly equipped to serve as their base of operations.

"First of all, we're watching the games on the TV, but that doesn't explain the multiple games that we needed to get to. What we would do is we'd have a producer call up the Chicago office and get all the scores from the Chicago office, and then transcribe them as best they could," Memolo said. "It wasn't 100 percent foolproof but it was the best we could do given the circumstances."

As the vermin were being taken care of upstairs, Memolo and his colleagues scurried from bar stool to phone booth, keeping Sports Phone in action for a full Saturday shift. Did they enjoy a few well-deserved cocktails while working?

"Yes, we did," Memolo confirmed.

————

Sports Phone Stories

Why the Fuck Would I Want to Talk to You?
(as told by Charlie DeNatale)

Sports Phone regularly sent staffers to press conferences, games, and other events, and as a result often had their own interview clips to play for callers. An employee starting in 1978, Charlie DeNatale sometimes covered spring training in the early '80s, filing audio from camps all around Florida. One of the more memorable stops for the media buyer and part-time actor was with the New York Yankees, where he had a not-so-pleasant encounter with Mr. October.

"Mike Farrell [who was the boss at the time] was kind enough to trust me to send me to spring training for two or three years, where I just went from city to city and covered every major league team. You know, got some tape, phoned it in and I was the guy down in Florida that was covering all spring trainings. I would say this was around '80, '81, '82."

"Here I am, a guy who comes from a radio background, and I'm showing up for example in the Yankee clubhouse, in the Yankee dugout, and I'm representing something called Sports Phone. Now, a lot of athletes knew what Sports Phone was, but there were many that did not."

"I'm on the field in Fort Lauderdale with the Yankees and they're doing their workouts and stuff. I'm there with my dopey tape recorder around my shoulder and this microphone in my hand. I'm figuring, you know what, I'm working for Sports Phone, I'm gonna get Reggie Jackson."

"So Reggie is trotting in from the outfield and I'm by the dugout. I say to him, and I figured this would carry some weight thinking he knows who Sports Phone is. I know he doesn't know who I am, but he knows Sports Phone. So I say, 'Hey, Reggie, I'm Charlie DeNatale. I'm from Sports Phone. I'd like to get a word from you.'

"So the first thing out of his mouth was, 'Why the fuck would I want to talk to you? What the hell do you want to know about me, and why the hell would you be interested in talking to me?'

"So that, right away, was my first real 'Holy shit, is this for real? I got to deal with this crap?' So that was a first experience with Sports Phone, and that was Reggie Jackson, who obviously had a reputation for being a little bit sassy with the media. For the most part, a great player, a terrific athlete, but not exactly a favorite of the media at times."

―――――

Sports Phone Stories

The Godfather of Sports Talk
(feat. Joe Benigno, Howie Karpin, Don La Greca, and Bob Papa)

A historian and writer whose storied career spanned four decades, Art Rust Jr. is known by many as the godfather of sports talk radio. Those who worked at Sports Phone, as well as some of its faithful callers, paid homage to the Harlem native.

Benigno: "You go back to the '80s, and the only sports show that I remember was Art Rust Jr. I called him a few times. I think that's where I found out about the Keith Hernandez trade, when Hernandez got traded to the Mets in '83. I think that's where I found out about that, with Arthur George Rust Jr. You had Sports Phone and you had Art Rust Jr. There really was nothing else, except the regular local sports reports at night on the news and the paper."

La Greca: "I worked in a pharmacy forever. I worked there from '85 to '96 part-time through college, and even my early years of Sports Phone and all that. One of the pharmacists loved Art Rust. This was before the FAN. God, he was so good. He always called Yankee Stadium the 'big ball orchard in the South Bronx.' He had [pitcher] Bob Tewksbury on. I'll never forget. 'Hey Tewks, how's the wing?'"

Papa: "In the early '80s, really the only major sports talk was Art Rust Jr. and the college kids. People would call into Art Rust Jr's show and they'd say, 'Well, I was listening on [Fordham University radio] WFUV this week,' and he would say, 'Well, they're just college kids.' I remember because I was covering a lot of Yankee games and using the credential that we had. I remember going up and introducing myself to him. When I

told him I was from Fordham, he kind of bristled at me a little bit or whatever, but the next thing you know we kind of developed a friendship out of
some commonalities. He invited me to WABC to sit in on his show. He put
me on the air for a couple of seconds at the end of the show, and then he
came on with Jack Curry and I on *One-on-One*, the Fordham show, one
night."

Rust Jr. holds a special place in Howie Karpin's heart, essentially
giving him a start in the business.

Karpin: "In January 1980, I began an internship at WMCA Radio,
working in the newsroom. I was pulling wire copy and doing all the
mundane jobs that an intern was responsible for. I was also writing sports
copy for Bob Grant, a renowned political commentator, who also dabbled
in sports. Bob was the first one who acknowledged my name on air.

"I learned that there was a sports talk show on Saturday that was
hosted by Art Rust Jr., who was a pioneer in sports broadcasting. Art
made his mark as the first Black TV sportscaster on WNBC-TV in the late
1960s into the early 1970s. Sports talk radio had gone out of vogue in the
late 1970s but Art helped bring it back, first on WMCA and then when he
went to WABC where he hosted a nightly show, five days a week.

"I asked if I could work on the show and I got the opportunity to work
with the producer, Steve Malzberg, and Art. Thanks to working on the
show, I met Jay Horwitz, the legendary Mets PR person who was just
beginning his tenure at that time, Mariners TV play-by-play voice Dave
Sims, and Rick Cerrone, the editor of *Baseball Digest*, to name a few.

"WMCA was the Islanders' flagship station, so my first professional
credential was an Islanders playoff game, but Art got me my first credential to cover a Yankee game. What a thrill it was walking onto the field with
Art, who seemed to know everybody. Sure, I was starry-eyed but, thanks
to being at the ballpark, I met Mike Farrell from Sports Phone, who told
me they were expanding and were going to need people."

"In July 1980, I was hired by Sports Phone and it couldn't have come at a better time. I was getting married in August so I invited Art and his lovely wife, Edna, and they came to my wedding."

———

 Sports Phone Stories

The Syndicate
(as told by Howie Karpin feat. John Martin and Tommy Tighe)

The first time that I covered a Yankee game for Sports Phone was in 1981.

Of course, I was excited to be assigned to cover my favorite team as a kid. I would get to sit in the press box, and I would get a chance to talk to the players, but I never imagined how I would be introduced to the business of covering sports.

At that time, Sports Phone was one of the few media outlets that had their own phone line in venues like Yankee Stadium and Madison Square Garden. There was a reporter from another media outlet who was using the phone to conduct his business on Sports Phone's dime, so I was instructed to not accept any collect calls for this reporter.

He worked for a radio outlet and was part of a group that was "controlling" the market, so to speak. There were so many local events to cover in the New York Metropolitan area. With radio stations needing sound from these events, stringers would be needed for coverage. This group, which we affectionately referred to as "The Syndicate," would set up the stringers but they would also take a portion of their fee for the sound.

This was part of the politics of working in one of the local press boxes. The stringers would usually be made up of students from Fordham University because they had access to the local events. Reportedly, the students would also be intimidated by this reporter.

The way the Yankee Stadium press box was set up, the writers were on the first base side and the broadcast media was located on the third base side. Sports Phone's seat was in the top row of a three-tier broadcast media section.

Sure enough, the phone rings and it was a collect call for this reporter. The person on the other end was Howie Rose, whom I did not know at the time, and I politely declined the call. The reporter had to go all the way to the other end of the press box to take the call from Rose. A colleague of mine was sitting next to me, and we both had our eye on this reporter as he made his way back from taking the call.

The reporter stops and is standing above me and says, 'If this wasn't the Yankee Stadium press box, I'd wire your fuckin' jaw.' Obviously, that didn't sit well with me, so I threw my pen on the desk and stood up right in his face. 'Don't fuckin' threaten me, motherfucker, and let's step outside.'

No blows were exchanged, and neither were any more words. I made my point. When I checked in with John Martin, who is like 6'4" and was the [Sports Phone] boss at the time, he said, 'Do you want me to come up to Yankee Stadium and kick his ass?' I said, 'No, the situation is well in hand.'"

This group included the infamous Howie Spira, best known for being hired by George Steinbrenner to dig up dirt on star outfielder Dave Winfield. This later led to a two-and-a-half-year federal prison sentence for Spira and a lengthy suspension from baseball for the Yankees owner. Spira was also confirmed to be an FBI informant against organized crime figures.

During his days as a stringer, Spira was a big gambler who often called Sports Phone, and always asked our press box reporters for out-of-town college football scores during September Saturday matchups at Shea Stadium or in the Bronx.

Sports Phone reporters in the field would have an opportunity to meet members of the media, famous or otherwise, while building a network of contacts to serve them well in the future. Sports media was highly competitive and not too many colleagues were willing to be helpful. That wasn't always the case, though, as Tommy Tighe got help from a notable media personality who had his back from day one.

"Kevin Harlan and I, he did Chiefs radio when he first started," Tighe said. "He wasn't doing play-by-play at the time. He was hosting and they had me come on and do it and I said, 'Okay, great. I'd love to. Any Giant game or Jet game that you need.' I'll put you on both, Tommy, I'll put you on both. So I do Shea [Stadium], I do Giants Stadium. Didn't make a difference to me, whatever it was."

"Anyway, [another member of "The Syndicate"] heard about this, so Mutual [Radio] started to sponsor it because he had an in with them. He told them, 'Make sure you get rid of Tommy [Tighe] and put me in there.' Harlan went to bat [for him]. He said, 'This is our network. It had nothing to do with Mutual. They're just sponsoring it. We're gonna keep that.'"

"So [the guy] says 'I'll do the Jets, you can let him do the Giants.' So what would he do? He'd be sitting in his bedroom, [expletive] and sending out an FUV [Fordham University's radio station] guy or whoever, and that guy wouldn't get paid. He'd get paid [instead] and he'd 'take care of them.' Kevin went off the wall and said, 'I don't want any of these people. I want a steady guy,' but every home game he's getting a different person, so he fought and I got it back.

"Kevin going to bat for me way back when, long before he became what he is now. I said I'll always remember that. 'Tommy, that's just the kind of guy I am.'"

———

Sports Phone Stories

Moves Like Jagger
(feat. Charlie DeNatale)

At one time New York Sports Phone covered all of the local teams in person, including the Cosmos of the North American Soccer League. This often gave young reporters like Charlie DeNatale an opportunity to meet celebrities from outside the sporting world, one that they didn't always take.

"The other assignment I had which I truly loved and became friends with Tommy Tighe at the time," DeNatale recalled. "Mike [Farrell] assigned me to the Cosmos back in the days when the Cosmos were really good. Tommy Tighe and I were kind of double-teaming the Cosmos because Tommy was doing freelance and I was doing for Sports Phone."

"So we'd go to the Meadowlands, we'd hang out in the press box and our favorite guy was Giorgio Chinaglia. I mean, we loved him and to interview him. Tommy and I would go to the press box, watch the game, and go down to the locker room. One night, me and Tommy are going down there and Giorgio talking to some guy that looks familiar and he's really, really short.

"I said to Tommy, 'Look at that guy over there talking to Giorgio. He looks really familiar.' He turns around and it's fucking Mick Jagger. I said to Tommy, 'That's Mick Jagger.' He [Tommy] said, 'Holy shit. Do you want to talk to him?'

"I said, 'No, I don't. I'd rather just go up to Giorgio and Ricky Davis.'"

———

Sports Phone Stories

85 Percent of the World is Working. The Other 15 [percent] Come Out Here!
(feat. David Schuster)

On April 29, 1983, Cubs manager Lee Elia orated an infamous tirade that has gained legendary status since. Sports Phone had two reporters at Wrigley Field that day — Les Grobstein (who recorded the sound) and David Schuster, who offered his account of the historic outburst.

Chicago had not finished above .500 in 11 seasons and dropped to 5–14 after losing to the Los Angeles Dodgers that day in front of less than 10,000 in attendance on Chicago's North Side. Suffice it to say, the vociferous Cubs fans gave the team a tough time for their performance and Elia answered back in a rant for the ages.

"They [the Cubs] were playing the Dodgers that day. [Right fielder] Mike Marshall, who's from Buffalo Grove, it's a local high school here, he's on the Dodgers," Schuster recalled. "Initially, I'm in the Dodgers clubhouse talking to him [after the game] and then I go down the left field line, which is where the old clubhouse was. So I came in there a few minutes after Elia started going crazy."

"I hope we get fuckin' hotter than shit, just to stuff it up those three thousand people that show up every fuckin' day," Elia said.

"Grobstein, God rest his soul, he was recording everything and I figured as long as he's recording, I didn't have to turn my recorder on, which was a mistake," Schuster said. "But I stood there, and Elia was going crazy. I had to turn my back to him because I started laughing to myself and I didn't want him to see me laughing."

Elia continued: "They're really, really behind you around here… my fucking' ass. What the fuck am I supposed to do? Go out there and let my fuckin' players get destroyed every day, and be quiet about it for the fuckin' nickel and dime people that show up. The motherfuckers don't even work. That's why they're out at the fuckin' game. They oughta go out and get a fuckin' job and find out what it's like to go out and earn a fuckin' living. Eighty-five percent of the fuckin' world's working, the other fifteen [percent] come out here, a fuckin' playground for the cocksuckers. Rip them motherfuckers! Rip them fuckin' cocksuckers like the fuckin' players. Got guys busting their fuckin' ass and them people boo, and that's the Cubs?"

"The whole thing was unbelievable," Schuster said. "After it was all over, after he [Elia] went crazy for about 15 or 20 [minutes], Les went upstairs and played the tape for [Cubs GM] Dallas Green. Dallas Green called Elia to his office and said, 'You know you're going to be in trouble,' blah, blah, blah. He didn't get fired. He actually got fired later in the season, but yeah, that was just comical."

The tirade went down as such a key piece of Chicago sports history that Grobstein's microphone, recorder, and tape used to capture Elia that day sold at auction in 2023 for $1,800.

———

Sports Phone Stories

Sonny at the Toll Booth
(feat. Bob Grochowski and Howie Karpin)

The Rangers were hosting Edmonton on March 17, 1993, when two former Sports Phone announcers were working on press row for other outlets.

Mark Messier was in his second year in New York and there were high expectations, but the club struggled and would eventually miss the playoffs. Stanley Cup–winning goalie Bill Ranford was in the net that night for the Oilers, with the Rangers attempting 59 shots.

Ranford made 56 saves, with the Rangers falling 4–3 in overtime.

"I think I did a wrap for the Canadian Broadcasting Company (CBC), who paid very well for voicers and stuff. Bobby G. was sitting next to me and I told him, 'I'm going to say 'Ranford took more shots than Sonny at the toll booth,'" Karpin recalled, referencing the scene from Mario Puzo's *The Godfather*, in which Sonny Corleone (played by James Caan) is trapped and gunned down at the Jones Beach Causeway toll plaza.

"No you won't," replied Grochowski, to which Karpin gave a confident "Yes, I will."

Shortly after, Karpin went on-air with CBC.

"When I got on their hockey show I said, 'Ranford took more shots than Sonny at the toll booth as he made 56 saves.' After I signed off, there was dead air for about five seconds or so," Karpin explained.

"The host was dying of laughter, and you could hear that was the case when he eventually got back on. That line has been repeated over and over at local venues for years."

———

 Sports Phone Stories

I Didn't Say That!
(feat. Gordon Damer and Don La Greca)

Ira Silver was well-liked around the Elmont office, and known for making his co-workers burst out in laughter. To appreciate this story, you need to first understand that Silver was Brooklyn Brooklyn, not some transplant with a Midwest inflection.

"I loved Ira. He was a funny guy," Don La Greca said. "He had a thick Brooklyn accent."

Brian McGovern was manning the Chicago Sports Phone line one shift in the '90s when the hometown Blackhawks were in action, with Silver responsible for collecting scores.

He was waiting for the Chicago hockey update to print when McGovern asked him for the details.

"I think it was Brian who asked for the [latest] goal scorer, and at that time we had a computer which was just the interface where you could go to each game. It wasn't [on] the internet. We had a ticker tape kind of system, which would print out just continuously, so we couldn't go and search the information. The information would just come up," Gordon Damer recalled.

"So Ira said to Brian, 'It didn't come over yet.'" But the way he said it, Brian took it to mean Tim Comeover, something like that. He's like, 'Tim Comeover. I've never heard of this guy.'"

McGovern wasn't familiar with this new skater for the Hawks, but he had an update to record.

"So Brian recorded, 'The goal scorer for Chicago, Tim Comeover.' and we're all like, 'Who the fuck is Tim Comeover?" Damer added.

The synthetic sharpshooter made it on-air, to the chagrin of that shift's supervisor.

"I'd have to listen to everybody's update to make sure the scores were right before they're allowed to go home. So I'm listening to the update and [McGovern] goes, 'Blackhawks win 4–2. Chelios, [other goal scorers], Tim Comeover,'" La Greca explained. "'Tim Comeover! Who's Tim Comeover?' He's like, 'He said Comeover, Tim Comeover!' And then Ira's like, 'I didn't say that! I said it didn't come over yet.'"

Damer had his own issues at times with some of the NHL's tougher monikers.

"In the days before the internet, it was tough to know how to pronounce certain people's names. The one name that I butchered and I'll never forget is when [Hall of Fame goalie] Martin Brodeur first came up," he reminisced. "I called him like, 'Mar-tin Bro-deer' or something ridiculous. It was not even remotely close to his name, and they're like who the hell is that? His name is Martin Brodeur, and I'm like, How the fuck am I supposed to know that?'"

 Sports Phone Stories

Stay Out There
(feat. Bob Grochowski and Howie Karpin)

On February 23, 1994, Howie Karpin and Bobby Grochowski were covering the Rangers at Madison Square Garden when coach Mike Keenan opted to punish right wing Alex Kovalev, who would remain on the ice when he was supposed to come off – deciding to play him for a seven-minute shift against the Boston Bruins.

"I remember being with you [Howie] at the Ranger game [after our Sports Phone days] with the Kovalev shit, and you said to me, 'Had you ever seen that before?' I said no, so of course with this guy [Keenan] being nuts, anything is possible." Grochowski recalled.

"You said to me, 'If I ask him if he ever did that before, do you think he would say something?' I said, 'Definitely. Wait 'til after all the writers are finished but tell him you don't cover hockey all the time.'"

Keenan had a reputation for being a loose cannon, so neither knew what to expect when Karpin sprung the question.

"I cover hockey all the time. I never fuckin' saw that," Grochowski added. "I remember you told me his eyes lit up. He was like a supervillain remembering the moment. He said he played some guy for the whole period in the Memorial Cup because he broke curfew?"

"He said he played a guy the whole game," Karpin clarified.

"The whole game, right," Grochowski noted. "He [Keenan] had a gleam in his eye. He was fucking nuts."

"Right, he was more reveling in the fact that the guy was super pissed at him," Karpin said.

———

Quickie Quiz

Q: Which All-Pro defensive end recognized Bobby G. on Third Avenue?

A: Mark Gastineau

Bob Grochowski: "I was at P. J. Clarke's… I ran across, on the Third Avenue side there's a payphone on the corner. I saw a Rolls Royce parked in front of that payphone and Gastineau was on the phone. He's waving to me. He doesn't know my name, of course, you don't have to. He knew my face, because he'd see me [at Hofstra practice facility] every fuckin' Wednesday. In those days, [the Jets] were still pretty decent."

CHAPTER 11
THE COMPETITION

L ike with any successful business, competition popped up all over in the form of similar services. One of these was run by Bronx-born Mickey Charles, whose Pennsylvania-based operation capitalized on the popularity of Sports Phone by snagging some very familiar digits for its national dial-up line.

THE 900 COUP

"[Phone Programs] initially launched the 900 [976-1313] number but it was a very competitive thing," Mike Farrell recalled. "AT&T had all sorts of people who wanted to do a national sports line, and I believe Phone Programs had it initially but didn't hang on to it."

Originally run out of a two-car garage in Huntington Valley, Charles employed an aggressive ad campaign that gained widespread recognition for his budding service.

"Mickey Charles took over the 1-900 number after Sports Phone started it," Tommy Tighe explained. "[He] took it down to his offices near Philly."

The details on exactly how and when Charles's outfit ended up with the 900-976-1313 number are a bit murky and vary depending on who you ask, as do whether or not his company did business solely under the moniker Dial Sports, or if they also co-opted Dial-It Sports as well (both can be found in old advertisements, interviews, etc.). One area not disputed is his national line's call volumes, generating millions of dollars in revenue per month at its peak.

"He had national aspirations," Mike Walczewski said. "He was a dirty word around Sports Phone."

As the number of callers grew, so did the need for more staffers and square footage.

"The operation shifted to Masons Mill Business Park as it became larger," noted Joe Delikat, a La Salle University communications student who began working for Charles in 1985. " I figured if I wasn't going pro in any sport, the next best thing was to announce the sports I loved."

As a former caller, Delikat had some experience with score phones.

"[Sports Phone] was on my radar, but that was way before I started working at Dial Sports," he said. "I used to call it as a kid to get score updates on my favorite football teams since there were not 100 channels on the television back then. It was my way of feeling connected."

Many of Delikat's stories mimic those that came out of Third Avenue and Elmont, in terms of environment.

"Those were some of the most carefree days. Very much like our own little sports team, 99.9 percent were young college guys who shared a passion for sports, but we also liked to talk about the ladies and go out drinking after our shifts were over," he reminisced.

"Since we had to stay until the very last game ended, this some-times meant drawing the unlucky Hawaii football game shift which would end very late at night, or in the morning if we're being techni-cal. Lots of 'locker room' banter as you can imagine, not very politi-cally correct back in the late 1980s."

They also shadowed Sports Phone in other ways, manning their own region-specific lines.

"On the score phone end, we had the national booth and the side booths serviced specific cities. I can recall Philadelphia, Pittsburgh, Chicago, and San Francisco, in particular, but there were some other major markets covered," Delikat described. "Those were just local area code numbers and the fee was assessed by the phone company for the call."

Now a professional handicapper for the four major sports and horse racing, Delikat moved to Atlanta in the mid-1990s to work on yet another score phone.

"It didn't have a branded name, but it was very similar to Dial Sports in that we covered the sports and announced the sports in the same manner," he said. "However, this scoreboard was more of an infomercial, as it was structured to include two or three quick ads for 900 numbers that would sell individual handicappers touting a play for the day for x amount of dollars, and that is how we generated revenue."

Phone Programs and Sports Phone would later launch another line that targeted a national audience, one that remained active well into the '90s.

TWO FOR THE MONEY

Another notable dial-up service that came to prominence was the Nevada Sports Schedule Scorephone, created by seasoned speculator Jim Feist and aimed specifically at those with gambling interests.

"What Sports Phone did for me is it gave me an opportunity and I saw a need for a very efficient, very accurate, and timely service," Feist explained. "That was the impetus to get started on being in the sports service industry."

Based in Las Vegas, Feist's main line provided scores and betting odds free of charge — a vehicle he used to advertise and upsell others that came with a price tag attached.

"It took quite a few people to run it. It was expensive to run, but it created a lot of traffic and allowed me to use it as an advertising piece-based model," he recalled.

"I also had a sports betting tip phone where people could call in and get plays. This was a pay service. We also had a newsletter that we sold and that was also a pay service. Eventually, the score phone got so large and so expensive [that] we also charged for premium service, although we did have a free service. It wasn't upgraded as the premium paid service was."

One of those people was former sportscaster Randy McGuire, who began working for Feist while attending UNLV in 1981 and went on to fill multiple roles within the organization.

"We started doing our local free scorephones, with advertising for various Jim Feist products, as early as 1981 when I first came on board there. The 900 numbers started in 1984," McGuire said.

"Since we had paid advertising our updates were never limited to just 60 seconds, but they were limited to how much time we had on our original recording technology, [which were] endless loop tapes. Once we were able to switch to recording with cassette tapes we had no such time limits anymore, and could fit all of the day's scores into every update."

Another on-air personality at Scorephone was longtime SiriusXM anchor and host Zig Fracassi, who saw time on both the free and premium numbers in the late '80s — the latter of which often featured picks from a 10-time World Series of Poker champion.

"A schedule book was done by the company, which was the official rotation for all Nevada sportsbooks, as well as those who subscribed for the schedule. The game order [on Scorephone] was the same as the scores and lines order," Fracassi described.

"[My job] was primarily the day shift, where the betting lines were updated once an hour and scores as they happened. Then I shifted over to our 900 number division as I was the voice on several numbers where people called in for picks on games from Jim Feist or Doyle Brunson, Frank Hall, etcetera."

Now behind the mic for three-plus decades, Fracassi's few years under Feist proved invaluable.

"It was one of the first paying gigs. I think it helped me in terms of timeliness, preparation, and trying to deliver information in as complete and concise a way as possible," he said. "They were also flexible in letting me work on the Scorephone, as I was between radio gigs."

Another veteran on-air voice who once worked in radio with Fracassi, Tony Cordasco was a Scorephone employee from 1988 to 1990.

"Looking back at how sports scores were consumed then, I feel Scorephone played a big role. We had to paint a picture for the listener," Cordasco reflected. "It really helped me in my sports delivery. I know a lot of sports fans relied on us. It was a very creative vehicle."

Just like the folks back east at Sports Phone, the desert-based unit had to get creative when it came to obtaining the latest info.

"I had people on the phone constantly calling radio stations and TV stations in local markets, giving us a rundown of what was happening in the games," Feist explained.

"Many times we would have people at the other end [who] would just put their phone next to the broadcast so we could listen to the game because, of course, you didn't have those feeds that you have today on the internet or television."

As the tech improved, so did the data-gathering process.

"We primarily used paid sports ticker services to get scores in the early days, prior to Jim buying five satellite dishes and installing them on our roof along with a dozen TV monitors so we could watch games and get live scoring updates on many of the games that way as well," McGuire said.

"In the early years, we'd do updates about every 10-15 minutes as the ticker scores came over, but once we added the satellites we were able to start updating as often as every five minutes, if not faster for days with a light schedule."

While the call volumes may not have matched Sports Phone at its peak, Feist's lines were seeing more than their respectable share of traffic.

"I am a bit hazy on exact numbers but 20-30,000 calls on the free local numbers sounds about right during football weekends," McGuire added. "And 4-5,000 or so daily weekend calls on the paid 900 numbers."

Those figures translated to significant profits.

"To give you some perspective as to how big this was. The gross revenue was a minimum of $3 million a year," Feist explained. "That's not spelling out what the expenses were but it was a profitable business and did generate pretty good money, but it took a lot of work and a lot of employees."

Scorephone's employees were quite aware of Sports Phone and its multi-city operation.

"We knew of the New York City-based 976 score phones, and later hired a salesperson in 1989 who'd actually worked at Sports Phone himself," McGuire said.

Some were even customers when on the road.

"I was aware of New York Sports Phone," Cordasco noted. "My family lived in New Jersey and whenever I went back there we would use the New York score phone for updates."

Others not as much.

"My mother sternly reminded me not to call it, as it cost too much money," Fracassi shared. "It was awesome. I'm sure there was some kind of model [at Scorephone] to 976-1313, as we also featured notable injury or weather information."

Another parallel to Sports Phone can be found in Scorephone's connections to a feature film.

"My favorite story was that of my friend and former Scorephone announcer Brandon Lang. The sports gambling movie *Two for the Money*, with Matthew McConaughey and Al Pacino, is a mostly true story based on Brandon's experiences working for me," McGuire revealed.

"[First] as a Scorephone announcer, later a pick phone handicapper, and subsequently in New York City handicapping for one of my sports tout advertising clients who hired him away from us to handicap for his company there. Pretty wild that my former employee and room-mate ended up getting a major Hollywood film made about his life."

INDEPENDENCE DAY

Many mid to large-market newspapers started to offer their own itera-tions of a score phone, often advertised below the fold alongside Sports Phone and some of its major competitors. Other independent lines popped up throughout the country, some managed by those most interested in the numbers game — an unofficial daily lottery that could be wagered on in local gambling spots.

"We called a 976 number for horse racing results. My friend, he owned that line," said Lefty, a New York-based gambling expert with 65 years in the industry (not the same Lefty referenced by Steve Finamore in Chapter 7). "That was strictly for the [daily] numbers. There were four or five exchanges for the 976."

These other exchanges were often used by bookmakers not only to take bets but also to provide odds, scores, and other pertinent informa-tion to their customer base.

CHAPTER 12
THE EVOLUTION OF LIVE SCORES AND NEWS

The mere mention of Sports Phone harkens back to a simpler era, one where waiting was just a part of life.

"The whole Sports Phone phenomenon just kind of reminds me of a time, because I was a big box score guy. In Westchester [County] we had the *Herald Statesman*. Every morning, looking at the box scores," Pat O'Keefe reminisced.

"I remember being very excited when they expanded their box scores at one point to include batting average, which is funny now because batting average itself is not as relevant as it used to be. Then of course, the best part of all that was the Sunday paper where they listed every qualifying batter and pitcher for the ERA and for the batting averages. The whole Sports Phone thing ties in with that."

Once callers got a taste of regularly recorded updates through Sports Phone, there was no turning back.

"In retrospect, I would have to say that this service introduced the public to live sports reporting," Jeff Melnik opined. "Waiting for the

Daily News, the [*Daily*] *Racing Form,* or *The Sporting News* to get stats was just a little too long for me. The phone suddenly became the gateway to current sporting reports."

Much of what we see today as far as the delivery of sports information is concerned can be traced back to what Phone Programs had implemented as early as 1972.

"If you were passionate about it and you wanted to find out what was going on before everybody else or hear the call, or whatever it might be. I would certainly back the thought that it set the table for the next step in information and immediacy," Eddie Olczyk acknowledged.

"It was before its time and certainly helped set the table for where we've come full circle where now it's instantaneous and it's live with the press of a button. Now we just happen to use our phones in our hands for getting information right now, where you used to call in and get the information."

In addition to competing dial-up services, the evolution of live updates began to take shape in other forms, many of which cannibalized swaths of Sports Phone's customer base.

"It broke the seal, so to speak," Jim Memolo said. "I'm not sure anybody realized that there was such a demand."

That demand continued to blossom, and the combination of technological advancements along with some old-fashioned creativity led to new methods of disseminating sports information to the masses.

THE FAN

On the afternoon of July 1, 1987, the world's first 24-hour sports radio station went on the air. Originally located on 1050 AM, New York City-based WFAN would change the way sports fans consumed content for decades to come.

"I was the first update. I was the first person on the air," noted Suzyn Waldman. "What I do remember is the updates were five minutes [long]. Those updates were five minutes every 15 minutes. And don't forget, no computers, this was rip and read at the finest hour."

Those updates were comprehensive, perhaps excessively so.

"They were five minutes because we had to cover everything. Somebody says you have to give the college scores, and I said nobody in New York cares about college scores. They tried to be a national station," Waldman recalled.

"Don't forget FAN was not successful until [Don] Imus came in and they brought in all New Yorkers, and got rid of all the national people that were on because they weren't quite sure what they were doing. The guy who ran FAN was running Enterprise [Radio Network], which was a national sports station that started earlier and failed, and a lot of those people came from there. They were trying to be everything to everybody."

While it certainly wasn't the station's main goal in the early going, leadership at WFAN seemed to have their eyes on Sports Phone's caller base.

"I never spoke directly to somebody in management that said we're going after Sports Phone, but I will say I remember an ad early on. I thought it was a bit over the top," Ed Coleman explained.

"It said something [like] 'We make Sports Phone obsolete.' or 'We make Sports Phone old news.' I can't remember exactly what it was but it was definitely a shot at Sports Phone, and to me, we were just getting started. Half of us didn't even know what the fuck we were doing. We're trying to get the radio station off the ground, the first sports station ever, and I thought it was a bit over the top."

The strategy may have been a bit premature.

"I understood what they were doing and saying, and I guess with your advertising campaign you have to go after somebody," Coleman said. "But I thought it was a shot across the bow before you were ready to do it. I always thought that was kind of funny. There's no question that Sports Phone influenced what we were doing."

As WFAN's identity became clearer, some of the updates were gradually pared down to a more digestible format. While the radio anchors didn't have the same time constraints as those working at Sports Phone, over the years they steered closer to the latter's bite-sized rundowns as opposed to a full five minutes read multiple times per hour.

"When I started at FAN our sports updates were twice an hour. We had top-of-the-hour and bottom-of-the-hour updates. We also had quick scoreboard updates at 15 and 45," Sweeny Murti described.

"The updates at the top of the hour and the bottom of the hour would be handled by an update anchor, and at 15 and 45 the producer would write out a quick couple of headlines and scores, hand them to the host and the host would read them. They would just break in roughly to whatever they were doing and do that. When that changed for us was in '93 when Mark Chernoff became program director."

The update format and frequency were condensed even further at this point, likely siphoning off a significant chunk of Sports Phone's customers as a result.

"What Chernoff implemented early on was the 20-20 flashes, and that changed our format on how we gave scores. Now it was three times an hour, every 20 minutes, and I remember we used to hammer home this idea of you'll get your scores and news every 20 minutes, bang, bang, bang, like clockwork. That was something that was heavily promoted on our station," Murti added.

"He took away our top and bottom full updates, and 15 and 45 scoreboards, and just made a top-of-the-hour full update and 20-40 scoreboard splashes. I can't say this for sure, but I have a feeling that is part of what started to pull down Sports Phone even more."

The timing of these updates was likely no coincidence.

"Certainly coming out of the school of Sports Phone," Dave Sims said. "We were doing updates at top-of-the-hour, 20 and 40 minutes."

The quick, concise delivery method heard on 976-1313 was later adopted by FAN and others.

"I think the idea was always a kind of rapid fire. I remember in the later days of Sports Phone, Don La Greca talking to me about the idea that you only had a certain amount of time to rip through these scores so that is what influenced the style," Murti said.

"The time constraint is what influenced the style is my recollection of what they told me. We kind of had that to a degree too, because at some point you just had to start ripping through scores."

For those anchors present in WFAN's initial stages, there's a clear contrast between the updates then and now.

"Probably when you listen back to updates from when the station started and you listen to them now, there's a couple of things [that stand out]. Brevity is one. They're much shorter," Coleman said.

"We used to do five-minute updates at the top of the hour, not during 15 and 30 and 45, but like top of the hour. There were a ton of games and you went into detail on all of that stuff. It's probably a little more relaxed now, too. It was probably a little more formal then. Give the scores, make sure you get them all in, that kind of thing. You can throw in this or throw in that and be a little looser I guess."

BOTTOM LINE

The Entertainment and Sports Programming Network launched on September 7, 1979, kicking off its telecast with the very first episode of *SportsCenter*. Available to select cable subscribers, ESPN was the first to bring round-the-clock sports programming into people's homes.

"ESPN was finally starting to become a thing, and I guess we all probably realized that's going to be the be-all and end-all," recalled Mike Weinstein. "Sports really should have its own channel, though I think we used to debate it. People were skeptical about it."

Even so, the network wasn't a big threat to Sports Phone's industry footprint, at least not early on. The majority of TV-viewing households weren't equipped for cable yet, with the tipping point of over 50 percent not reached until almost a decade later. In addition, ESPN was not typically offering real-time scores, injuries, and so on throughout the day and night.

"I always tell people, Sports Phone didn't get killed by WFAN. We weren't going to get killed by them," Bob Grochowski explained. "What killed Sports Phone was the college football crawler on the bottom of the screen. That's when the call volumes started to deteriorate completely."

A form of that revolutionary crawler debuted on sister station ESPN2 in 1995 and featured the latest scores, news, and other near real-time details that had made Sports Phone so popular. It would later be branded the BottomLine and incorporated into the main channel as well, but by then 976-1313 was already a thing of the past. There was even a version of the BottomLine ticker created for personal computers, which ran on the Windows 98 and Windows XP operating systems.

"Sports Phone did set the tone for the early stages of what you're seeing today in sports talk, when that started, and ESPN with the BottomLine," said Linda Cohn, a *SportsCenter* fixture since '92.

"[When] they instituted the BottomLine, myself and several anchors, we were like, 'What? How can you give the final score at the bottom of the screen before we even talk about it and show the highlights?' It was like, 'Are you crazy?' People wanted to know the score immediately and who did what."

As more people signed up for cable TV, dialing 976-1313 happened less and less.

"They started putting the scores at the bottom of the screen. More and more people get cable," Murti said. "Now you have ESPN putting all of your scores on the bottom of the screen, and that's another way of making irrelevant picking up a telephone and calling somebody for scores."

Other networks featured their own versions of live update graphics.

"When home I looked at the old weekend sports ticker on Headline News or the old channel SportsChannel America, which when not broadcasting had computer graphic sports scores and news," Frank Fleming shared. "I also remember a little later in the '90s, SportsChannel America became NewSport, a 24-hour sports news channel."

Sports Plus Network on SportsChannel actually ran its own rudimentary ticker well before ESPN debuted theirs. In later years CBS, NBC, and Fox Sports would integrate scrolling updates as well.

"The ticker in the bottom of every crawl, the crawl at the bottom of the screen," Scott Engel commented. "That's Sports Phone in television form."

WORLD WIDE (W)EB

Between continuous TV ticker scrolls and radio score updates broadcast every 20 minutes, Sports Phone was looking like a punch-drunk boxer in a standing eight count, barely holding on but still in the fight.

The knockout blow would land soon after, as home internet access became readily available throughout most of the country. Even in their infancy, services like America Online and Prodigy brought affordable connectivity to the masses, which in turn allowed the public to dial in and retrieve a wealth of information right from their computer whenever they desired.

This included the latest scores, stats, and breaking news along with plenty of other details about your favorite players or your three-team parlay. Not only were these updates now available at the press of a button, but much of their content was updated in real-time through data feeds from companies like STATS, Inc.

In many cases, stats stringers (also known as datacasters) would be at the venue with a laptop connected to a phone line, keying in the action as it happened in front of them. This meant that updates could be delivered by the second, refined to include every pitch to a batter, pass to a wideout, and personal foul on a pick and roll.

With updates now available through several convenient methods, those doing their bidding for outlets like Sports Phone were a dying breed.

"I recall being in the press box during the waning days of this and being fascinated that people were there to call in scores that could pretty easily be obtained elsewhere," explained industry professional and former datacaster Joe Stillwell.

"I could tell by the conversations that parties on both ends of the phone knew they were doing it just to tick a box, even though technically it wasn't necessary. A lot of these folks had two roles in the press box, and they were squeezing this one in on the side during breaks."

The days of dialing a number to get the scores were slipping into the rearview, with the stretch of road between nostalgia and technology growing longer in a hurry.

"I can tell you a memory from 1993, right at the cusp of the internet, when I was living in Springfield, Missouri, and the Orioles played a West Coast game in Seattle. It was too late for the evening news, and the papers didn't have it the next morning," Stillwell added.

"I literally called the paper to find out the score. Then I tried it a second time another day and they asked me not to call again. There were other times that, due to bad timing, I'd wait a whole day to get a score."

Other companies would glean their data through different methods, but it was clear that the demand for immediacy had become widespread and there was no reversing course.

"When I arrived at SportsTicker in 2001, pitch-by-pitch was transmitted via a phone headset. NBA and NHL updates were called in at the specified times," Larry Fleisher said. "By the end, it had evolved to using instant communication tools like AOL Instant Messenger. Same thing with [transmitting] starting lineups."

Although the advent of smartphones was still a long way off, these up-to-the-second data feeds birthed other on-the-go devices — which many bettors clipped to their belts or pants pockets.

"You had a beeper, and you'd press a button and it would tell you what time the game starts. Another button, who was pitching, and then the line on the game, who was injured," said longtime gambling insider Lefty (not the same Lefty referenced by Steve Finamore in

Chapter 7). "That's as far as it went, and then later on they updated it with the weather and all that BS."

The combination of the live data and the devices used to access it helped tip the scales to one side of the wagering equation, although the house will always have the advantage.

"To be frank with you, the way they got it instituted today, it's given a better percentage of how to bet because they got more updates, injuries, weather, wind, you know, all that stuff," Lefty added.

"The listing of each batter that's playing that particular day, when you didn't know who was playing day to day [pre-internet], so you've got a better perspective. A bettor today has more of an advantage. More information has helped the bettor, not the bookmaker."

Datacasting and other information-gathering roles continue to evolve to this day, with MLB and the NFL taking over much of the collection and dissemination duties previously handled by STATS, SportsTicker, and the like. With the rise of legalized gambling, the speed and accuracy in which these updates are entered and delivered has reached new levels of scrutiny, where perfection is the expectation.

In-home internet access also meant the end was nigh for Phone Programs' other offerings, in particular their high-grossing 900 numbers.

"The computer brought on the entertainment age. Now you can be easily entertained. Before the computer, before the web, people were hungry for entertainment — so much so they were paying $1.20 a minute to get on the phone and listen to Bobby The Brain Heenan or John Entwistle," Joe Gauci commented.

"That was their outlet across the country. Sports Phone, they gobbled it up over the phone. Not just bookies, everybody, but as soon as the computer came along there was no way that the 900 systems —

unless it was porn — were going to compete. Shortly after that, porn 900 couldn't compete because you can get porn for free. You don't need Ma Bell anymore."

ISLAND IN THE STREAM

Another development that coincided with expanding internet access was the ability to stream audio and eventually video content, with sports-related broadcasts being the main driving force at first.

Now a billionaire several times over with a multitude of successful ventures under his belt, Mark Cuban and business partner Todd Wagner were just getting started in 1995 when they began running the day-to-day operations for AudioNet, with the company's initial mission focused on letting users listen to sporting events online.

The Indiana alums' combined vision started with a relatively elementary desire, wanting to hear Hoosiers games and other sports-related content while in their new hometown of Dallas.

"Absolutely," Cuban explained in response to the notion that there had to be plenty of other sports-starved fans out there with a similar want. "And not just games, but sports talk radio as well."

Tired of relying on newspapers, *SportsCenter*, and what passed for updates in the internet's nascent stage, the Dallas duo created a platform that began with a lone server and an ISDN line and rapidly became an industry titan that played a key role in the development of audio and video streaming technology so prevalent today.

"It started the entire streaming industry," Cuban said of the company, which later became known as Broadcast.com. "That's a big 'what comes next!'"

With current ventures ranging from an affordable prescription medication service to still controlling basketball operations for the

Mavericks, a club in which he sold his majority stake in late 2023, Cuban helped create and pioneer a market that wasn't recognized before, and contributed to its significant growth — not unlike Phone Programs and Sports Phone did in the decades prior.

"We made it so any fan with a computer could get anything multimedia," the former *Shark Tank* star acknowledged.

ECHOES OF THE PAST

With all this immediacy comes a litany of advantages, but some things have gotten lost to progress as we've advanced.

"My two favorite moments of the week as a sports fan growing up were getting *The Sporting News* in the mail, usually on Thursday, and getting the Sunday paper, particularly during baseball season. You get the box scores from the day before except for maybe the West Coast, but you get those late Friday games so there were more box scores in the Sunday paper. I think we appreciated it more," Ricky Cobb reflected.

"Some guys, the All-Star Game was the only time that you would see them all year. Growing up in Kentucky, I was getting a few Cincinnati Reds games and I was getting the Cubs and the Braves. I was getting the NBC *Game of the Week* and ABC's *Monday Night Baseball* when they still did it. I wasn't getting any regular American League coverage, so I would go the entire season and I might never see the Texas Rangers or the White Sox or the Oakland A's play not even once," Cobb added.

"The guys' baseball cards were a big deal, particularly in the '70s when it was just Topps. The NBA was barely on TV at all, and so you're following by the newspaper. You're following by what information you can pick up on television, and then you're following by however you can creatively. At the time, the Sports Phone numbers were probably the best other source that you had."

It wasn't just nostalgia that took a hit.

"The internet has changed everything. I can remember when I first started covering the Mets what an advantage sports radio had over newspapers because they couldn't print until the next day," [Ed] Coleman explained. "There was no internet at that time. There was no Twitter. There were no phones. You had it first and that was great, but that obviously changed over time."

Moreover, universal access to information presents a double-edged sword for broadcasters.

"Well, it makes it easier and harder, easier because the information is at your fingertips. So anything that pops into your head, you can pretty much look it up within seconds. It also makes it harder because anyone can do that. It's not like this information is only available to me, it's not like this information is only available to professional broadcasters," Pat O'Keefe mused.

"So when you're doing a game, or where you're hosting a show, and you're the person who's in charge of giving information, you now have to go above and beyond. You can't just give information that's available to everyone. You've got to dig deeper, and you have to use that information to craft a story that is still relevant and is still interesting to people, fans, listeners, viewers, whatever, who are coming to this with a lot more knowledge than they would have a generation ago."

As with any industry, change is the only constant, and when it comes to sports information it seems nothing can slow down this bullet train.

CHAPTER 13
CLOSING TIME

8-tracks, Walkmans, CD players… VHS tapes, Blu-ray discs, DVDs… AOL, Napster, Myspace.

Depending on your age, some of these may have been integral parts of your life at one point, to the extent that you might not have been able to envision a world without them. Yet as we learn over and over again, something new inevitably comes along and before we know it we've forgotten all about that trusty iPod and the countless hours its tunes kept us company.

Sports Phone and the stories of its competitors was no different. What was once the only method to get updated scores at any time of day or night fell victim to progress, with technological advancements and ingenuity turning the once-revered service into just another relic of time.

"As far as score phones are concerned they are now obsolete, just like Blockbuster went out of business [due to] Netflix," Jim Feist said. "There's a million ways to get scores and lines."

The downsizing began when Chicago Sports Phone shuttered operations in 1990, with Detroit's office closing up shop less than a year later. Like many other out-of-town lines, their numbers remained active but were handled out of New York.

Around that same time, Sports Phone left its pricey Manhattan headquarters behind for the more cost-effective Elmont, Long Island, location — which served as its home base for about a decade. It was during this time when many of the aforementioned methods to get scores and other updates began to gain steam.

Even with these competing avenues draining call volumes at a rapid rate, Sports Phone remained viable for several more years. The team-centric hotlines still offered something exclusive for a spell, as did Sports Phone Live. There was also the convenience of picking up a payphone on the go when radio, TV, or the web weren't in reach.

As the '90s came to a close, however, Sports Phone was on its last legs.

END OF THE ROAD

"In about late '98 or early '99, Fred [Weiner] brought us all into the office and he started interviewing everybody. We didn't know what it was about. Just asking us how we can trim the fat, how we can save a lot of money, and at that time there was a lot of things we didn't need anymore," Don La Greca recalled.

"I was giving them my ideas on how they could trim the fat, so just before they started laying off people they approached me. Fred said, 'Would you be interested if I paid you? Would you be interested in running Sports Phone?' I forget how much he was gonna pay me, like one hundred grand or two hundred grand for the year."

Weiner's basic plan was to close the Elmont office, slim down to a barebones staff, and have La Greca run things from the location of his choice.

"I was just working at WFAN at the time, doing updates on the weekends and filling in here and there. I'm like, 'Oh, that's good money. I'll do it.' I signed a year contract," La Greca explained.

"I rented an office in Franklin Lakes, New Jersey, got the satellite, DirecTV. I hired Gordon Damer, Bill McNulty, and a couple of other people on the side. I think I actually had Jerry Recco doing some stuff for me. I did it and I just paid the guys. I did the taxes and everything. I was way in over my head. I had no idea what I was doing, but it was a way to kind of keep a paycheck going."

Not only was the staff smaller, but the cadence and frequency of updates changed as well.

"There was a guy Chris Catania, McNulty, Damer, and myself. It was pretty much just us four consistently, and I did a lot of it myself too, because I lived not that far away. We were no longer doing the two minutes on Sundays anymore and all that," La Greca said.

"I also did a lot of stuff from home too. It just showed you how ridiculous it was because I could be sitting home, getting the scores off of the BottomLine or off the internet, and then updating the phone. Like, why is anybody calling when I'm getting the information at home the same way anybody else could? The writing was on the wall at that point."

Perhaps those who were still calling 976-1313 had just gotten used to doing so, and some could have been averse to change.

"A 25-year-old sports fan in 2000 is not calling Sports Phone. It's just the older crowd. You weren't getting new subscribers. All you were doing was recycling the old people who had it in the '70s and '80s and were still, they were probably the Luddites. They were still buying newspapers. They weren't tech-savvy or didn't want to be tech-savvy, and that's the people who were still hanging on to Sports Phone. That was all you were getting, is my guess," Sweeny Murti opined.

"It's like anything else. Like today, I work with a group of people now who are all in their twenties. Facebook is a joke. Facebook is what their parents use. Every technology ages out or has a demographic to it, and AM radio was the same thing... If you had metrics available to you, it would probably tell you that your demographic was skewing very old on Sports Phone by that time."

The Franklin Lakes crew became accustomed to one-man shifts, with some treating it like a fireman's schedule.

"It was like a house that was broken up into different offices and we had the upstairs floor. I think we maybe had like four guys at that point and you just got like a block, you got a two-day block," Damer recalled.

"I lived in Long Island at the time. Say it was like Tuesday-Wednesday. I would drive out, work Tuesday night into Wednesday, and sleep there overnight. I'd get up Wednesday and do Wednesday all day and then I'd leave at the end of the shift."

With the twenty-first century underway and an insignificant group of stragglers likely the only ones calling, Weiner and Phone Programs chose to bow out completely.

"When the contract ran out Fred said, 'Listen, we're not going to renew it, because it's obviously dead at this point.' We're already into 2000 now so there's the internet, the BottomLine on ESPN. It's not working out," La Greca explained.

"I kept everything going. I was getting faxes from horse tracks around the country and doing that. I was keeping the Ranger and

Knick hotlines alive. I was doing that all kind of by myself. I did it for a year and then it just died its death."

THE FOREST WAS SPORTS PHONE

The advancements in radio, television, and computing are what eventually relegated Sports Phone to the history books. Despite that, the real, not-so-hidden gem of the service was the people who comprised its ranks.

Sports Phone saw decades of success, but one of its original employees still feels that the company could have done much more with its rare collection of talent.

"Sports Phone was a wonderful opportunity for everybody who was involved in it. It was also an incredible missed opportunity for the people who owned it. You didn't have sports talk radio. You didn't have all these other sports information sources," Mike Farrell said.

"They could have taken the personalities that they developed and marketed them because that's the business they were in. They were media buyers. They know how to buy and sell media time. They could have taken a King Wally, for example, and turned him into the biggest thing in New York sports. They could have syndicated them on radio. At the end of the day, I don't think they fully appreciated what they had, and what they let kind of slip through their hands."

Phone Programs certainly had their share of profitable lines aside from Sports Phone, a fact that may have clouded their judgment.

"When the 900 numbers opened up and everything else happened, they got smitten with the fact that they were creative people and they could create all sorts of telephone information programs but really didn't appreciate fully the impact they could have had," Farrell added.

"They had these visions of being many things to many people, and sports to them, that was kind of the playpen. They could have owned New York sports. They had that much influence. But they thought, well, we get into Dial-A-Joke, we do this, we do Dial-A-Recipe, we do Dial-A-Prayer. Well, okay, but maybe you're kind of grabbing onto the trees and not seeing the forest. The forest was Sports Phone. That was the umbrella over everything."

CHAPTER 14
FINAL THOUGHTS

W hile we were able to cover many of those who worked at Sports Phone in our book, it was not possible to include everyone who filled out a slate, cut a tape, or recorded a score rundown over the service's decades-long lifespan.

RECOGNIZING THE REST

Below are some not mentioned in earlier chapters, each who made their impact on Sports Phone at one point or another.

Al Abrams, Glenn Appleyard, Jerry Barmash, Pat Benkowski, Ed Berliner, Chris Boden, Jim Brumfield, Bill Bryson, Eddie Caggianelli, Lou Canellis, Evan Carter, Joe Castellano, Bill Collins, Steve Courtney, Howard Gill, Ron Gleason, Mark Goldman, Rich Gross, Tom Green, Fred Heumann, John Imbriale, Jaan Janes, Jeff Joniak, Fred Kortmann, Tom Kelley, Rich Kincade, Dave LewAllen, Steve Loscher, Matt Loughlin, Chris Madsen, Jared Max, Joe Mazzone, Bruce Nathanson, Michael O'Donnell, Steve Olken, Ed Randall, Ted Robinson, Kevin Rogers, Steve Silver, Brian Wheeler, Jim Volkman, and Ed Vucinic.

There are others not listed above who were also part of Sports Phone history, and while it was certainly not our intention to leave them out we apologize for doing so nevertheless.

NOTABLE QUOTABLES

You've made it this far, so we want to thank you for reading our book. We hope you've enjoyed it!

To finalize our journey, we've compiled some standout quotes from our extensive list of 100-plus interviewees, thoughts and memories not incorporated into the previous chapters.

"It was just a remarkable time, remarkable people, a remarkable experience. You had all this enthusiastic young energy getting funneled into doing the thing they loved doing, which was reporting on sports. From there so many people were able to take that initial experience and plateau it out into so many different areas of play-by-play, of print reporting, of doing updates, hosting shows, producing. People were just able to just take it and run with it. That was the initial seed that was able to sprout, and you see how many sprouts, how much bloomed, from what was there initially." — Mike Farrell

"It was an incredible group and a lot of eclectic people, but every-body had good hearts. That was the most important thing, and every-body tried to help each other out." — Bob Papa

"I remember moving to Florida in the late '90s and calling a similar type of service, but I can't remember what it was… I wanted to know if the Seahawks were gonna make the playoffs and thinking, I need something like Sports Phone out here. What's going on? I felt lost without it when I moved." — Scott Engel

"We played basketball and softball… We played against the Bulls front office. We played against the Cubs front office. We played at old

Comiskey and at Wrigley. So we had some really good times and I wouldn't have traded that for anything. I loved working at Sports Phone back then." — David Schuster

"I think it was impossible for us to understand what the long-term effect and the influence that something like Phone Programs and Sports Phone was going to have." — Robbie Caploe

"The sports fans of the '70s and '80s, they needed that voice. They needed that voice to trust, to keep putting the dime back in, and getting what they want." — Steve Cangialosi

"When I mention it to people, even years later, everybody still knows what Sports Phone is of a certain era. I don't think we ever had a sense of how big it was, which was probably good. You'd be walking around with swelled heads. We were just excited to be doing something. It was one of those ideal times I could have never dreamed of happening but happened, and so it was great." — Denis McNamara

"Al [Trautwig] was terrific to work with. Matter of fact, he did this satirical commercial regarding the [New York] Cosmos... In the end, he said something like, 'Come out and see the fuckin' Cosmos!'" — Andy Roth

"Right before the pandemic, I saw Chuck Cooperstein and we grabbed brunch at the hotel he was staying at, and it was fun when [NBA Hall of Famer] Dirk Nowitzki walks up and says hi to him. It's cool seeing how everybody's managed to follow their dream in one way or another" — Mike Weinstein

"It felt like a brotherhood. Everybody was pulling for each other. We figured we were getting paid to watch sports and talk about it, and I think everybody was generally always in a good mood. It just seemed to me that everybody that walked through those doors certainly realized the unique opportunity that it presented, but they also knew that when it came time to chase the bigger goals and dreams they had the confidence to do it." — Alan Sanders

"The uniqueness of it was, obviously ESPN and cable was just starting. They're in their younger days. There wasn't that accessibility of instant sports updates like there was with Sports Phone. It was the groundwork for what became sports radio as we know it today." — John Cwikla

"I can't even call it the minor leagues to broadcasting because it was something, a sports analogy was something that was way out of left field. What do you call someone who had been on Sports Phone?" — Peter Newman

"It was the beginning. It was the forerunner of a lot of things to come." — Lisa Wernick

"I was always very aware that if I screwed up, some little girl was not going to get a chance. I'm sure that Linda [Cohn] felt that way too. I was really clear that when I sat in that seat at Yankee Stadium, if I screwed this up someone wasn't going to have a chance." — Suzyn Waldman

"My wife was looking at something online. It was a T-shirt with the old Sports Phone logo of the guy calling up the 976-1313 and she said to me, 'That's a really cool flex to be able to say you were part of something that was kind of on the cutting edge.' All the people that filtered through that place over decades, it's definitely cool to know that you were part of it. It's weird ever explaining it to someone because it feels like any time you use the sentence 'before the internet existed,' it's like, yeah, and when we got done with that we rode our dinosaurs home at the end of the night. But it is a cool flex to be able to say that you were a part of that." — Gordon Damer

"I just think that we were part of the pivotal history of sports in its entirety, and I can look at it and I can think of what it meant to sit there and to cut that tape up … One of the other great magics of our work is we had people out in the field, and the synergy between the folks in the field getting the tape, getting the sound, and then getting it into Sports Phone, it's something that I think we took for granted how good we were at it." — Cedric Dew

IN MEMORIAM

We'd like to recognize the following Sports Phone/Phone Programs employees, contractors, and stringers who are no longer with us. May they rest peacefully.

Glenn Appleyard
Carl Beane
David "Blackjack" Brown
Les Grobstein
Guy LeBow
"Bullet" Bob Meyer
Kurt Schneider
Ira Silver
Dave Wills

THROUGH THE LENS OF HISTORY

Before we part ways, let's take a final look back at Sports Phone and those who played a role in it — through snapshot memories of days gone by and relics of that past…

Sports Phone keychain, button, and magnets. Credit: Scott Orgera

1984–85 Chicago Bulls Sports Phone poster. Courtesy of Troy R. Kinunen collection

1981 Detroit Lions pocket schedule, sponsored by Sports Phone. Credit: Scott Orgera

Cuba Gooding Jr. (left), Leigh Steinberg, and Tom Cruise on the set of *Jerry Maguire;*
This scene was shot at a Los Angeles hotel decorated to look like the site of the NFL
Draft. Credit: Leigh Steinberg

1981 Cleveland Indians pocket schedule, sponsored by Sports Phone. Credit: Scott
Orgera

Sports Phone print ad. Credit: Charlie DeNatale

Mike Walczewski (left), Charlie DeNatale, and Cory Eisner in Eisner's Sports Phone office. Credit: Charlie DeNatale

919 Third Avenue in Midtown Manhattan, the home of Sports Phone from 1972–90.
Credit: Charlie DeNatale

1978-79 Seton Hall men's varsity basketball pocket schedule,
sponsored by Sports Phone. Credit: Scott Orgera

SETON HALL UNIVERSITY
1978-79 MEN'S VARSITY BASKETBALL SCHEDULE

SPORTS PHONE· 999-1313
New Jersey Bell customers a dime at a time
within your area code

1978-79 Seton Hall men's varsity basketball pocket schedule,
sponsored by Sports Phone. Credit: Scott Orgera

Sports Phone softball team; Fred Weiner (holding clipboard), Bob Meyer (looking at
clipboard), Howie Rose, and others (background). Credit: Charlie DeNatale

Sports Phone T-shirt. Credit: Charlie DeNatale

Sports Phone jacket. Credit: Charlie DeNatale

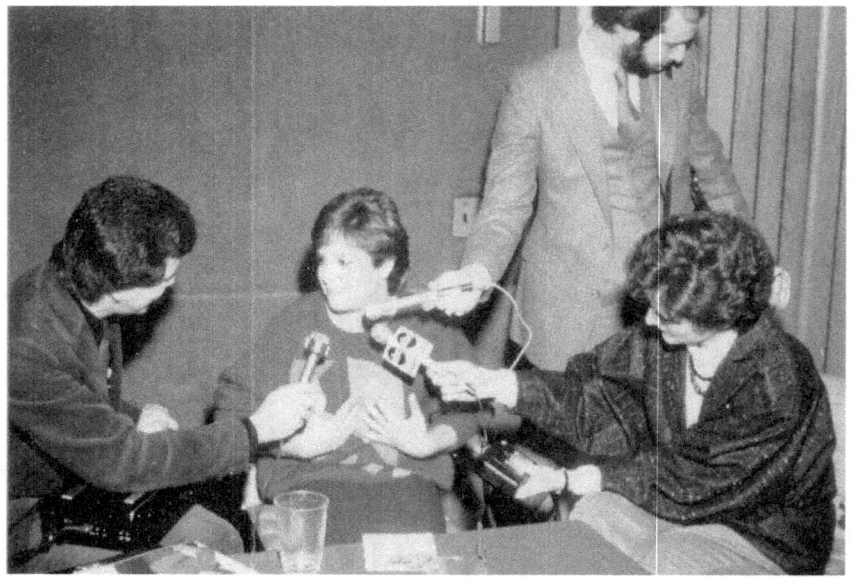

Olympic gymnast Mary Lou Retton on Sports Phone in December 1984. Credit: Sports Phone Facebook Group

Don La Greca at Sports Phone's Elmont office. Credit: Don La Greca

Fran Capo live on WFAN radio in NYC. Credit: Fran Capo

Jim Memolo (left) and Jim Berman. Credit: Sports Phone Facebook
Group

Al Abrams(left), Mike Walczewski, and Mike Weinstein during the 1981 Strat-O-Matic Dream Series. Credit: Sports Phone Facebook Group

P. J. Clarke's. Credit: Sports Phone Facebook Group

Andy Roth interviewing Julius Erving (Dr. J). Credit: Andy Roth

Sports Phone microphone cube. Credit: Andy Roth

Sports Phone logo. Credit: Charlie DeNatale

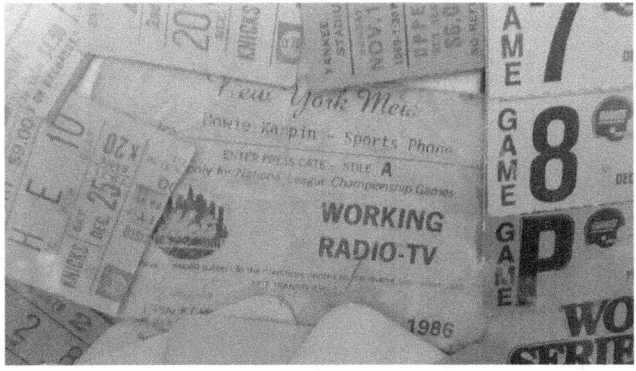

A group of press credentials, including one for Sports Phone during the Mets' 1986 championship season. Credit: Howie Karpin

Now the people who bring you the latest time and weather, bring you the latest sports.

By calling Sports Phone,® you can get the latest sports stories and scores when you want them. Exclusive interviews. Late-breaking stories. Immediate reports direct from the scene of the action. Twenty-four hours a day, seven days a week. And since reports are updated as often as four to times daily, you not only get the latest, you get it the fastest.

Introducing Sports Phone.
Call 936-1313

 Illinois Bell

Sports Phone print ad. Credit: Scott Orgera

Co-authors Howie Karpin and Scott Orgera have a combined 75 years of sports media experience between them.

Credit: Howie Karpin

Credit: Scott Orgera

BIBLIOGRAPHY

Associated Press. "Former Pro Star Provides Results." *Naples Daily News*, November 12, 1972 (accessed via Newspapers.com).

———. "Sports Phone: New Service Offers Fast Results on Results." *Corpus Christi Times*, November 12, 1972 (accessed via Newspapers.com).

———. "Sports Phone Spurred by Off-Track Betting." *San Bernardino County Sun*, November 8, 1972 (accessed via Newspapers.com).

———. "Yanks Win Game One from Mets." *Asbury Park Press*, June 24, 1981 (accessed via Newspapers.com).

Atkin, Ross. "Dial-a-Scoop." *Brandon Sun*, October 7, 1976 (accessed via Newspapers.com).

Bender, Bill. "This Notre Dame vs. Boston College Game Has Eerie Similarities to Legendary 1993 Upset." *The Sporting News*, November 14, 2020. https://www.sportingnews.com/us/ncaa-football/news/notre-dame-boston-college-1993/9wtk91hc94z014swuwd7thjrr.

Berry, Matthew. "Untold Stories of 40 Years of Fantasy Baseball." ESPN, March 4, 2020. https://www.espn.com/fantasy/baseball/story/_/id/28838799/untoldstories-40-years-fantasy-baseball.

Bill Holmes & Associates. "Forensic Analysis Report." *The Dowd Report*, May 8, 1989. https://www.thedowdreport.com/EXHIBIT_084.pdf.

Bogaczyk, Jack. "Need Latest Scores Quickly? Call Sports Phone." *Roanoke Times*, March 29, 1980 (accessed via Newspapers.com).

Calabria, Pat. "Sports Phone: A 58-Second Fix." *Newsday*, July 25, 1982 (accessed via Newspapers.com).

———. "Hey Mister, Have You Got a Dime, Please?" *Buffalo News*, August 7, 1982 (accessed via Newspapers.com).

———. "Dial-It Sports Phone a Hit with Bettors." *Valley* News, July 29, 1982 (accessed via Newspapers.com).

Cohen, Andy. "AC's Archive: Don Shula Looks Back at His Record-Setting Win." Miami

Dolphins.com, January 4, 2020. https://www.miamidolphins.com/news/donshula-looks-back-at-his-record-setting-win-philadelphia-eagles-1993.

Costello, Brian. "Miracle, Misery and Memorable Jets Moments at Giants Stadium." *New York Post*, January 3, 2010. https://nypost.com/2010/01/03/miracle-miseryand-memorable-jets-moments-at-giants-stadium/.

deputay. "1981 Dial Sports - Sports Phone commercial." YouTube, July 31, 2018. https://www.youtube.com/watch?v=I_HpM5eqZuA.

Diamond, S. J. "Most 1-900 Numbers Don't Deliver What They Advertise." *Los Angeles Times*, November 17, 1989. https://www.latimes.com/archives/la-xpm-1989-11-17-fi-1629-story.html.

Faraudo, Jeff. "The Cal 100: No. 23—Leigh Steinberg." Cal Sports Report, July 16, 2023. https://www.si.com/college/cal/news/no-23-leigh-steinberg#:

Fitzgerald, Ryan. "Dan Okrent Is the Father of Fantasy." *Provincetown Independent*, July 30, 2020. https://provincetownindependent.org/community/2020/07/30/dan-okrent-is-the-father-of-fantasy/.

Fosmoe, Margaret. "Throwback Thursday: Notre Dame Dreams Died In '93 Loss to Boston College." ND Insider, November 19, 2015. https://www.ndinsider.com/story/sports/football/2015/11/19/hrowback-thursday-notre-damedreams-died-in-93-loss-to-boston-college/45836051/.

Frank, Jay. "Ma Bell Now Talking Sports." *Daily Oklahoman*, March 9, 1980 (accessed via Newspapers.com).

FSGA. "Industry Demographics." Fantasy Sports & Gaming Association, n.d. https://thefsga.org/industry-demographics/.

Goldaper, Sam. "John F. X. Condon, Announcer for New York Knicks, Dies at 75." *New York Times*, October 15, 1989. https://www.nytimes.com/1989/10/15/obituaries/john-f-x-condon-announcer-for-new-york-knicks-dies-at-75.html.

Gurtner, George. "Stories Still Told of Legendary Racetrack Figure." NOLA.com, November 30, 2014. https://www.nola.com/entertainment_life/stories-still-told-of-legendaryracetrack-figure/article_82752141-5650-5d74-838b-fb4e929658df.html.

Hansen, Chris. "Lady in the Lake." NBC News, January 3, 2007. https://www.nbcnews.com/id/wbna16446018.

Henderson, Joe. "Sports Phone: If You Just Can't Wait." *Tampa Tribune*, October 7, 1978 (accessed via Newspapers.com).

Hoffer, Richard. "Dial-It Answers Fans' Immediate Desire." *Kenosha News*, June 9, 1981 (via Newspapers.com).

———. "The Score According to Wally." *Tucson Citizen*, June 13, 1981 (accessed via Newspapers.com).

Holdship, Deborah. "A League of His Own." *Michigan Today*, May 8, 2021. https://michigantoday.umich.edu/2021/05/08/a-league-of-his-own/.

"Hot Lines; Help of All Kinds by Phone." *New York Times*, October 17, 1993. https://www.nytimes.com/1993/10/17/nyregion/hot-lines-help-of-allkinds-by-phone.html.

"How Fantasy Became Reality: Rotisserie's Rise from Yoo-Hoo Showers to Yahoo! Dollars." *New York Daily News*, March 29, 2009. https://www.nydailynews.com/2009/03/29/how-fantasy-became-reality-rotisseries-rise-fromyoo-hoo-showers-to-yahoo-dollars/.

Joey Diaz Clips. "Joey Diaz on Being Addicted to Gambling." YouTube, April 8, 2019. https://www.youtube.com/watch?v=YJttpuC-5s8.

Kaiser, Jacqueline. "Let Your Fingers Do the Walking for Latest Scores." *La Crosse Tribune*, December 31, 1980 (accessed via Newspapers.com).

Ketcham, Diane. "Hello, Santa? Wrong Number." *New York Times*, December 16, 1984. https://www.nytimes.com/1984/12/16/nyregion/hello-santa-wrongnumber.html.

Ladson, Bill. "Touch 'Em All, Joe! Revisiting Carter's Iconic World Series Homer." MLB.com, October 20, 2023. https://www.mlb.com/news/revisiting-joe-carter-s-iconic-world-series-home-run.

Leahy, Sean. "How Al Michaels Ended Up Calling the 'Miracle on Ice.'" NBC Sports, February 22, 2020. https://www.nbcsports.com/nhl/news/how-al-michaels-ended-upcalling-the-miracle-on-ice.

Lev, Michael A. and Barbara Rose. "Pink Slip for Holidays? It's Not That Uncommon." *Chicago Tribune*, December 25, 2007. https://www.chicagotribune.com/news/ctxpm-2007-12-25-0712240942-story.html.

Lidz, Franz. "If You Don't Know the Score, Sports Phone Services Will Give It to You." *Sports Illustrated*, April 25, 1983. https://vault.si.com/vault/1983/04/25/ifyou-dont-know-the-score-sports-phone-services-will-give-it-to-you.

"Listen Back: Suzyn Waldman's First Update & The Beginning of WFAN." WFAN.com, July 1, 2020. https://www.audacy.com/wfan/articles/suzyn-waldmans-first-update-the-beginning-of-wfan.

"Longest Game in Organized Baseball History." https://www.baseball-reference.-com/bullpen/Longest_game_in_Organized_Baseball_history#Line_and_Box_Score.

Mackinder, Matt. "Coach Kurt an Innovator before His Time." Slam Wrestling, February 13, 2009. https://slamwrestling.net/index.php/2009/02/13/coach-kurt-an-innova-tor-before-his-time/.

Mainville, Max. "On This Day: Boston Bruins Attack the Stands in 1979." Black N' Gold Hockey, December 23, 2020. https://blackngoldhockey.com/2020/12/on-this-dayboston-bruins-attack-the-stands-in-1979/.

Michigan Department of Corrections. " Offender Tracking Information System (OTIS)—Inmate Profile for Mark Steven Unger. https://mdocweb.state.mi.us/OTIS2/otis2pro file.aspx?mdocNumber=611081.

"Mickey Charles Interview on Sports Phone (July 6, 1982)." YouTube, July 6, 1982. https://www.youtube.com/watch?app=desktop&v=gVTtXDeHAVM.

"Mike Walczewski's Top Five Moments at Madison Square Garden." Fordham News, October 25, 2015. https://news.fordham.edu/fordham-magazine/mike-walczewskis-top-five-moments-at-madison-square-garden/.

Mugalian, Art. "Sports Phone—What Hath Bell brought?" Daily Herald, November 11, 1977 (accessed via Newspapers.com).

Oliver, Greg. "Journalist, Photographer Blackjack Brown Dies." Slam Wrestling, July 30, 2022. https://slamwrestling.net/index.php/2022/07/30/journalist-photographer-blackjack-brown-dies/.

Paltrowitz, Darren. "Denis McNamara on WLIR, Northport, the Long Island Music Hall of Fame, NYM & More." No Place Like Long Island, February 9, 2017, podcast. https://www.noplacelikelongisland.com/podcast/2017/2/9/denis-mcnamara.

"Phone Calls Are Listed in Point-Shaving Case." New York Times, November 6, 1981. https://www.nytimes.com/1981/11/06/sports/phone-callsare-listed-in-point-shav-ing-case.html.

Pollard, Stu. "900-976-1313 - Dial-IT Commercial (80's)." YouTube, November 17, 2017. https://www.youtube.com/watch?v=lWlm03aJW7Y.

Purdum, David. "The Rise of Dial Sports and Pre-Internet American Sports Betting." ESPN, August 15, 2015. https://www.espn.com/chalk/story/_/id/13423573/the-rise-dial-sports-pre-internet-american-sports-betting-chalk.

Quan, Jay. "5 Essential Moments from 'He's the DJ, I'm the Rapper.'" Rock the Bells,

March 29, 2023. https://rockthebells.com/articles/rtb-rewind-5-essential-moments from-hes-the-dj/.

Robb, Rick. "Sports Phone Is Calling All Score Freaks." *Miami Herald*, February 26, 1980 (accessed via Newspapers.com).

Rosenthal, Phil. "Sports Phone an Early Game-Changer." *Chicago Tribune*, November 17, 2017. (accessed via Newspapers.com).

Seide, Jeff. "Darryl Sittler's Magical 10-Point Game." The Hockey Writers, September 18, 2023. https://thehockeywriters.com/darryl-sittler-record-10-point-nhl-game/.

SI Staff. "Willie's Firing Evokes memories of Odd Exterminations from the Past." Sports Illustrated, June 18, 2008. https://www.si.com/mlb/2008/06/18/strangefirings.

"Sports Phone Begins for the Fans." *Ridgewood News*, April 6, 1977 (accessed via Newspapers.com).

Spotnitz, Frank. "Boxing Great Muhammad Ali Underwent a battery of hospital..." UPI, September 19, 1984. https://www.upi.com/Archives/1984/09/19/Boxing-great-Muhammad-Ali-underwent-a-battery-of-hospital/2773464414400/.

Steer, Howard. "'Dial-It' Offers Up-to-the-Minute Scores." *Virginia Chronicle*, December 28, 1983. https://virginiachronicle.com/?a=d&d=SNH19831228.1.7&e=-------en-20--1--txt-txIN--------.

Strat-O-Matic Staff. *Strat-O-Matic Review: Volume 11*, September 1, 1981. https://strat-digital-museum.s3.amazonaws.com/Strat+Review/Strat-O-Matic+Review+September+1981.pdf.

Terranova, Justin. "Mad Dog Revels in Giants World Series Win." *New York Post*, November 2, 2010. https://nypost.com/2010/11/02/mad-dog-revels-in-giants-worldseries-win/.

"The Bell System Announced Thursday That a New Telephone..." UPI, September 26, 1980. https://www.upi.com/amp/Archives/1980/09/26/The-Bell-System-announced-Thursday-that-a-new-telephone/6425338788800/.

US Court of Appeals for the Second Circuit. "Case Files, Briefs, and Appendices, 1891–1993." Record Group 276. National Archives at Kansas City. National Archives Identifier: 577901. https://catalog.archives.gov/id/577901.

Verdi, Bob. "Hawks Threaten to Decay into Fiscal, Artistic Flop." *Chicago Tribune*, January 2, 1977 (accessed via Newspapers.com).

———. "Rose Looking Ahead, Not Back." *Chicago Tribune*, August 10, 1981 (accessed via Newspapers.com).

Vidonic, Bill. "Radio Anchor Gets Prison in Child Pornography Case." *The Times Online*, January 21, 2008. https://www.timesonline.com/story/news/2008/01/22/radio-anchor-gets-prison-in/18366525007/.

Vorva, Jeff. "Is Anything just a Phone Call Away?" *Northwest Herald*, July 26, 1988 (accessed via Newspapers.com).

Wigglesworth, Valerie. "Author Jim Dent Gets 10-Year Prison Sentence after 10th DWI." *Dallas Morning News*, April 15, 2015. https://www.dallasnews.com/news/2015/04/15/author-jim-dent-gets-10-year-prison-sentence-after-10th-dwi/.

Witsil, Frank. "Unger: The Family's Legal Saga Full of Twists." *Detroit Free Press*, October 25, 2004 (accessed via Newspapers.com).

ABOUT HOWIE

Howie Karpin has worked in sports media for the past 45 years. Howie is a sports update anchor at SiriusXM and is an accredited Major League Baseball official scorer in New York. He has worked on numerous radio stations as an anchor and reporter and has authored or co-authored 14 books.

Howie is a columnist for nysportsday.com and is a contributor to *Baseball Digest*.

He lives with his wife, Kathy, in Riverdale, New York. They have two married sons, Danny and his wife, Emmy, and Jake and his wife, Anita, and granddaughter Maddy.

Howie worked at Sports Phone from 1980 to 1992.

facebook.com/howie.karpin
x.com/howiekarpin
linkedin.com/in/howie-karpin-a1719b38

ABOUT SCOTT

Scott Orgera is a sportswriter and statistician with three decades of experience under his belt. He has covered thousands of MLB and NFL games and events during that time. His reporting has extended to Division I college sports, professional soccer, the NBA, and the NHL. Orgera's bylines include the Associated Press, *Baseball America*, Baseball Prospectus, FanGraphs, *Forbes*, and The Hardball Times, among others. He has also contributed to several editions of Baseball Prospectus's bestselling books, serving as an associate editor, proofreader, and writer.

Formerly a highly rated reporter for STATS for 25 seasons and an MLB.com datacaster, Scott is a Baseball Writers' Association of America member, managing social media for their New York chapter. He graduated summa cum laude in Analytics from Purdue University. Beyond sports, Orgera has authored over 1,500 computing and technology articles for Lifewire (formerly About.com), co-written the children's book *Mikey and the Magic Medicine,* and has over a quarter-century of experience in software development, quality assurance, and technical writing for multiple Fortune 100 companies.

instagram.com/scottorgera

x.com/scottorgeranyc

linkedin.com/in/scottorgera

facebook.com/ScottOrgeraNY

ACKNOWLEDGMENTS

HOWIE KARPIN ACKNOWLEDGES...

I dedicated this book to the women in my life, now the men: I am so proud of my sons, Danny and Jake Karpin. My brother-in-law, Barry, who has been a huge supporter throughout my life. My nephew Israel and my great nephew, Alex. Of course, my co-author, Scott, who did a wonderful job writing, designing, and inspiring me to go for this. I want to thank my colleagues who have worked side by side with me along the way. I am blessed with so many friends, that to thank all of them here would fill up an encyclopedia, but I must thank each and every one of them because I don't have this career without my family and friends.

SCOTT ORGERA ACKNOWLEDGES...

Since this is my first full-length book and might be my last, I'm using this section to acknowledge as many people as I can who've positively impacted my journey at one point or another. It's been a long road, and without the friendship, guidance, mentorship, and support I've received from so many, I'd never be in a position to live out this dream. While I did my best to include everyone, there will be some who were inadvertently omitted, and to each of you, I apologize. Also, some names belong in more than one section here, but to save ink in what was already a hefty tome I only listed each person once.

To start, I want to thank my co-author Howie Karpin, without whom this book wouldn't have been possible. It's been an honor and a privilege to work alongside Howie all of these years, and I'm proud to call him not only a colleague but also a good friend. We did it, buddy! I also want to thank Howie's wife, Kathy, as well as his sons, Danny and Jake, both former AP stringers who I had the pleasure of sharing a press box with over the years.

No trek begins without family, and in that area, I've been abundantly blessed throughout these 47 years. It's difficult to express what those closest to me have meant without rambling stream-of-consciousness style and taking up too much of the page, but I'll try my best.

My parents, Betty and Rich Orgera, have been in my corner since they first brought me home to Devoe Terrace in the Bronx way back when. Their unconditional love and support have never wavered, even though I haven't always been the easiest son to deal with. Through all of my bullshit, they made sure I had what I needed to keep on pushing.

When I had an opportunity to cover a couple of games for STATS, Inc. in 1995, they didn't hesitate to buy me a laptop, knowing that it might just be those two days and nothing more, but also knowing that it could be the opportunity of a lifetime. Money doesn't grow on trees on the west side of Yonkers, but they stepped up to support my dream — like they always did before, and continue to do to this day. I walked into the Yankee Stadium press box as a shook-up teenager, and the rest was history. I'd need another book's worth of pages to truly thank you both properly, so I'll just hope that I do a good enough job of that in our daily lives. I count my blessings every day that the folks who created me just happen to be amazing people.

To Deano, my first editor and easily the smartest person I know, your figurative giant red pen has undoubtedly been the most important tool in getting me to this point. There was a time when I could barely get through writing a passable article, let alone a book, and you always got me to the finish line. We've been through so much that I can't do any of it justice in such a limited medium, but I think I can summarize it with this. I've never been and most likely never will be prouder of another human being than I constantly am of you, and I'm lucky to call you my brother. Us, always.

To Lizzie, my sister-in-law, who became family long before it was made official, I'm forever grateful that you and your fam are part of ours. Since day one I knew you were my kind of people, and the years have just strengthened that notion. Thank you for always being there, and for always being you, making everyone around you better. I couldn't ask for a better sister.

To Abby Rose and Henry Man, I had often heard that being an uncle was the best job in the world, but I feel like that statement undersold how life-changing and flat-out fun it is. I love you both more than anything, and spending time with you is my favorite part of life, hands down. I didn't think a pair of kids could have such big hearts, but you're each living proof that there's still so much good in the world.

To the rest of the family, sending much love to all of you: Aloysius Burke, Douglas Orgera, Dougie Orgera, Kelly Harrington, Brian Harrington, Kaitlyn Orgera, Sarah Harrington, and Ella Harrington.

To the family members we've lost along the way, I hope you're at peace and happier than you've ever been: John Burke, Elizabeth Louise Burke, Sally Orgera, Ann Orgera, and Cameron Orgera.

To the extended members of superfam: Shaun Bauer, Annie Bauer, Lily Bauer, Ava Bauer, Paulie Faia, Claire Faia, Grace Faia, Tommy Faia, Paul Faia Sr., Patricia Faia, Kathy Philp, Robert Philp, Katie Brown, Ashley Pitrulle, Timothy Pitrulle, Camden Pitrulle, Sienna Pitrulle, Bubba Philp, Bobby Philp, Derek Philp, Ella Philp, Elyssa Philp, Jason Philp, Jordan Philp, Maggie Philp, Matty Philp, Molly Philp, Peyton Philp, Timmy Philp, Tom Philp, Brian Wright, and Cristen Wright.

This next list is a long one, but what do you expect when the number of interviewees tops a hundred? For everyone who contributed directly to this book, my hat's off to every one of you. What Howie and I were able to pull off here was something special, but without your contributions, we'd be left with what would have amounted to a pretty boring read!

Because of this, I feel an extreme debt of gratitude to each of the following people: Rich Ackerman, Shelley Adler, Kenny Albert, Jeff Allen, Joe Benigno, Jim Berman, Lindsay Berra, Joe Bomrad, Stepan Bybyk, Liz Callaway, Steve Cangialosi, Robbie Caploe, Fran Capo, Chris Carrino, Jim Cerny, Ricky Cobb, Harlan Coben, Gary Cohen, Linda Cohn, Ed Coleman, Rocco Constantino, Chuck Cooperstein, Tony Cordasco, Rich Coutinho, Mark Cuban, Jack Curry, John Cwikla, Gordon Damer, Ricardo De Leon, Joe Delikat, Charlie DeNatale, Cedric Dew, Jared Diamond, Joey Diaz, Eric Egan, Kevin Egan, Doug Ely, Scott Engel, Chris Erwin, Drew Esocoff, Mike Farrell, Jim Feist, Steve Finamore, Larry Fleisher, Frank Fleming, Butch Forte, Zig Fracassi, Bobbito Garcia, Jeff Garlin, Joe Gauci, John Giannone, Phil Giubileo, Amy Lennard Goehner, Don La Greca, Erin Green, Bob Grochowski, Ed Guevara, Andy Hall, Pat Harris, Fred Huebner, Bill James, Jim Johnson, Scott Kaufman, Dave Keane, Brian Kilmeade, Elisa Kim, Diane Kraut, Stephen LeBow, Lefty, Pat Leonard, Bebe Lerner, Clare

Livingston, Laura Llamas, Michael Margolis, John Martin, Tony Matteo, Nat Mauldin, Edward McDonald, Randy McGuire, Denis McNamara, Timothy Meade, Castle Conrad Media, Jeff Melnik, Jim Memolo, Charles Miller, Fred Miller, Sweeny Murti, Peter Newman, Charles O'Brien, Daniel Okrent, Eddie Olczyk, Paul Olden, Pat O'Keefe, Jerry O'Neil, Bob Papa, CJ Papa, Bismark Pierre, Kevin Reece, Adam Richman, Hal Richman, Adam Romero, Howie Rose, Andy Roth, Christopher Russo, Ken Samelson, Alan Sanders, David Schuster, Peter Schwartz, Ellie Seifert, William Sherman, Dave Sims, Michael Skarka, Charlie Slowes, Connor Smith, Leigh Steinberg, Joe Stillwell, Tommy Tighe, Steve Torre, Jeffrey Townes, Lynette Townes, Mike Walczewski, Rick Walczewski, Suzyn Waldman, Mike Weinstein, and Lisa Wernick.

And for those who contributed indirectly, which includes anyone else who spent time giving feedback on my ideas for the book, offered encouragement when the 14-hour days were beating me down, provided support with software, publishing, or promotion, connected me with an interview subject, or just listened to me ramble on about one thing or another during the writing process: Alex Alcantara, Reggie Barge, Andy Cullen, Jesse DePalma, Rich Deubel, Michael D'Oyley Sr., Kenny Egan, Eric Epps, Antonio Fernandez, Doug Fischer, Mike Gaspar, Tony Giannelli, Nicole Strecansky Gonzalez, Schorrod Haynes, Bryan Herity, Gina Jackson, Chris Kiers, Dave Latty, Joe Licht, John Licht, Jesse Maher, Jade McSpedon, Mark Mueller, Kevin O'Rourke Jr, Brian O'Shea, Jay Pagano, Monica Pinho, Bruce Rivera, Nelson Roldan, Jacob Santiago, Dave Seery, Raymond Sosa, Arwen Thomas Belloni, Jeffrey Vick, Johnny Villacis, Ryan Waszylenko, Eric Yagasits, Jen Lorio Yedowitz, Dean Yurcho, and Rich Zarychta.

There were other potential interviewees that I talked to, either one-on-one or through a third party, who were also willing to contribute but didn't have much experience in the areas that we were focusing on so chose to pass. I appreciate you as well for taking the time to at least consider the project and for getting back to me. They include Bill Burr, Steve Buscemi, David Cross, Chris DiStefano, Michael Imperioli,

Michael Rapaport, Vincent Pastore, Steve Schirripa, Vince Vaughn, and Denzel Washington.

Before diving in any further, I wanted to dedicate some space to all of those who are gone but never, ever forgotten. You'll forever be remembered in these pages and beyond: Gerry Beatty, Patrick Biller Jr., Marlon Bryant, Pat Burke, Andrew Ciccarelli, Maurice Covington, Michael Deubel, Carmine Dipasquale, Jamie Egan, Tom Eyler, Liz Fernandez, Shannon Forde, Rick Freeman, Alyssa Freeman, Jimmy Galligan, Joao Gaspar, Tommy Goff, Daniel Gordon Jr., Arthur Jackson, Stanley Kieltyka, Ralph Kiner, Robert Kocur, Lloyd G. Latty Sr., Eddie Layton, John Lobianco, Ed Lucas, Norman Mac Lean, Carlton Major, Tim McCarver, Steve McDonnell, Rob McQuown, Vincent Mueller, Bobby Murcer, Deborah Murphy, Marty Noble, Fran Nolan, Andrea Nolan, Michael Nolan, Kim O'Dell, Christine Kenney O'Rourke, Michael Pantoja, Martin Peterson, Pat Quinn, Jorge Rivera, Georgiana Robinson, Mary Teague, Frederick Patrick Seery, Bill Shannon, Bob Sheppard, Thomas Sledge, Raymond Thomas Jr., Dennis Wasylenko, and Kelly Wynne.

For everyone who's made a mark when it comes to my career in sports, starting in the early '90s covering TV games as a backup, to my 30th season donning press credentials. At the top of the list have to be those who took a chance on me at each juncture, whether that was letting me run with the ball or preparing me for new responsibilities, as well as those who paid it forward: Billy Altman, Darius Austin, Jerry Beach, Ron Blum, Marc Carl, Steve Curtis, Kate Feldman, Lawrence Fischer, Mike Fitzpatrick, Jake Fox, Dave Freeman, Dominic French, Doug Gould, Bryan Grosnick, Kevin Kernan, Brett Knight, Vince Lara-Cinisomo, Jonathan Libman, Rob Mains, Chuck Miller, Jack O'Connell, Brendan Riley, Howie Rumberg, Jake Seiner, Jordan Sprechman, Bob Trainor, and Ben Walker.

In a competitive sports industry that constantly finds ways to humble you, it's the people around you that keep you going: Kristie Ackert, Ellen Adair, Bernard Aguinaldo, Chris Ahmad, Laura

Albanese, Nathalie Alonso, Dom Amore, Christian Arnold, Joe Auriemma, Mark Barry, Tyler Barton, Zack Becker, Ted Berg, Justin Birnbaum, Matthew Blittner, Erik Boland, Michael Bonner, Peter Botte, Kaitlyn Brennan, Smith Brickner, Craig Brown, Maury Brown, Kevin Burkhardt, Homer Bush, Josh Cabrera, Pete Caldera, Liam Carroll, Paul Cartier, Rick Cerrone, Bobby Ciafardini, Shaun Clancy, Jay Cohen, Rachel Cohen, David Cone, Travis d'Arnaud, Ken Davidoff, Tomasso DeRosa, Anthony DiComo, Lou DiPietro, Nick Diunte, Kevin Doyle, Rich Dubroff, Julio Eduarte, Robert Ellis, Daniel Epstein, Angel Erikson, Mark Feinsand, Alex Feuz, Spencer Fordin, Noah Frank, Rob Friedman, Stephanie Geosits, Robert Giese, Curtis Granderson, Larry Hardesty, Coley Harvey, Mark Healey, Tim Healey, Mark Herrmann, Dennis Hetrick, Brian Heyman, Sonny Hight, Kyle Hightower, Bryan Hoch, Doug Hogue, Tyler Holmes, Jay Horwitz, Phil Hughes, C. Sven Jenkins, Kim Jones, Phil Joseph, Harold Kaufman, Bob Klapisch, Luke Knox, Roch Kubatko, John Labombarda, Bill Ladson, Jon Lane, Jason Latimer, Kenny Leandry, Jim Leyritz, Susan Lulgjuraj, Bill Madlock, Mike Mancuso, Rich Mancuso, Matthew Mankiewich, Joe Maracic, Abbey Mastracco, Wallace Matthews, Mike Mazzeo, Anthony McCarron, Matt Meffe, Howard Megdal, Jeffrey Melnik, Bill Meth, Jerry Milani, Doug Mittler, Lauren Moran, Michael Moriarty, Rob Morse, Ray Negron, Melissa Newhart, Ray Norberto, Jose de Jesus Ortiz, Meghan Ottolini, Arlenis Peña, John Perrotto, Ken Powtak, Ron Przybycien, John Quirk, Gershon Rabinowitz, Ed Randall, Joe Rivelli, T. J. Rivera, Gio Rodriguez, Mark Rosenman, John Sasman, Bret Sayre, Cory Schwartz, Ginny Searle, Chris Shearn, Gary Shiff, Steve Simineri, Amy Sisoyev, Leif Skodnick, Claire Smith, Dave Smith, Ryan Spaeder, Alex Santos II, Alex Santos Sr., Wally Stampfel, Margo Sugarman, Mark Suleymanov, Mary Jean Sunshine, Dan Szymborski, Wes Tervo, Bob Tewksbury, J. T. Torenli, Adry Torres, Justin Toscano, Joe Trezza, Alexandra Trochanowski, Benjamin Tuliebitz, Tim Virgilio, David Waldstein, Bob Walters, Bob Waterman, Zach Weber, Collin Whitchurch, Hank Widmer, Ethan Wilson, Billy Witz, and Jason Zillo.

I've been burning the candle at both ends since I was a kid, so I also need to acknowledge those who've helped in my computing and technology path, many of whom have contributed to me being the man I am today. Some served as mentors, confidants, and friends, making it easier to navigate a pressurized corporate world: Shrinidhi Badiger, Albert Bangs, Vince Brophy, Phil Cavino, Anil Chebolu, Somanna Chengappa, Mike Cianciulli, Ruben Diaz, Charles Emmons, Octavio Hernandez Garcia, Phil Gukowsky, Nicole Hammeral, Prasadbabu Konduru, Sanjay Krishna, Andrew Kutzy, Dipit Mandloi, Cheryl Martin, Donna McCaffrey, Cathleen Meade, Peter Nemarich, Sai Santosh Venkatrao Parasa, Angel Pena, Bruce Phillips, Mohan Rajaraman, Rakshitha Rajendra, Renita Reddy, Zaniah Renner, Mike Rhodes, Rita Rightmire, Don Saxton, Carlos Solorzano, Debra Sundaram, Sanjay Suratran, Pavan Thotireddy, and Samira Virani.

And all the others who've played a memorable part in my tech career: Abha Abraham, Tim Ackroyd, Krishna Aduri, Asha Aggarwal, Monique Alicea, Nicola Allen, Mohit Bajpai, Vijeth Balarama, Guy Bevente, Bibin Bharath, Ravi Bhusurapu, Amanda Blake, Lew Blum, Tony Bonvolanta, Yogesh Borse, Nora Buckley, John Cappelli, Santosh Cheela, Sundararasan Chellamuthu, Alex Chin, Venkata Chitti, Jeff Coffin, Charles Colpitts, Sandra Coria, Jennifer Corvino, Andre Crenshaw, Cameron Crews, Justin Criswell, Frank Dandreano, Dave Dunmire, Andy Fryefield, Tommy Gambrell, Anne Gehrmann, Subhadip Ghosh, Billie-Ann Grant, Adam Green, Robert Green, Jason Gulick, Abhishek Gupta, Nagesh Gurrala, Lucy Hein, Adriana Hernandez, Keith Hernandez, Preeti Hess, Jason Hughes, Roy Jos'-Land, Sibin Joy, Nilakantha Kar, Edward Karim, Balaji Kayaroganam, Seena Khatter, Uthay Kumar, Alok Kumar, Senthil Kumar, Jared Likes, Durga Madiraju, Rahul Malik, Stu Mark, David Marvin, Lois Mazziotta, Kevin McCaffrey, Juan Carlos Mejia, Karthikeyan Muthukrishnan, Ajith Nair, Senthil Kumar Natarajan, Subramanian Natesan, Kashyap Nayak, Zakir Patrawala, Noe Petrón, Madhuri Ponugoti, Madhu Purushothaman, Arthur Quarequio, Sandeep Reddy, Shubhra Rode, Diana Rodriguez, Suman Roy, Daniel Rozinsky, Dawne Rushkarski, Karthik Sankaran, Heidi Williamson Sargent, Kelly Schneider, Drifa Segal, Ambrish Sharma, Damodar Shenoy, Abhishek Singh, Joann Sparks, Ashok Srinivasan, Pavan Srinivasan, Pavan Tammana,

Mounika Thota, Sampoornam Velusamy, Ranjani Venkatasan, Travis Vogel, Polina Volodina, Rob Vrshek, Kelly Walters, Sudheer Yallam-reddy, Rashida Zaidi, and Ali Zeeshan.

On a personal level, countless other individuals have had a supportive influence throughout these many years, including memorable co-workers at one of the many jobs I've held since that first paper route. Whether it was offering a helping hand, teaching me something new, sharing something I wrote, lending an ear, having my back, or just spreading some love when it was most needed, I wanted to acknowledge them and their families as best I could: Marisol Acosta, Ricky Acosta, Paul Agostino, John Albano, Ed Almonte, Deven Alvarado, Crystal Anderson, Keith Applewhite, Margaret Areizaga, Chris Balezentis, Jill Balezentis, Marty Ball, Joseph Banome, Amir Barge, Irene Barge, Louis Barge, Tyrone Barge, Dawn Basli, Joe Bassi, Mario Bassi, Steve Bastien, Tarik Bastien, Carrieann Beddows, Ed Beglane, Kerry Bello, Ray Bello, Ben Belloni, Ike Bethune, Ali Bishrav, Abby Blair, Sheldon Blair, Erica Bleakley, Carol Boothe, Rolando Bosque, Nick Bottone, Brian Bracken, Meghan Bracken, Gavin Bradley, Larry Bray, Billy Brembs, Johnny Brembs, Jim Breuer, Philip Brocking-ton, Lynn Brooker, Rich Brooker, Eugene Brown, Mary Brown, Terian Buckner, Billy Burke, Kelly Corbett Burke, Tom Burke, Tim Burney, Elizabeth Green Burrell, AnnMarie Butler, Sylvia Butrymowicz, Mike Caballo, Nicole Caldropoli-O'Connor, Cecilia Cameron, Keith Campion, Frank Cangelosi, Mike Cangelosi, Jeffrey Cardwell, John Carr, Carlos Casal, Melina Casal, Dennis Casey, Angelo Castagnozzi, Hugo Castro, Gina Cerone, Dennis Chach, Kate Chapman, Meagan Fitzpatrick Chiappa, Rolando Chumaceiro, Fred Ciappetta, Freddy Cisneros, Victor Coaxum, Jermaine Cockfield, Anthony Cognatello, Dennis Cokley, Yahaira Cokley, Jay Colombos, Jen Colombos, Mary Anne Connaughton, Kevin Cooper, Brian Coote, Eddie Corbett, Felix Costa, Matt Courtien, PJ Creegan, Tim Cremins, Ryan Crews, Anthony Cruz, Lino Cruz, Sonia Cruz, Tania Cruz, Tony Cuello, Pat Cullen, Tricia Cullen, Jessica Cunnington, Michelle D'Avanzo, Michael Dawkins, Raiya De Leon, Riyar De Leon, Ruby De Leon, Yandery De Leon, Nick DePalma, Issa Debien, Katie Murphy Dedde, Ryan Delaney,

Louie Delgiudice, Mike Delgiudice, Joe Demchak, Brian Denneny, Nancy Devitt, Sean Devitt, Arlindo Dias, Michelly Diaz, Pete DiMeglio, Antaun Jones-D'Oyley, Leah D'Oyley, Micah D'Oyley, Michael D'Oyley, Sean Drain, Cameron Druitt, Ronni Druitt, Dina Dunn, Hailey Egan, Hedy Egan, Jayden Egan, Jim Egan, Marie Ann Egan, Hector Faneytt, Junior Faneytt, Kori Faneytt, Maximus Faneytt, Vada Faneytt, Kelly Farling, Anthony Fava, John Federico, Matt Fedor, Jennifer Feliu-Illa, Jean-Jacques Fequiere, Jose Fernandez, Jaxson Fischer, Pete Fischer, Billy Fitzpatrick, Kevin Fitzpatrick, Molly Fitzpatrick, Jerry Foley, Kara Forcelli, Skip Forte, Vin Frazier, Marlene Galizi, Ann Gallo, Katie Gallo, Mike Gallo, Paul Gallo, Kevin Galvin, Mike Galvin, Chris Gamby, Steve Gardner, Sobha Gavani, Joe Gebbia, Frank Girdauskas, Mike Girdauskas, Ed Girduaskas, Jesus Gomero, Jovan Gonzalez, Bobby Gorman, Denis Gorman, Jason Gorman, Jeanne Gorman, Dave Graham, David Graham Jr., Heather Graham, Jamie Graham, Janet Graham, Doug Gray, Ralph Greathouse, Carl Green, Nealon Greene, Sandeep Gulati, Jennifer Gurreri, Jimmy Gurreri, Rich Gurreri, Asia Hackett, Jordan Hackett, Brian Halladay, Mike Harrison, Dermot Hayes, Seamus Hayes, Robert Haynes, Sarah Haynes, Schorrod Haynes Jr., Tasheema Haynes, Chris Heinrich, Chris Heinrich Jr., Denise Heinrich, Steve Heinrich, Patrick Herber, Kerry O'Brien Hess, Rob Hess, Melissa Hlewicki, Kaitlyn Hold, Nicole Hold, Nomi Holland, Tim Holland, EJ Horney, Brian Horton, Jaclyn Hugg, Jamar Hunt, Norm Hutchins, Angelina Iannuzzi, Nicole Intervallo, Toriano Jackson, Walter Jackson Jr., Dennis Jacobi, Kim Jacobi, Matt Janeczko, Larry Jemison, Samantha Jenkins, Alvin Johnson, Brendan Johnson, Joe Johnson, Tommy Johnson, Chuck Jones, June Junjulas-Colombos, Dara Kane, Sheri Kaplan, Kenny Katz, Neil Katz, Debbie Keane, Sinead Keane, Tommy Keane, Geoff Keating, Suzanne Keating, John Keavney, Mary Keavney, Janel Kerson, Joe Kieltyka, Liz Kieltyka, Nichole Kieltyka, Victoria Kieltyka, Daniel Kiers, Lisa Kiers, Mike Kiers, Vanessa Perez-Kiers, Alan Klein, Nick Kowal, Nicole LaVista, Roxanne Marji Lafontant, Harvey Lanot, Rich Latty, Joe Lecoq Jr., Calvin Lee, Darren Lefever, Jessica Flores Leto, Michael Leto, Eddie Lewis, Eddie Lewis Jr., Vinny Liberatore, Alison Licht, Ashley Licht, Avery Licht, James Licht, McKenzie Licht, Tierney Licht, Tyler Licht, Phil Lobue, Rich Lombardi,

Joe Loughlin, Dawn Lozito, Gary Lozito, Lorraine Lozito, Pete Lozito, Troy Lumpkin, Mike Mackay, Joe Madden, Kevin Madden, Gary Magner, Bill Maher, Chase Maher, Jasmin Maher, Ken Maher, Kirk Maher, Kurtis Maher, Laura Maher, Linda Maher, Mia Maher, Payton Maher, Skylah Maher, Zoey Maher, Sheldon Major, Denise Makar, Kyle Makar, Kristin Malachuk, Rahmelo Malik, Christina Mangione, Sean Manning, Bill Mannix, Danny Mannix, Jay Maolini, Justin Mapps, Katia Marques, Richie Marques, Janine Marsigliano, Rob Martin Jr., James Martinetti, Megan Martinetti, Nora Martinetti, Milena Martinez, Joe Matthews, Brendan Mayer, Kathy Mayer, Sean Mayer, Pat McCormack, Gerard McCoy, Courtney Mcdermott, Kevin Mcdermott, Matt Mcdermott, Mike Mcdermott, Molly Mcdermott, Rory Mcdermott, Sean Mcdermott, Tim Mcdermott, Vinny Mcdermott, Tom McDonald, Rob McDonough, Hondo McGivern, Andrew McGowan, Colm McHugh, Raul McKenzie, Andrew McKeown, Conor McKeown, Andrea McLynn, Brandon McLynn, Brian McLynn, Dylan McLynn, Jack McLynn, Jay McLynn, Kylie McLynn, Michelle McLynn, Mikey McLynn, Matt McMahon, Kyle McPhillips, Duane McQuay, Artie McShane, George McShane, Dennis H. McSpedon, Dennis N. McSpedon, Matt McSpedon, Frank Meade, Kevin Meade, Donna Meehan, Keith Melnik, Kerrie Meyer, Arshama Middleton, AnnMarie Miele, Nick Miele, Edwin Milan, Darlene Mitchell, Amy Burney Mitrakos, Dana Monaco, Dominic Monaco, Joe Monaco, Michelle Monaco, Brian Mosiello, Chrissy Mueller, Jane Mueller, Sheila Mueller, Tommy Mueller, Carolyn Muller, Julie Muller, Kevin Muller, Paul Muller, PJ Muller, Ryan Muller, Christina Mundo, Brian Murphy, Emmett Murphy, J. Emmett Murphy, Jennifer Murphy, Kieran Murray, Sheila Murray, Jennifer Marques Napolitano, Nnamdi Nedd, Noreen Nezaj, Rob Nezaj, Richard Nicholas, Shayne Nichols, Andy Nicolas, Felicia Nicolas, Ryan Nicolas, Michele Nolan, Sean Norwood, Sean Nugent, Chris O'Connell, PJ O'Connell, Sean O'Connor, Jessica O'Dell, Mike O'Dell, Karen O'Gorman, Kristen O'Leary, Mike O'Neill, Rich O'Neill, Tara O'Neill, Jenna O'Rourke, KJ O'Rourke, Kali O'Rourke, Katelin Gorman O'Rourke, Keegan O'Rourke, Kevin O'Rourke Sr., Susan O'Rourke, Brian O'Shea Jr., Christian O'Shea, Dermot O'Sullivan, Atticus Oelkers, Chris Oelkers, Jennifer Oelkers, Mike Osborn, Joe

Osika, Anthony Packer, Ike Padilla, Anita Pagano, Christina Pagano, Eddie Pagano, Elessia Pagano, Jason Pagano, Bonnie Brown Panaro, Isabella Papillon, Nick Pappalardo, Sal Pappalardo, Andrew Peat, Anita Peat, Ellen McPhillips Pellegrino, Dana Perillo, Darren Perillo, Tommy Perillo, Angela Peterson, Claire Peterson, Marty Peterson, Jason Philips, Fernando Pinho, Maria Pinho, Marilyn Barros Pires, Danny Pivak, Chris Planell, Mike Planell, Rich Popovich, Joe Prestigiacomo, John Price, Brian Pugsley, Joanette Pugsley, Liz Pugsley, Rajendra Rampersaud, Kurt Rauber, Samantha Rauber, Bill Reed, Bree Reed, Serenity Reed, Skylar Reed, Stormy Reed, Yazmin Reed, Kim Regan, Ernie Di Renzo, Trisha Ricci, Andrew Rice, Catherine Rice, Mary Rice, Paul Rice, Sue Rice, Timmy Rice, Amanda Riley, Louisa Riley, Dean Riolo, Denise Riolo, Gary Riolo, Justin Rivas, Aracelis Rivera, Cynthia Rivera, George Rivera, Germania Rivera, Harry Rivera, Bill Robertson, Giovanni Rodriguez, Victoria Ross, PJ Rowan, Tim Rowan, Lee Ruddy, Sean Rudolph, Agron Rugova, Driton Rugova, Jimmy Rugova, Skel Rugova, Gina Ruocco, Mike Ruth, Abraham Said, Arthur Said, Brittany Said, Kenny Samoyedny, Paul Samoyedny, Lourdes Sanchez, Ava Santavicca, Dennis Santavicca, Laura Santavicca, Jessica Sarfaty, Pat Sava, Ghassan P. Sayegh, Sarah Scalet, Annie Schianno, Christopher Seery, Frances Seery, Isabella Seery, Karen Seery, Nicole Seery, Kristy Segal, Paul Selby, Beth Shapiro, David Shapiro, Rob Shasta, Carrie Shaw, Dorothy Shepard, William Shepard, Chris Siano, Pearl Siano, Leroy Simmons, Erica Slanzi, Liz Slanzi, Tim Slanzi, Vinny Smith, Gwen Soba, Derek Soohoo, Jessica Soto, Mike Spano, Ross Sparno, John Spring, Terrance Springer, Justin Stanford, Steve Stanislawczyk, William Stanislawczyk, Troy Stewart, Marie Stone, Tommy Stratigakis, Tim Suchy, Cathy Sullivan, Joe Sylvestri, Brian Teague, Caitlin Teague, Kevin Teague, Kristin Teague, John Teti, Dana Thomas, George Thomas, Mary Ann Thomas, R. J. Thomas, Rich Thompson, Rashimir Tucker, Yolanda Turner, Chris Urban, Marisa Uzzi, Lorean Valentin, Anthony Vares, Claire Vargo, Margie Vazquez, Jack Velasquez, Angela Vetrano, Jackie Vetrano, Ricky Vetrano, Flor Villacis, Johnny Villacis Jr., Luis Alfredo Villacis, Jason Villafana, Denise Viviano, John Viviano, Stephanie Viviano, Ralph Walker, Keith Walker, Al West, Bob Williams, Donald Williams, Janae Williams,

Janice Williams, Joseph Williams, Michelle Williams, Mike Williams, Rob Williams, Raymond Wooten, Joe Wynne, Ryan Wynne, Shannon Wynne, Sharon Wynne, Timmy Wynne Jr., Carolyn Yagasits, Joe Yedowitz, Josie Yedowitz, Tommy Yedowitz, Stacie Youket, Adriana Yurcho, Deeana Yurcho, Derrick Yurcho, Diane Yurcho, Dylan Yurcho, Jason Yurcho, Jason Yurcho Jr., Jayden Yurcho, Michael Yurcho, Rebecca Yurcho, Rocco Yurcho, Samantha Yurcho, Blase Zaino, Mark Zaino, Myrna Zaino, Paul Zaino, Jackie Zappia, Johnny Zappia, Jason Zarychta, Jenna Zarychta, and Michelle Zarychta.

To the bands, brands, and businesses that have provided support in one form or another, including Trish, Tracy, Kaitlyn, and the rest of the team at Francey Brady's, Bronx Ale House, Andira and the crew at Bronx Public, Direct Physical Therapy, Dobbs Ferry Lobster Guys, Game Day Sports Bar, Get Fresh Yonkers, Juice House of Tuckahoe, the Irish American Baseball Society, Owen and the staff at La Sensacion, Maggie Spillane's, Mary Anne's Irish Design Shop, Nugent's Pub, One Pier Steakhouse, Rory Dolan's, Ruff Ryders, SHAV Lather Bar, Since 1982, Shilelagh Law, Signatures for Soldiers, Southern Westchester Courier, Team Greene Athletics, The Hogue Foundation, Tryon Public House, and Urge Burger.

To the many teachers and professors who saw potential in me from Sacred Heart Grade School and High School, Westchester Community College, Pace University, Purdue University, and others who taught what feels like countless tech courses these past few decades.

Finally, to the city of Yonkers, the place that built me up and broke me down, just to end up building me back up again. It's been said that there's a black cloud over the west side even on the brightest of summer days and that we're all just crabs in a bucket, trying to get over while knocking each other down in the process. What isn't said enough is how strong our bonds can be when you've got the right people in your circle, and how those that come from our neck of the woods are capable of achieving just about any damn thing if we're driven enough. What they don't talk about is how the support from those in the town is something you can actually feel, physically, in your bones. How it's palpable when you're trying to achieve something big, and how it can serve as that secret ingredient to get you over the finish line, even when you're gasping for just one more breath of air and your legs have already given out. From Odell to Caryl and everywhere in between, Warburton, Broadway, Palisade, Nepperhan, Kinsley Park, the North End, Lake Ave, High Street, Glenwood, Riverdale, NYBG, the Amackassin, the Post, and all the ballfields, bars, and back blocks that have welcomed me and bought into my dreams these many moons. I see you. To everyone who supported me in the DPW, Yonkers Public Schools, YFD, and YPD, you have my thanks. When our backs are against the wall, we shine the most. I found myself there while working on this book, and in the end, I hope I've done you proud. I love you and I hate you, Yonkers, and isn't that the way it's supposed to be? Until next time, keep shining…

www.ingramcontent.com/pod-product-compliance
Lightning Source LLC
Chambersburg PA
CBHW060849120626
46553CB00001B/19